ARCHAEOLOGY HOTSPOT FRANCE

Archaeology Hotspots:
Unearthing the Past for Armchair Archaeologists

Series Editor: Paul G. Bahn, independent archaeologist and author of *The Archaeology of Hollywood*

Archaeology Hotspots are countries and regions with particularly deep pasts, stretching from the depths of prehistory to more recent layers of recorded history. Written by archaeological experts for everyday readers, the books in the series offer engaging explorations of one particular country or region as seen through an archaeological lens. Each individual title provides a chronological overview of the area in question, covers the most interesting and significant archaeological finds in that area, and profiles the major personalities involved in those discoveries, both past and present. The authors cover controversies and scandals, current digs and recent insights, contextualizing the material remains of the past within a broad view of the area's present existence. The result is an illuminating look at the history, culture, national heritage, and current events of specific countries and regions—specific hotspots of archaeology.

Archaeology Hotspot Egypt: Unearthing the Past for Armchair Archaeologists, by Julian Heath (2015)

Archaeology Hotspot Great Britain: Unearthing the Past for Armchair Archaeologists, by Donald Henson (2015)

ARCHAEOLOGY HOTSPOT FRANCE

Unearthing the Past for Armchair Archaeologists

Georgina Muskett

ROWMAN & LITTLEFIELD
Lanham • Boulder • New York • London

Published by Rowman & Littlefield
A wholly owned subsidiary of The Rowman & Littlefield Publishing Group, Inc.
4501 Forbes Boulevard, Suite 200, Lanham, Maryland 20706
www.rowman.com

Unit A, Whitacre Mews, 26-34 Stannary Street, London SE11 4AB

British Library Cataloguing in Publication Information Available

Library of Congress Cataloging-in-Publication Data

Names: Muskett, G. M. (Georgina M.), author.
Title: Archaeology hotspot France : unearthing the past for armchair archaeologists / Georgina Muskett.
Description: Lanham, Maryland : Rowman & Littlefield, 2018. | Series: Archaeology hotspots | Includes bibliographical references and index.
Identifiers: LCCN 2017051842 (print) | LCCN 2017052316 (ebook) | ISBN 9781442269231 (Electronic) | ISBN 9781442269224 (cloth : alk. paper)
Subjects: LCSH: France—Antiquities. | Excavations (Archaeology) —France. | Historic sites—France. | Archaeology—France.
Classification: LCC DC31 (ebook) | LCC DC31 .M95 2018 (print) | DDC 936.4—dc23
LC record available at https://lccn.loc.gov/2017051842

Printed in the United States of America

CONTENTS

ACKNOWLEDGMENTS

I should like to thank my editor, Paul Bahn, for his help, advice, and encouragement throughout. I would also like to thank the staff at Rowman & Littlefield for their support and practical assistance with this book. My greatest thanks are due to Richard Dunsford, who commented on the text and by whose thoughtful advice it has benefited greatly.

LIST OF ILLUSTRATIONS

DATES FOR ARCHAEOLOGICAL PERIODS IN FRANCE

Lower Paleolithic	800,000–300,000 BP
Middle Paleolithic	300,000–40,000 BP
Upper Paleolithic	40,000 BP–9600 BC
Mesolithic	9600–6000 BC
Neolithic	6000–2200 BC
Early Neolithic	6000–4600 BC
Middle Neolithic	4600–4100 BC
Late Neolithic	4100–3500 BC
Final Neolithic	3500–2200 BC
Bronze Age	2200–800 BC
Early Iron Age	800–450 BC
Later Iron Age	450 BC–50 BC
Gallo-Roman	50 BC–end of fifth century AD
Merovingian	sixth and seventh centuries AD

PREFACE

France has been a unified nation for many hundreds of years, its rich heritage supported by a vibrant and varied collection of archaeological sites and monuments.

The geographic area covered in this book principally corresponds to that of modern-day mainland France, although in antiquity this boundary, of course, was not recognized. For administrative purposes, France is divided into 101 départements, of which ninety-six are in mainland France and Corsica (figure 0.1) and five are "outre-mer"—that is, overseas. The mainland départements are grouped into thirteen régions. The smallest administrative division is known as a "commune." The usual convention to describe a location, which is followed in this book, is to quote the place name followed by the département name in brackets.

The chronological span covered by the book is from 1.3 million years ago, when humans were first attested in France, until AD 800, the coronation of Charlemagne as Holy Roman emperor.

The book starts with an account of the development of archaeology in France, from the early sixteenth century until the early twenty-first century. It continues with a chapter providing a chronological overview of significant sites and discoveries from the prehistoric period in France, between 1.3 million years ago and 2500 BC. The subjects include the earliest known humans, art from the Upper Paleolithic period, Neolithic monuments in Brittany, Neolithic and Bronze Age "lake villages," and Bronze Age hoards

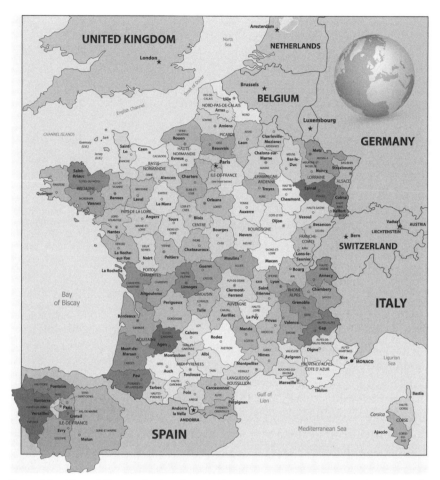

Figure 0.1. Map of France, showing the administrative areas known as départements. istock, 538776758

found in France. Chapter 3 outlines the archaeology of Iron Age, Gallo-Roman, and Early Medieval France, beginning with evidence of contact with the Mediterranean world during the seventh century BC. It continues with the indigenous settlement during the Iron Age, the changes that resulted from the Roman conquest of Gaul, evidence of maritime trade from shipwrecks, and archaeological evidence of the influx of non-Gallic people and the establishment of the Merovingian dynasty. The next chapter considers the way in which archaeologists working in France have made a significant contribution to our knowledge of the past. Innovations of French archaeology, particularly the naming of type sites for phases of the Paleolithic period, the development of underwater archaeology, the use of aerial photography in archaeology, and the application of archaeological science in France, also are discussed. Chapter 5 considers the debates, controversies, and scandals that have occurred in French archaeology, some of which have led to changes in practice or interpretation, whereas others continue to be debated. Finally, there is a selective review of archaeological discoveries of the twenty-first century that have made a significant impact on our knowledge of the archaeology of France. Many of these have been the result of archaeological excavation in advance of infrastructure projects, particularly discoveries resulting from the extensive development of the high-speed railway network in France.

Join me in a journey of discovery through the fascinating story of French archaeology, from "household names," such as the Lascaux cave, the megalithic monuments of Carnac, and the Roman aqueduct-bridge of Pont-du-Gard, to the lesser-known but no less captivating aspects that are part of France's archaeological heritage.

The story is enlivened by some extraordinary characters, including the inventor of the Turkish towel, the author of *Carmen*, the Emperor Napoleon III, and a little dog. All played a part in the archaeology of France during the nineteenth and twentieth centuries.

Bon voyage!

❶

THE DEVELOPMENT OF ARCHAEOLOGY IN FRANCE

The chapter presents an account of the development of archaeology in France, from the early sixteenth century until the early twenty-first century.

THE ORIGIN OF ARCHAEOLOGICAL STUDY IN FRANCE

An interest in France's past began in the early sixteenth century, when certain learned individuals assembled collections of ancient Gallo-Roman objects. One of the earliest recorded collectors of antiquities was Claude de Bellièvre, who was born in Lyon in 1487. A member of a distinguished family, Bellièvre had received legal training at the University of Toulouse before becoming an advocate for King François I. He became a leader of the civic government in Lyon and subsequently the first president of the Parlement du Dauphiné at Grenoble. In later life, Bellièvre focused on the study of the history of Lyon and displayed his collection of Roman inscriptions in his "Jardin des antiquités," which was open to other antiquarians for study.

The most renowned object associated with Bellièvre is a bronze plaque known as the Table Claudienne. Measuring 193 centimeters by 139 centimeters, it has Latin text inscribed in two columns. The inscription is a proclamation made in AD 48 by the Roman emperor Claudius to the Senate, outlining the privileges given to Lugdunum, modern-day Lyon. Originally displayed in the Sanctuary of the Three Gauls, discussed in chapter 3 as the site of the persecution of Christians in the late second century AD, the Table Claudienne was found in 1528 during the construction of a house in the Croix-Rousse area of Lyon. The discovery was brought to the attention of Bellièvre, who purchased the plaque on behalf of the city in the following year. The Table Claudienne, of which only the lower portion survives, was found in two parts, both of which are now in the Musée gallo-romain de Lyon-Fourvière.

Around the same time, the antiquary Guillaume du Choul, also from Lyon, was noted for his collection of coins. His manuscripts on Roman society were dedicated to King François I and King Henri II, and he also published books on Roman baths, military camps, and religion.

However, archaeology in the modern sense did not begin until the later seventeenth century, when Jacob Spon (1647–1685) used the term "archeologia." Spon, who was a doctor and scholar from Lyon, also adopted a critical method for the study of inscriptions and supported the use of archaeological evidence. Accordingly, Spon distinguished archaeology from the practice of collectors.

There also had been antiquarian interest in Gallo-Roman architectural remains, which had remained visible in the landscape. Many of the more spectacular were in southern France and, as discussed in chapter 3, the scenae frons of the theater at Orange attracted the admiration of King Louis XIV (reigned 1643–1715), and the king also had commissioned a survey of the Gallo-Roman villa at Saint-Cyr-sur-Mer (Var). However, Gallo-Roman remains in the rest of France also attracted antiquarian interest. For example, the settlement site of Champlieu, in the commune of Orrouy (Oise), had been recognized from at least the end of the sixteenth century. It was described in detail by l'abbé Claude Carlier in his work *Histoire du duché de Valois*, written in 1764. As discussed below, the site also attracted the attention of the emperor Napoleon III.

The Cabinet des Médailles in Paris, more formally the Département des Monnaies, Médailles et Antiques de la Bibliothèque nationale de France, can be described as the oldest museum in France. Originally known as the Cabinet des rois de France, its origins lie in the rare and precious objects collected by the kings of France, and it was not until the reign of Henri IV (1589–1610) that it became a national, rather than personal, collection. The collection expanded in the reign of Louis XIV, who moved it to the palace of Versailles, although it returned to Paris in the eighteenth century. Individual collections were added, such as the extensive collection of antiquities owned by the Comte de Caylus, which was bequeathed to the Cabinet des

Médailles on his death in 1765. Works of art from religious institutions, such as the Sainte-Chapelle, donated as taxes during the French Revolution, also were added to the collection. In 1917, the Cabinet des Médailles moved to its present premises on the rue de Richelieu in Paris, in the Bibliothèque nationale de France.

THE DEVELOPMENT OF THE ARCHAEOLOGY OF NEOLITHIC FRANCE

The Neolithic monuments in France remained largely visible in the landscape, and the dolmen tomb known as La Pierre-Levée in Poitiers (Vienne) attracted many visitors. A sixteenth-century sketch of the tomb showed the signatures of visitors carved on the monument. In addition, the tomb was mentioned in Rabelais's comic novel *Pantagruel*, written in 1532, emphasizing the tomb's renown.

The first recognized excavation in France is of a dolmen tomb in 1685. The tomb was discovered at Cocherel, in the commune of Houlbeck-Cocherel (Eure), during a search for building stone on land owned by Robert le Prévôt, a local aristocrat. On the discovery of human remains, le Prévôt assembled a team of workmen and commenced the careful excavation and recording of the tomb and its contents. He discovered twenty skeletons, one with a hole in the skull, together with objects including polished stone axs under the heads of the skeletons, beads, bone needles or points, and three pottery vessels that contained cremated remains. The account of the discovery of the tomb was reported by le Prévôt in 1686 in the Philosophical Transactions of the Royal Society in London. The tomb and its contents were later described in detail in 1719 by Bernard de Montfaucon, followed by Pierre de Brasseur in 1722 and Jacques Martin in 1727. An appendix to Brasseur's 1722 publication *Histoire civile et ecclésiastique du Comté d'Evreux* included a drawing of the tomb showing eight articulated skeletons.

A group of Neolithic monuments that attracted early antiquarian interest is found in Brittany at sites such as those in the Carnac area (Morbihan), discussed in chapter 2. The visibility of the monuments in the landscape had been recognized by antiquarians from the 1720s onward. Between 1727 and 1737, Christophe Paul de Robien (1698–1756), president of the Parliament of Brittany, made a study of the megalithic monuments of Locmariaquer and Carnac. Robien recorded their descriptions, accompanied by illustrations by a painter named Huguet, in an unpublished manuscript preserved in the library at Rennes (Ille-et-Vilaine). Although the initial focus of the scholar the Comte de Caylus (1692–1765) was classical archaeology, he also had an interest in the archaeology of France. Caylus's major work, *Recueil d'antiquités* égyptiennes, étrusques, *grecques, romaines et gauloises* (Collection of Egyptian, Etruscan, Greek, Roman, and Gallic antiquities), included drawings and descriptions of megalithic tombs in France.

In a paper read to the Institut de France, the historian and antiquarian Pierre Legrand d'Aussy (1737–1800) introduced the use of the terms "menhir" and "dolmen," taken from the Breton language, to describe the standing stones and tombs, terminology still in use.

Other early excavations were those undertaken by Armand-Louis-Bon Maudet de Penhoët, accompanied by an M. Renaud, at the tombs known as La Table des Marchands in 1811 and Les Pierres Plates in 1813, discussed further in chapter 2. Indeed, the earliest known drawings of engraved decoration from inside a megalithic tomb were those made by Maudet de Penhoët in 1814 in La Table des Marchands (figure 1.1) and Les Pierres Plates (figure 1.2).

Archaeological awareness of the Neolithic monuments in Brittany increased following the appointment in 1834 of Prosper Merimée, better known today as the author of the novella *Carmen*, to the post of Inspecteur général des monuments historiques (inspector general of historic monu-

Figure 1.1. Tomb known as La Table des Marchands, Locmariaquer. istock, 617888194

Figure 1.2. Tomb known as Les Pierres-Plates, Locmariquer. istock, 116008032

ments), a post he held until 1853. In 1835 Merimée undertook a tour of Brittany, publishing his notes the following year. He recorded that he deplored the destruction of the monuments by dislodging and removing the stones, whether to search for "treasure" or to reuse as paving stones.

In the early 1870s, the Abbé Jean-Joachim Collet had excavated at the foot of seven of the standing stones at Le Ménec in the Carnac area, where he found charcoal, a few pottery sherds, and stone tools. Collet, who was a member of the Societé polymathique du Morbihan, writing articles on archaeology, engaged in correspondence with prehistorians including Emile Cartailhac. However, the first major excavations of a group of menhirs were undertaken in 1877 and 1878 at Kermario (figure 1.3) by the Scottish antiquary James Miln (1819–1881). Miln's account of his excavations at Kermario, also in the Carnac area, were published posthumously following his death in Glasgow in 1881. At this time, Miln's archaeological collection was given to the town of Carnac, where his brother, Robert Miln, established the James Miln Museum. Zacharie le Rouzic, who had been Miln's assistant from a very young age, became keeper of the museum and continued his archaeological work. From 1927, the museum in Carnac-Ville has been named Le Musée James Miln-Zacharie le Rouzic, following le Rouzic's donation of his own archaeological collection.

Figure 1.3. Kermario alignment, Carnac. istock, 503668088

THE DEVELOPMENT OF THE ARCHAEOLOGY
OF EARLY MEDIEVAL FRANCE

Between the sixteenth and eighteenth centuries, few French scholars focused on archaeology of Early Medieval France. Knowledge of the Merovingian period in France was based on a few texts from the sixth to eighth centuries. It is believed that the earliest excavation of a Merovingian cemetery began in 1830 by Henri Baudot at the commune of Charnay (Saône-et-Loire). However, it was not until 1840 that the cemetery at Charnay was recognized as Merovingian, and subsequent discoveries at other sites enabled similar identifications. By the middle of the nineteenth century, chance finds of Merovingian cemeteries were made during church repairs and the construction of railways and roads. These continued in the second half of the nineteenth century, when the increased industrialization of France led to further discoveries and the foundation of new archaeological societies.

Although the speed of expansion of the railways in France in the second half of the nineteenth century resulted in some newly found sites being looted or destroyed, others subsequently were excavated using the archaeological methods current at the time. An example of this took place in 1863, when workers constructing the railway found a large Merovingian cemetery at Hardenthun in the commune of Marquise (Pas-de-Calais) during construction of the railway line between Boulogne-sur-Mer and Calais, apparently plundering about 120 graves. Abbé Daniel Haigneré, then the archivist of the town of Boulogne-sur-Mer and president of the Departmental Commission of Historic Monuments of Pas-de-Calais, was able briefly to stop the railway construction, allowing the excavation and publication of finds from the remaining part of the cemetery. By then Haigneré was an experienced archaeologist, having undertaken his first excavation in 1857—a Merovingian cemetery at Pincthun, in the commune of Echingen (Pas-de-Calais). The exploitation of a quarry revealed a cemetery of forty-nine tombs, the first Merovingian cemetery to have been found in the area of Boulogne-sur-Mer. This was followed by many other excavations by Haigneré in the Boulogne area, mostly Gallo-Roman or Merovingian cemeteries.

The acquisition and sale of finds from late nineteenth- and early twentieth-century discoveries of Merovingian cemeteries were frequently controversial and, in some cases, was little more than looting of archaeological sites. Among the most notorious characters were Jean-Baptiste Lelaurain and Léandre Cottel. Lelaurain had received some archaeological training from his father, who had conducted excavations at the behest of the emperor Napoleon III. It is alleged that Lelaurain had excavated more than twenty thousand graves from the Late Roman and Merovingian periods, none of which were recorded properly. One of the largest Merovingian cemeteries excavated by Lelaurain was north of the commune of Marchélepot (Somme), where he excavated approximately four thousand graves. Until his death in 1905, Lelaurain earned a living from the sale of objects retrieved from graves, which were acquired by collectors. These included John Evans, whose collection was presented to the Ashmolean Museum in Oxford in 1909 by his son Arthur Evans, a former keeper of the museum who was renowned for his excavations on Crete. Léandre Cottel, a primary school teacher who was an associate of Lelaurain, also had a reputation as an excavator who did not record his discoveries. Cottel's finds from the cemeteries he excavated also were sold to collectors and museums.

THE DEVELOPMENT OF THE ARCHAEOLOGY OF PALEOLITHIC FRANCE

The nineteenth century was a key period in the development of the study of Paleolithic stone tools and art in France and, above all, the true age of these objects.

Paul Tournal, originally a pharmacist from Narbonne, conducted excavations in the Grande Grotte de Bize (Aude) in 1827. As a result of these excavations, Tournal suggested the significance of discoveries of objects fashioned by humans alongside the bones of humans and modern and extinct animals, an idea that was considered heresy at that time. In 1833, the same year he founded the Musée archéologique in Narbonne, Tournal used the term "antehistoric" to describe the period before recorded history; in other words, before the Bible. This was perhaps the first indication of the existence of prehistory.

In the 1840s, Jacques Boucher de Perthes explored the gravel quarries of the river Somme, where he found chipped stone tools in association with the fossilized bones of extinct animals deposited in the Ice Age. This was key to the breakthrough in determining the age of these objects. Boucher de Perthes published his findings in the first volume of his three-volume work *Les Antiquités Celtiques et Antédiluviennes*, the title confirming that the term "Celtic" was in general use to describe pre-Roman antiquities and additionally suggesting that the association between the stone tools and extinct animal remains indicated that humans had existed long before the biblical flood. The view of Boucher de Perthes was not widely accepted, but attitudes were changing. New archaeological discoveries in France and England, together with the publication of Charles Darwin's *On the Origin of Species* in 1859, altered ideas on the age of worked stone tools. The conclusions of Boucher de Perthes were supported by geologists and antiquarians, including Charles Lyell, Joseph Prestwich, and John Evans, who confirmed the concept of the antiquity of humans.

The study of stone tools in France continued in the later part of the nineteenth century, with a large number of "type sites" for phases of the Paleolithic period in Western Europe and beyond being named from sites in France. This is discussed further in chapter 4.

The identification of the age of Paleolithic art was not made until the late nineteenth century, following many finds whose true age had not been recognized immediately.

Images, both painted and engraved, had been noticed in caves from at least the seventeenth century, indicated by dated graffiti on cave walls. However, the first reported finds of portable art that would only later be identified as dating from the Ice Age had been made in the first half of the nineteenth century, several decades before cave art. An early specialist in Paleolithic art, Edouard Lartet, reported that Paul Tournal had found a piece of antler engraved with chevrons in the Grande Grotte de Bize (Aude), but the details of the object were never published, and it is now

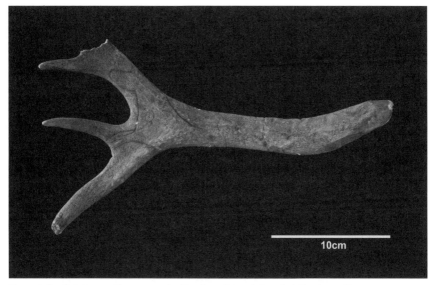

Figure 1.4.   Reindeer antler, engraved with a horse's head, found at Neschers. Alamy

lost. The first attested decorated tools were found around 1833 in the Salève quarries in the commune of Etrembières (Haute-Savoie), across the border from the Swiss municipality of Veyrier, by François Mayor, a doctor from Geneva. They were a harpoon, made from antler to resemble a plant with buds along its stem; and a baton, also made from antler, pierced at one end and with a simple engraving, perhaps representing a bird. A reindeer antler, engraved with a horse's head (figure 1.4), which had been found at the open-air site of Neschers (Puy-de-Dôme) by Jean-Baptiste Croizet, the local priest, is believed from documentary sources to have been found between 1830 and 1848. The antler was acquired by the British Museum in 1848 and transferred to the Natural History Museum in London when the latter became independent from the British Museum.

In 1852, a reindeer foot bone engraved with two female deer was found by André Brouillet and Charles Joly Leterme at the Grottes du Chaffaud (Vienne). A drawing of the bone was made by Prosper Merimée, then Inspecteur général des monuments historiques, who enclosed it with a letter to Jens Worsaae, the Danish archaeologist It is believed to be the earliest known drawing of Ice Age art. The bone, which is 13.5 centimeters long and 3.7 centimeters wide, was donated to the Musée de Cluny in Paris where, without an awareness of Paleolithic art, it was documented as being Celtic.

By the 1860s, the existence of Paleolithic art was accepted through the discovery of engraved and carved bones and stones found in several caves and rock shelters by Edouard Lartet and Henry Christy, whose contributions to French archaeology are further discussed in chapter 4. Through their finds of decorated objects in association with Paleolithic stone and bone tools together with the bones of Ice Age animals, Lartet and Christy discovered evidence that humans had existed alongside animals that by that time were extinct. In 1864, an image of a mammoth engraved on a mammoth tusk was found by Lartet and Christy at the Abri de la Madeleine, near Tursac (Dordogne). At about the same time, the first discovery of an Ice Age figurine was made, a statuette of a young woman, 7.7 centimeters tall. The figurine, given the name "Vénus impudique" (Immodest Venus) and made from mammoth ivory, was found at the Abri de Laugerie-Basse (Dordogne) by Paul Hurault, Marquis de Vibraye.

By 1867, sufficient interest prompted a display of prehistoric objects to be included in the Exposition universelle held in Paris.

Evidence of cave art began to be reported in increasing numbers in the late nineteenth century, although its date had yet to be recognized. In 1878, Léopold Chiron made early photographs of engravings in the Grotte Chabot, near Aiguèze (Gard); the following year he wrote to the archaeologist Gabriel de Mortillet to report the engravings he had recorded, associated with the presence of stone tools. However, Mortillet, who recognized the importance of Paleolithic portable art, did not believe that cave walls were decorated in the same period and did not present Chiron's information in the journal he published.

Debate continued regarding the age of the decoration on the cave walls. Crucial discoveries proved to be at La Grotte de la Mouthe in Les-Eyzies-de-Tayac-Sireuil (Dordogne), hereafter referred to as "Les Eyzies," where in 1895 Emile Rivière found engravings in a gallery that had been blocked by archaeological deposits from the Paleolithic period, indicating that the engravings were also Paleolithic. The following year, François Daleau noted engravings of animals including horses and aurochs in the Grotte de Pair-non-Pair, in the commune of Prignac-et-Marcamps (Gironde), which had been discovered in 1881. The authenticity of Paleolithic cave art was established by discoveries shortly after at Les Combarelles and Font-de-Gaume, both close to Les Eyzies (Dordogne). Two caves are at Les Combarelles, designated Les Combarelles I and II, although only the former is now open to the public. Les Combarelles II and the entrance to Les Combarelles I were excavated by Emile Rivière between 1891 and 1894. However, it was not until 1901 that Denis Peyrony, Henri Breuil, and Louis Capitan entered Les Combarelles I and found hundreds of engravings, many overlapping. Breuil recorded that he had initially identified almost three hundred en-

Figure 1.5.   Engraving of a feline from Les Combarelles cave. Jean Vertut, P. Bahn collection

gravings, and many more were recognized subsequently. The images include stylized female figures and many animals, especially horses and deer, with a particularly striking image depicting a feline (figure 1.5).

The discovery of the engravings at Les Combarelles encouraged Denis Peyrony to visit the nearby La Grotte de Font-de-Gaume to check whether it, too, was decorated. His instinct was correct; the cave was found to be decorated with more than two hundred figures, including more than eighty bison, some rendered in black, brown, and red, dated between 14,000 and 10,000 BC. La Grotte de Font-de-Gaume is now the only decorated cave in France with polychrome paintings that remains open to the public. The discoveries, which suggested the paintings and engravings dated to the Paleolithic period, paved the way for the studies that continue to the present day.

ARCHAEOLOGY IN FRANCE IN THE LATE EIGHTEENTH AND NINETEENTH CENTURIES

The former learned societies of l'Ancien Régime, pre-Revolutionary France, had been dissolved in 1793, along with other royal institutions. Their place was taken by the Institut de France, a learned society, which was established in Paris in 1795 by the Convention nationale, the third government of the

French Revolution. L'Institut de France, which still exists, groups together five Académies: the Académie française, the Académie des inscriptions et belles-lettres, the Académie des sciences, the Académie des beaux-arts, and the Académie des sciences morales et politiques. To some extent this fostered the discussion of archaeology, and in 1799 Pierre Legrand d'Aussy, who had introduced the use of the terms "menhir" and "dolmen" to describe the megalithic monuments in Brittany, presented to the Institut de France a "Memoir on ancient burials . . . and a project for excavations to be carried out in our départements." This proposal did not, however, progress. Indeed, from the end of the eighteenth century until the middle of the nineteenth century, the only officially appointed archaeologist was the curator of the Cabinet des Médailles in Paris, although this role required only a classical education rather than any archaeological experience.

The restoration of the Bourbon monarchy in 1814 did not see a great revival in the promotion of the material remains of French history. However, in 1816 the king ordered the return to the Basilica of Saint-Denis of most of the architectural fragments from the royal tombs. The tombs in the Basilica of Saint-Denis had been desecrated by revolutionaries in 1793, although Alexandre Lenoir succeeded in removing some of the architectural remains, including statues and stained glass. These subsequently were housed in the Musée des monuments français, founded in Paris in 1795 by Lenoir.

The role of Inspecteur général des monuments historiques (inspector general of ancient monuments) had been created by the politician François Guizot in 1830; Ludovic Vitet was the first holder of the post, succeeded by Prosper Merimée. This was followed in 1834 by the foundation by Guizot of a Comité historique, whose role was to compile an inventory of historical monuments. It is apparent, however, that the committee initially was dominated by architects, whose focus was on standing remains.

In 1858 the Emperor Napoleon III convened the Commission de la topographie des Gaules, who undertook excavations on his behalf, including at Merdogne, now known as Gergovie (Puy-de-Dôme) and Alise-Sainte-Reine (Côte-d'Or), the presumed sites of Julius Caesar's battles at Gergovie and Alésia, respectively; and at Bibracte (Saône-et-Loire), where Caesar wrote his *Commentarii de Bello Gallico* (Commentaries on the Gallic War). The Commission de topographie des Gaules also was charged with producing the publication *Dictionnaire archéologique de la Gaule*, although the project was adjourned in 1878 and not revived until 1894.

One of Napoleon III's objectives was to locate Alésia, the site of the crucial battle during the final conquest of Gaul by Gaius Julius Caesar, in the "Gallic Wars" that took place between 58 and 52 BC. In his *Commentarii de Bello Gallico*, Caesar records his final struggle against Vercingetorix, who by 52 BC had become the leader of all of the indigenous tribes from the river Seine in the north to the river Garonne in the southwest. Caesar wrote that the struggle against Vercingetorix culminated in the final battle at Alésia, the capital of the Mandubii tribe, a hill fort where Vercingetorix and his troops had taken refuge. The site of Alésia was not known, and Napoleon III decreed that archaeological excavations should be undertaken on Mont-Auxois, near Alise-Sainte-Reine (Côte-d'Or), which he believed could be identified as Alésia. It is recorded that the imperial administration employed approximately fifty laborers, each of whom was paid three francs per day. Between 1860 and 1862, a team led by Alexandre Bertrand, who was the first secretary of the Commission de la topographie des Gaules, made preliminary excavations on Mont-Auxois. The excavations, which began in June 1861, were directed by Colonel Eugène Stoffel. Stoffel's interest in the campaigns of Julius Caesar was reflected by his 1887 publication titled *Histoire de Jules César*. In 1864 Napoleon III issued an official decree that Alésia was indeed located on Mont-Auxois and, accordingly, he commissioned a colossal statue of Vercingetorix from the sculptor Aimé Millet to overlook the presumed site of the battle (figure 1.6).

In addition, Napoleon III requested excavations at the Gallo-Roman site of Champlieu, in the commune of Orrouy (Oise), close to his palace at Compiègne. The remains at the site, which has been designated a historic monument since 1846, comprise a theater, able to accommodate up to three thousand people, baths, and a sanctuary.

In 1862 Napoleon III also initiated the conversion of the former royal residence at Saint-Germain-en-Laye, which had been in decline during the eighteenth and nineteenth centuries, to be the "Musée des Antiquités celtiques et gallo-romaines." The chateau became a historic monument shortly afterward and was restored to give the appearance it would have had in the reign of King François I, in the first half of the sixteenth century, involving the removal of later additions. This work was planned and begun by the architect Eugène Millet, who formerly had been assistant to Eugène Viollet-le-Duc, the architect who had led the Gothic revival in France. Although restoration work continued at the chateau until 1907, the first exhibition galleries had been opened in 1867 by Napoleon III; Alexandre Bertrand, who had been involved in the initial excavations on Mont-Auxois, became its first curator. By 1898 the museum had more than thirty-five thousand objects in its collection, displayed in thirty-eight galleries. The museum still exists, as the Musée d'Archéologie nationale- Domaine national at Saint-Germain-en-Laye (Yvelines), hereafter referred to as the Musée d'Archéologie nationale (figure 1.7). The museum was founded to house archaeological objects that the Musée du Louvre did not collect, including

Figure 1.6.   Statue of Vercingetorix on Mont-Auxois. Alamy

Figure 1.7. Musée d'Archéologie nationale-Domaine national at Saint-Germain-en-Laye. Alamy

those from the excavations at Alésia and the stone tools collected by Jacques Boucher de Perthes.

It is noteworthy that many of the early prehistorians were self-taught, originally soldiers, clergymen, or wealthy individuals who were prominent in their local communities. Furthermore, those with an interest in the past who had a university education often were students at the French Schools in Athens or Rome, discussed further below, and conducting fieldwork in Greece or Italy rather than excavate in France. One such individual was Charles Ernest Beulé, who, as discussed further in chapter 4, excavated on the Acropolis in Athens and at Carthage. It should be noted, however, that although Alexandre Bertrand had studied at the Ecole française d'Athènes in 1849, his appointment in 1858 as secretary of the Commission de topographie des Gaules apparently gave him the desire to develop archaeology in France.

FRENCH ARCHAEOLOGISTS OVERSEAS IN THE NINETEENTH AND TWENTIETH CENTURIES

The Commission des Sciences et des Arts de l'armée d'Orient was a group of around 150 scholars, artists, scientists, and engineers, collectively known as savants, who accompanied Napoleon Bonaparte's invasion of Egypt between 1798 and 1801. Their findings, including records of archaeological remains, were published in their complete form in 1829 in the *Description de l'Egypte*. Napoleon's commission not only provided a wealth of information about ancient Egypt, it also provided the model for expeditions to Greece, Persia, Algeria, and the Levant.

French overseas schools of archaeology were established from the middle of the nineteenth century; the Ecole française d'Athènes was founded in 1846, followed in 1875 by the Ecole française de Rome. Continuing interest in Egyptian archaeology was reflected with the foundation in 1880 of the Ecole du Caire, which became the Institut français d'archéologie orientale du Caire in 1898. The same year saw the foundation of the Mission archéologique d'Indo-Chine in Saigon, which became the Ecole française d'Extrême-Orient in 1900. The Ecole française d'Extrême-Orient, usually abbreviated to EFEO, now has its headquarters in Paris and, as well as in Vietnam, has centers in India, Thailand, Malaysia, Indonesia, China, Taiwan, South Korea, and Japan. The five French schools of archaeology overseas also include the Casa de Velázquez in Madrid, established in 1928, which evolved from l'Institut français d'Espagne, founded in 1913. It focuses on the archaeology of North Africa.

The network named Instituts Français de Recherche à l'Etranger (French overseas research institutes), usually abbreviated to IFRE, currently consists of twenty-seven institutions and seven branches, operating in thirty-four countries. IFRE is under the joint authority of the Ministère des Affaires étrangères (Ministry of Foreign Affairs) and the Centre national de la recherche scientifique (National Centre for Scientific Research), usually abbreviated to CNRS. There also are 125 French archaeological missions abroad. The IFRE network was begun in the late nineteenth century, with the creation in 1890 of the French Archaeological Mission in Persia, which was the forerunner of the French Institute in Iran. Other overseas institutes and missions include those in Afghanistan, founded in 1923; and in Istanbul, founded in 1930. Decolonization led to new locations for French institutes and missions, including Pondicherry and Ethiopia, both in 1955. Political changes in the late twentieth century led to the foundation of other institutes and missions, including in 1992 of l'Institut français d'études sur l'Asia centrale (Institute for Central Asian Studies) in Tashkent, Uzbekistan.

PROTECTION OF SITES AND MONUMENTS IN FRANCE

In 1913, the Assemblée Nationale passed legislation giving protection to historic monuments. However, this was not comprehensive, and sites as a whole or monuments that were buried were not included in the legislation. Accordingly, archaeological work conducted by individuals was not subject to any control. In addition, public funding for archaeological work was restricted to small grants made by the Comité des travaux historiques, and such excavations largely were conducted under the auspices of learned societies. This had been the case for many years; the excavation of the cemetery at Charnay (Saône-et-Loire), believed to have been the earliest excavation of a Merovingian cemetery, had been funded from 1830 until 1860 by Henri Baudot, a lawyer who was a member of the Academy of Sciences in Dijon (Côte-d'Or). In 1904, the private society known as La Société française des fouilles archéologiques had been founded, as it had been recognized that the French government could not increase funding for archaeological research or excavations. Accordingly, this allowed the instigation of important excavations and research, such as at Trophée des Alpes at La Turbie (Alpes-Maritimes), the Roman baths at the Gallo-Roman town of Gisacum, in the commune of Vieil-Evreux (Eure), Alise-Sainte-Reine (Côte-d'Or), and Saint-Bertrand-de-Comminges (Haute-Garonne).

It was not until 1941, during the Vichy regime, that Jérôme Carcopino, Minister of National Education and Youth, introduced what became known as the Lois Carcopino (Carcopino Laws). The law prohibited any excavations in France, including on one's own land, without a specific permit issued based on scientific and logistic competencies. In addition, it required people to declare any objects they found and enabled the state to undertake excavations on private land, without the owner's permission, albeit with compensation. France was divided into areas known as circonscriptions, each with a director. In addition, the journal *Gallia* was founded to publish the results of excavations.

One result of these changes was that the role professional archaeologists took increased at the expense of amateurs. Within each circonscription was one director for prehistoric archaeology, another for historic archaeology, mostly recruited from universities, notable exceptions being the prehistoric archaeologists Denis Peyrony and Saint-Just Péquart. Since the time of Napoleon III, large sites such as the oppidum of Gergovie had been excavated by nonprofessional archaeologists, often belonging to archaeological societies. However, from 1941, these excavations were taken over by Jean-Jacques Hatt, chair of national archaeology at l'Université de Strasbourg (Bas-Rhin).

The development of rescue archaeology—archaeological work conducted in advance of development—led to the foundation in 1977 of FIAS, Fonds d'intervention pour l'archéologie de sauvetage (Intervention Fund for Rescue Archaeology). The same year saw the adoption of article R.111-3-2 of the Urban Planning Code, which withheld permission for construction if it would jeopardize the preservation of an archaeological site. In 1979, a subdirectorate of archaeology was founded in the Ministry of Culture, and archaeological services were now run as local branches of the Ministry.

In 1973, AFAN, l'Association pour les fouilles archéologiques nationales (National Association for Archaeological Excavations), was created. AFAN's role was taken over by Inrap (Institut national de recherches archéologiques préventives), founded in 2002. Inrap, which currently has over two thousand collaborators and researchers, is the largest archaeological research organization in France. Alongside partners in the public and private sector, it undertakes evaluation and excavation of more than two thousand sites per year in mainland France and its overseas territories.

France was the first country with a government department for underwater archaeology with the founding of Le département des recherches archéologiques subaquatiques et sous-marines (Department of underwater and undersea archaeological research), usually abbreviated DRASSM, based in Marseille. The organization was created in 1966 by André Malraux, then minister for culture in the French government. In 1996, DRASSM merged with the CNRAS: Centre national de la recherche archéologique subaqatique (National Centre for Underwater Archaeological Research), which had been created in 1980 to manage and protect France's cultural heritage in inland waters. In 2010, DRASSM established a preventive conservation unit. DRASSM's original ship *L'Archéonaute*, which mapped around one thousand archaeological sites, was replaced in 2012 by a new vessel named *André Malraux*. Since its creation, DRASSM has excavated around fifteen hundred archaeological sites, ranging in date from prehistory to the present.

France is a signatory of the European Convention for the Protection of the Archaeological Heritage, generally known as the Valetta Convention of 1992, which came into force in 1995. The emphasis of the convention shifted from the perception of threats to the archaeological record predominantly being from unauthorized excavation to that of major construction projects and, in particular, made an obligation for the prior evaluation of a site before development starts. The Convention set guidelines for the funding of excavation and research work and publication of research findings. Another important aspect of the Convention is the requirement for the development of public awareness of archaeological heritage.

In France, preventive archaeology is treated as a necessary element of development. On sites above 3000 square meters, developers pay a fee known as the "redevance d'archéologie préventive" whose purpose is to fund an archaeological evaluation. If the evaluation indicates the likely presence of archeological remains that may be affected by the development, a full excavation would take place.

"ARCHÉOSITES": POPULARIZING ARCHAEOLOGY IN FRANCE

Reconstructions are a familiar feature of archaeology in France, which since the 1970s has fostered the construction of re-creational parks known as "archéosites," whose role is the dissemination of archaeology to the general public. Archéosites usually include extensive re-creations of structures from antiquity, with the aim of educating visitors as much as exercises in experimental archaeology.

A pioneer in this field was the Archéodrome de Beaune opened on the area of Beaune on the A6 autoroute, in the commune of Merceuil

Figure 1.8.   Reconstruction of fortifications at the MuséoParc Alésia. Alamy

(Côte-d'Or). The Archéodrome, which was developed by La Société des Autoroutes Paris-Rhin-Rhône and the regional archaeological service of Bourgogne, opened in 1978 but closed to the public in 2005 as a result of low annual visitor numbers, which had fallen from 250,000 to 40,000. The goal of the site was to demonstrate to visitors various construction methods used up to AD 1000 by re-creations of various types of buildings from the past. One of the best-known reconstructions was a section of the Roman fortifications that would have surrounded Alésia (figure 1.8). One of the reasons given for the demise of the Archéodrome de Beaune was a lack of investment and the failure to update or replace any of the buildings since 1994. A secondary activity at the Archéodrome was its use as a center for experimental archaeology, discussed further below.

Le Parc Samara, which opened in 1983 in the commune of La Chausée-Tirancourt (Somme), was inspired by the Archéodrome de Beaune, but it has proven to be much more successful. It combines a natural park with archaeology, allowing a visit to an excavated oppidum site with the opportunity to see reconstructed buildings. A range of structures from prehistory to the Early Iron Age have been presented—namely, a circular tent based on evidence from the site of Buisson Campin in the commune of Verberie (Oise) to illustrate a hunting camp of the Magdalenian period, and houses from the Neolithic, Bronze Age, and Early Iron Age based on examples from Cuiry-lès-Chaudardes (Aisne), Choisy-au-Bac (Oise), and Glisy (Aisne), respectively. The original reconstruction of an Early Iron Age house was based on an excavated example from Villeneuve-Saint-Germain (Aisne), but it was decided to dismantle it in 2013 and reuse the materials in a new reconstruction. Its replacement was a large house with a ground plan measuring 7.8 meters by 6.6 meters, based on discoveries made at Glisy (Aisne) in 2006 of buildings dating from the end of the fourth century BC. In recent years, Le Parc Samara has hosted an annual event in which archaeologists have conducted various exercises in experimental archaeology. In 2013, three pottery kilns, based on archaeological discoveries from Gallo-Roman sites around Arras (Pas-de-Calais), were reconstructed, and pottery made using Gallo-Roman techniques. The following year, archaeologists re-created Iron Age ovens, used for the boiling of brine, which results in the production of salt. The reconstruction drew on new research as it was based on examples found in 2010 in advance of road construction at the commune of Gouy-Saint-André (Pas-de-Calais). By chance, a few weeks previously a team of archaeologists had found a very similar salt-making workshop at the commune of Saint-Quentin-la-Motte-Croix-au-Bailly (Somme), which confirmed their experimental work.

Also in northern France, Le Parc archéologique Asnapio is situated in the commune of Villeneuve-d'Ascq (Nord). Excavations in advance of construction in the 1970s of the "new town" of Villeneuve d'Ascq revealed remains from the prehistoric and Early Iron Age. The themes of the Parc archéologique, which was first established in 1988 and inaugurated in 2001, partly draw on local archaeological discoveries. As at Le Parc Samara, a range of dwellings have been reimagined, including a tent from the Magdalenian period, based on the excavations of André Leroi-Gourhan at Pincevent (Seine-et-Marne), discussed in chapter 4. As at Le Parc Samara, the Neolithic houses found at Cuiry-lès-Chaudardes (Aisne) provided the model for the reconstructed example at Asnapio, and the reconstructed Bronze Age house was based on a round house found at the site of Haut-de-Clauwiers in the commune of Seclin (Nord). Various Early Iron Age buildings have been re-created, including houses and a granary, plus a reconstructed Gallo-Roman villa. Le Parc archéologique Asnapio also includes reconstructions of medieval buildings.

Local archaeological discoveries are also part of the Parc archéologique européen/Europäischer Kulturpark Bliesbruck-Reinheim, which is partly in the French commune of Bliesbruck (Moselle) and partly in the German municipality of Gersheim (Saarland). Opened in the late 1980s, the park incorporates the site of an Iron Age female burial accompanied by lavish grave goods (the "Celtic Princess of Reinheim"), excavated in 1954, together with several Gallo-Roman buildings, excavation of which has been continuing. Several buildings have been re-created in the park, including the "Tomb of the Celtic Princess," Early Iron Age houses, and partly reconstructed Gallo-Roman buildings, including a villa and baths.

Equally inspired by local archaeology is the Muséoparc Alésia in Alise-Sainte-Reine (Côte-d'Or), spread over an area of seven thousand hectares. The Muséoparc includes the remains of the Gallo-Roman settlement, discussed in chapter 3, and the statue of Vercingetorix by the sculptor Aimé Millet mentioned earlier in this chapter. An interpretation center, housed in a striking cylindrical building designed by the noted French-Swiss architect Bernard Tschumi, opened in 2012 and presents detailed information on the Roman conquest of Gaul and, in particular, the siege at Alésia. A hundred-meter-long section of the Roman fortifications is re-created (figure 1.8), based on the account by Julius Caesar and the excavations conducted at the behest of the Emperor Napoleon III. An archaeological museum is scheduled to open on the site in 2018.

Slightly different in nature is the Coriobona Village Gaulois in the commune of Esse (Charente), founded by the reenactment group Les Gaulois d'Esse in 2003. The aim was to re-create a small oppidum of the first century BC, basing the reconstructed buildings on discoveries from archaeological sites such as Saint-Gence (Haute-Vienne) and Tintignac (Corrèze); the oppidum of Corent (Puy-de-Dôme) is providing the model for the planned "tavern" at Coriobona. Activities demonstrated at Coriobona include plowing, metalwork, textile production, and pottery making.

It is less common for Late Roman and Early Medieval buildings to be reconstructed. An archéosite whose buildings are based on archaeological discoveries on the site is the Archéo'site Les Rues des Vignes, in the commune of Les Rues des Vignes (Nord), which opened to the public in 1991. The original site was excavated between 1979 and 1986, and discoveries included cellars from the Late Roman period, almost 350 Merovingian tombs and postholes from the construction of Carolingian buildings, which have formed the basis of various reconstructions, including a Merovingian necropolis, barn, and workshops, together with a Carolingian settlement whose construction began in 2005.

An archéosite that focuses on the Merovingian period is the Musée des Temps Barbares-Parc archéologique in the commune of Marle (Aisne), which was opened in 1991. The catalyst for the new museum and archéosite was the discovery of two Merovingian cemeteries at the commune of Goudelancourt-lès-Pierrepont (Aisne), to the southeast of Marle. The site was excavated between 1981 and 1987, revealing more than 450 burials dating to the sixth and seventh centuries AD. From 1988, surveys in the area adjacent to the cemeteries discovered habitation sites, including a farm, from the same period. In 1991, a museum opened in Marle, housed in a renovated mill building originally constructed in the twelfth century but damaged in the eighteenth century. The displays of finds from Goudelancourt-lès-Pierrepont include a rare example of a Merovingian decorated stone sarcophagus lid. Reconstructions on the archaeological park, which is located on more than four hectares of land adjacent to the museum, feature Early Medieval buildings, including a Merovingian farmhouse, erected in 1993, based on an example found at Goudelancourt-lès-Pierrepont. When the park was extended in 2006, it was decided to re-create a Frankish village. The buildings are based on discoveries by Didier Bayard during his excavations at the site of Le Gué de Mauchamp in the commune of Juvincourt-et-Damary conducted between 1984 and 1990 in advance of the construction of the A26 autoroute. Unusually, the smaller of the two Merovingian cemeteries at Goudelancourt-lès-Pierrepont, which contained 134 burials, also has been reconstructed.

Le Musée de Préhistoire des Gorges du Verdon in the commune of Quinson (Alpes-des-Haute-Provence) has a second site, the "Village préhistorique de Quinson," situated on the bank of the river Verdon. The "village préhistorique" includes not only reconstructions of five prehistoric structures from France, but also a re-creation of the circle of stones found at Olduvai in Tanzania, which the paleoanthropologist Mary Leakey believed to have been the remains of a hut created from branches secured at their base by stones. The buildings re-created in the "village" includes one of the huts from the site of Terra Amata in Nice (Alpes-Maritimes), discussed in chapter 2, although another, more complete, reconstruction of this type of hut can be seen in Le Musée de Terra Amata in Nice. As at Le Parc archéologique Asnapio, a tent from Pincevent has been reimagined. Two Neolithic dwellings have been reconstructed, one based on the type of houses found at Charavines (Isère), discussed in chapter 2, and the other based on the houses found at the site of Cambous in the commune of Viols-en-Laval (Hérault). Unlike most Neolithic houses, those discovered at Cambous, which date from between 2800 BC and 2400 BC, were made in the dry stone technique. The excavations, which began in 1967, found four groups of houses, each with between eight and ten structures. The archaeological site at Cambous also incorporates a reconstruction of one of the houses. Another reimagined Neolithic structure in the "village préhistorique" is a dolmen tomb, based on those found in the geographical region of Provence in southern France.

Several of the archéosites combine reconstructed buildings, some generic in nature, with demonstrations of ancient technology, including metalworking, pottery making, and weaving. Such archéosites include Le Village Gaulois in the commune of Rieux-Volvestre (Haute-Garonne), which focuses on the Iron Age; and the Parc Archéologique de Beynac in the commune of Beynac-et-Cazenac (Dordogne), which has attempted to re-create Neolithic, Bronze Age, and Early Iron Age life.

Other archéosites concentrate on specific aspects of life in the past, such as the Archéosite de Montans (Tarn). In the first and second centuries AD, Montans was important as one of the production centers of a type of South Gaulish terra sigillata pottery, found in western Gaul and modern-day northern Spain, with smaller quantities in Britain. The focus of the Archéosite de Montans is the reconstruction of the activities of the Gallo-Roman potters who worked in the area.

Archéosites should be distinguished from experimental archaeology projects. In addition to being a tourist attraction, the ultimately ill-fated Archéodrome de Beaune also served as a center for experimental archaeology. The site was used to conduct experimental archaeological activities on a wide range of material, including flint, metal, bone, textiles, and ceramics. In addition, experimental work was done to increase knowledge of ancient construction techniques.

The reconstruction of a Neolithic house from Cuiry-lès-Chaudardes (Aisne) in 1977 was the catalyst for the subsequent foundation of the Centre d'archéologie experimentale in the commune of Chassemy (Aisne) in 1980. One of the early projects was the reconstruction of an Iron Age farm based on excavations undertaken at Villeneuve-Saint-Germain (Aisne), although the Centre probably is best known for a two-year project, conducted since 1981, on experimental agricultural techniques in the Aisne valley during the Neolithic period.

As discussed in chapter 2, an experimental archaeology project was undertaken in 1988 at Lake Chalain (Jura), where two Neolithic houses were constructed, with part of the work carried out using Neolithic technology. The houses are no longer in existence, having collapsed in 2000.

Other reconstructions of Neolithic buildings were undertaken at CEPA (Centre expérimental de préhistoire alsacienne) in the commune of Holtzheim (Bas-Rhin). Experimental archaeological work took place at CEPA until the late 1990s, when the reconstructed houses were destroyed by fire, which signaled the end of the Centre's activities.

A more unusual experimental archaeology program was the reconstruction of a Gallo-Roman barge that had been discovered in 1808 while digging for peat in the commune of Fontaine-sur-Somme (Somme). The barge was excavated by Laurent Joseph Traullé, who was curator of the Museum des antiques in Abbeville (Somme). The barge, dated from pottery and coins to the second century AD, was twelve meters long and three meters wide, and could have carried seven tons of cargo. Although no physical remains of the barge survive, Traullée's description, together with more recent discoveries of similar vessels, have enabled reconstruction by the Ambiani Project.

Interest in the material remains of France's past started in the sixteenth century through chance discoveries investigated by interested and informed individuals. The excavation of the dolmen tomb at Cocherel paved the way for investigation of other archaeological remains, whether visible in the landscape or accidental discoveries. Recording and publishing of such discoveries became more common, leading to the establishment of learned bodies promoting interest in the material remains of the past. By the nineteenth century, the widespread construction of railways and roads throughout France revealed many more archaeological sites. Around the same time, the personal interest of Napoleon III led to a more systematic approach to the remains of the past. In the twentieth century, archaeology in France, both terrestrial and maritime, emerged as a true scientific discipline. The turn of the new millennium has seen no respite in archaeological discoveries in France, in part due to developments in infrastructure, with a statutory requirement to investigate sites prior to development.

2

CAVES TO LAKE VILLAGES

The Archaeology of Prehistoric France

The chapter provides a chronological overview of significant sites and discoveries from the prehistoric period in France. The chronological span is from around 1.3 million years ago until around 2500 BC. The focus is on five main topics from distinct geographical areas of France. The chapter initially will consider evidence of the earliest known humans in France, from the southern sites of Bois-de-Riquet at Lézignan-la-Cèbe (Hérault), Tautavel (Pyrénées-Orientales), and Terra Amata in Nice (Alpes-Maritimes). Second, one of the unusual features of the archaeology of France is the wealth of art from the Upper Paleolithic era, both cave art from sites such as Lascaux (Dordogne), Chauvet (Ardèche), and Pech Merle (Lot); and portable art, such as tools and figurines, with a particularly fine collection in the Musée d'Archéologie nationale in the western suburbs of Paris. The third focus will be the significant archaeological monuments in Brittany, the "megaliths" dating from the Neolithic period at sites such as Carnac and Gavrinis (both Morbihan). Attention then will turn to another type of archaeological site, the Neolithic and Bronze Age "lake villages" such as Charavines (Isère). Finally, discussion will focus on the archaeology of the Bronze Age in France, particularly the hoards found during the period.

Ongoing archaeological research in France continues to reveal important new sites and allows reinterpretations of existing sites. These discoveries are considered in chapter 6.

THE EARLIEST-KNOWN HUMANS

Prior to the sole human presence of *Homo sapiens*, a number of types of humans existed who have left evidence of their presence in modern-day France, from the end of the geological epoch known as the Early Pleistocene. The most recent discovery is from a site known as the Bois-de-Riquet in the commune of Lézignan-la-Cèbe, close to the town of Pézenas (Hérault). The site is in an abandoned basalt quarry, which stimulated interest in the 1990s with the chance discovery of a mammoth tusk. The first systematic excavations by a team led by Laurence Bourguignon took place in 2008 and produced mammal fossils and, most strikingly, stone tools dating from between 1.1 million and 1.3 million years ago.

Other evidence of humans who predate *Homo sapiens* in France has been found at two Lower Paleolithic sites in southern France: La Caune de l'Arago, close to Tautavel (Pyrénées-Orientales); and at Terra Amata in Nice (Alpes-Maritimes).

La Caune de l'Arago, also known as La Grotte de Tautavel, is a cave about three kilometers from the village of Tautavel (Pyrénées-Orientales) on the banks of the River Verdouble, which runs through the Corbières massif. Approximately 150 human fossils have been found in the archaeological levels that date from between 560,000 and 300,000 years ago, especially the levels of 450,000 years ago. Excavations began at the site in 1964 by a team of archaeologists led by Henry de Lumley, the catalyst being the discovery of early stone tools by Jean Abélanet in the previous year. The first major discovery was made in July 1969 of the almost complete fossilized mandible, with six teeth, of a female aged between forty and fifty-five at death. In July 1971, with further fragments found in July 1979, archaeologists discovered part of the fossilized skull of a male aged no more than twenty, estimated to have lived some 450,000 years ago (figure 2.1). The male, identified as *Homo heidelbergensis*, now generally is known as the Homme de Tautavel (Tautavel Man), and his skull fragments have enabled reconstruction of his face. The discoveries at Tautavel led to the establishment of the Musée de Préhistoire de Tautavel Centre Européen de Préhistoire. The main exhibits of the museum are a facsimile of La Caune de l'Arago and a reconstructed skeleton of Tautavel Man, made from fossil remains from Tautavel and casts of fossils found at other sites. Excavations continue at La Caune de l'Arago, and in 2015 a human tooth was found in levels in the cave dating to 560,000 years ago, more than 100,000 years older than the other human fossils in the cave. In addition, archaeologists have found tools made from

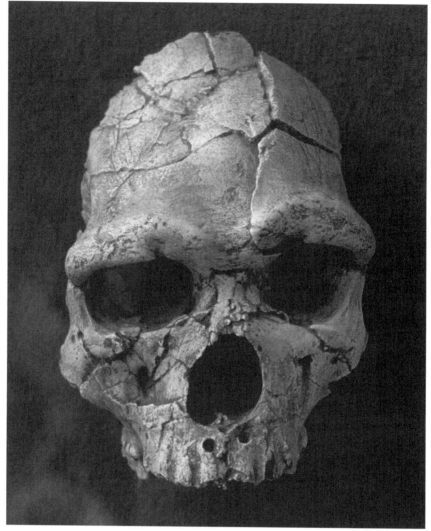

Figure 2.1. Skull of "Tautavel Man." Alamy

animal bones, especially horses, reindeer, and bison, which provide good evidence for the animal species in this part of France during this era.

Henry de Lumley also undertook excavations at two sites that are in the city of Nice (Alpes-Maritimes): Terra Amata and La Grotte du Laza-ret. Terra Amata, which dates to about four hundred thousand years ago, was discovered in 1966 during a construction project at the port of Nice. The site appears to have been a group of shelters on what was a beach in prehistory. Terra Amata is notable for producing early evidence of the domestication of fire and the use of pigment. Around seventy-five pieces of pigment in yellow, brown, red, and purple, many of which have traces of artificial abrasion, plausibly were introduced to the site as they do not occur naturally at Terra Amata. La Grotte du Lazaret is in the eastern suburbs of Nice. The cave, which is thirty-five meters long and between four and fourteen meters wide, was used as a shelter by early types of humans during the later part of the Lower Paleolithic period, between 200,000 and 130,000 years ago.

A site with a long history of occupation is La Grotte de la Baume Bonne at Quinson (Alpes-de-Haute-Provence). The cave was discovered and initially excavated in December 1946 by Bernard Bottet and his son Bertrand. Excavations continued by Henry de Lumley from 1957 to 1968 and recommenced in 1988 under the direction of Jean Gagnepain and Claire Gaillard. The earliest evidence from Baume Bonne dates from the Lower Paleolithic, some four hundred thousand years ago. Occupation continued into the Middle Paleolithic, the evidence being stone tools from this period. Objects found in the cave are displayed at the Musée de Préhistoire des Gorges du Verdon. The cave, a little over an hour's walk from the museum, can be visited.

The people known as "Neanderthals," the species *Homo neanderthalensis*, sometimes are described as our closest extinct human relatives. Evidence of Neanderthals can be found in various sites in France, most notably at Biache-Saint-Vaast (Pas-de-Calais), the Grotte de Bruniquel (Tarn-et-Garonne), La Chapelle-aux-Saints (Corrèze), La Ferrassie (Dordogne), and the Grotte du Renne (Yonne). The importance of the site of Le Moustier in the village of Peyzac-le-Moustier (Dordogne) is discussed further in chapter 4.

Fossilized human remains were found at Biache-Saint-Vaast (Pas-de-Calais) during rescue excavations conducted between 1976 and 1982 on the site of an iron foundry. The many fossilized faunal remains included those of humans from the Middle Pleistocene epoch, between 200,000 and 175,000 years ago. Of particular interest were the three cranial fragments from the same individual, which the excavators named Biache-Saint-Vaast 2 (BSV2), which were identified among other faunal remains in 1986. Analysis of BSV2 indicates a number of anatomical similarities with Neanderthals, suggesting that the people at Biache-Saint-Vaast in this period were members of an early European Neanderthal group. Blache-Saint-Vaast is also a significant site for evidence of the early use of composite tool technology, in particular the attachment of a worked stone tool to a handle. This technology increases the efficiency of the tools, accordingly making foraging and hunting more productive. The debate is whether this technology was devised independently in Europe by Neanderthals or spread from Africa into Europe.

The Grotte de Bruniquel (Tarn-et-Garonne) first was accessed in 1990 by cavers; archaeological work started in the early 1990s, followed by a more recent project that began in 2013. The archaeologists found that the only evidence of human presence in the cave are two round structures made from whole and broken stalagmites associated with four smaller piles of stalagmites and traces of burned bone. The position of the structures deep in the cave is interpreted as the marking of symbolic or ritual space. Dating undertaken by the more recent projects indicates that the largest of the structures was built between about 175,000 and 179,000 years ago. Although no human remains were found, the Neanderthals were the only human people in this area at this time. The investigations at the Grotte de Bruniquel indicate a high level of sophistication, including the use of deep areas within caves, the exploitation of the stalagmites in the caves for construction, and the use of fire.

The fossilized skeleton of a male Neanderthal, named by archaeologists La Chapelle-aux-Saints 1—sometimes referred to colloquially as le Vieillard ("Old Man")—is considered to be the first relatively complete Neanderthal skeleton found in a secure archaeological context. The skeleton was found in August 1908 by Jean Bouyssonie, with his brothers Amédée and Paul and their colleague Louis Bardon in a small limestone cave called Bouffia Bonneval near the commune of La Chapelle-aux-Saints (Corrèze). A large proportion of the skeleton, which is about sixty thousand years old, was retrieved: the well-preserved skull, jaw, most of the vertebrae, several ribs, most of the long bones of the arms and legs, and some of the small bones of the hands and feet. The remains were bought by the Muséum National d'Histoire Naturelle in Paris, where an early reconstruction was undertaken by the geologist, palaeontologist, and physical anthropologist Marcellin Boule. The reconstruction now is considered to be extremely misleading, although it strongly influenced the former popular perception of Neanderthals as primitive and brutish. A new excavation of the Bouffia Bonneval took place in 2011 and 2012. This work enabled archaeologists to conclude that the burial of La Chapelle-aux-Saints 1 was intentional and conducted quite rapidly. In addition, more fragments of La Chapelle-aux-Saints 1 were found, together with the remains of a second adult and two young individuals. A replica of the burial of La Chapelle-aux-Saints 1 is on display at the local museum of Le Musée de La Chapelle-aux-Saints "Jean Bouyssonie."

Another notable group of Neanderthal burials were discovered in the rock shelter at La Ferrassie in Savignac-de-Miremont (Dordogne), found in 1909 by Louis Capitan and Denis Peyrony, with additional excavations conducted by Henri Delporte between 1968 and 1973. Both excavations discovered fossilized human remains of both adults and children, seemingly buried intentionally. The best-preserved remains were those of an adult male, designated La Ferrassie 1. His leg and feet bones indicated that he walked upright, strongly contradicting the incorrect suggestion made by Boule. La Ferrassie also provided an example of Neanderthal art, as a limestone block above one of the child burials was decorated with a series of small hollows known as "cupules" or "cup marks." Excavations at La Ferrassie between 2010 and 2014 and reevaluation of one of the child skeletons from La Ferrassie are discussed in chapter 6.

Perhaps the most striking example of Neanderthal art is the proto-figurine found during excavation at the site of La Roche-Cotard in the commune of Langeais (Indre-et-Loire). The cave of La Roche-Cotard was found in 1912 by François d'Achon, although the proto-figurine was not found until 1975, when further archaeological work revealed an intact occupation layer where about seventy-five thousand years ago people, in all likelihood Neanderthal, stopped on the bank of the river Loire, lighted a fire, and prepared food. The proto-figurine, often referred to as a "mask," is a piece of retouched flint some ten centimeters tall. It has a natural conduit through which a piece of reindeer bone some 7.5 centimeters long carefully was inserted and held in place with small stones, giving the impression of eyes.

Pigments have been found at Neanderthal sites, including red pigment associated with human remains at Le Moustier (Dordogne) and La Chapelle-aux-Saints (Corrèze). At Le Pech-de-l'Azé in the commune of Carsac-Aillac (Dordogne), more than five hundred pieces of pigment, dating from between sixty and fifty thousand years ago, have been found. Most were manganese dioxide, which produces a black and blue pigment; some were pieces of iron oxide. Some were rounded or polished into a shape that suggests their possible use for drawing onto a soft surface.

Important evidence regarding the demise of Neanderthals comes from La Grotte du Renne, one of a group of caves in Arcy-sur-Cure (Yonne). The cave yielded deposits dated between fifty and thirty thousand years ago, containing evidence of both Late Neanderthal and *Homo sapiens* activity. Objects made by Neanderthals included bone awls, the canine teeth of wolf and fox, together with a fossil shell, all with incised grooves suggesting they were used as pendants; a fragment of bone with a wide carved hole; and a fossil with a hole bored through the center.

PALEOLITHIC ART

The Upper Paleolithic period, sometimes referred to as the "Ice Age," is noted for evidence of artistic production. Portable art and jewelry were created from about 40,000 BC, and caves with decorated surfaces are found from around 30,000 BC. However, most of the known art dates to the latter part of the Ice Age, around 10,000 BC. The vast majority of caves with decorated walls have been found in the southwest of France, in the départements of Ardèche, Dordogne, Lot, and Ariège.

Ardèche département: La Grotte Chauvet-Pont d'Arc

The group of paintings in the Grotte Chauvet-Pont d'Arc, near the commune of Vallon-Pont d'Arc (Ardèche), once were thought to be the oldest known cave paintings in France. The cave is close to the natural rock arch created by the river Ardèche known as the Pont d'Arc, which is thought to be the largest natural arch in Europe, standing sixty-six meters high, with a span of thirty-four meters.

The cave was found in December 1994 by three cavers: Jean-Marie Chauvet, after whom the cave was named; Eliette Brunel Deschamps; and Christian Hillaire. It was found in the course of the team's systematic survey of the Ardèche gorge, which they had been conducting since 1991. The team already had located new cave sites, some of which had been decorated in the Paleolithic period. Study of the Grotte Chauvet-Pont d'Arc began in 1998, led by Jean Clottes. Following the deterioration of paintings observed at Lascaux, the cave has never been open to the public, and accordingly a replica cave, known as the Caverne du Pont d'Arc, was constructed close to the original. The question of public access to painted caves and the views on replication, are discussed in chapter 5.

The Grotte Chauvet-Pont d'Arc is very large, around four hundred meters long, and almost certainly had more than one entrance. It can be divided into fifteen discrete areas, with decoration on the walls throughout the cave, apart from the initial section. The most elaborate decoration is in the Salle du Fond, deep in the cave. A large range of animals are depicted, fourteen different species, a greater number than found in the caves at Cosquer (eleven species), Lascaux (nine species), and Niaux (six species). In addition to the animals that appear frequently in other Paleolithic caves, such as horses, bison, and aurochs (a type of early cattle, now extinct), there are images of animals rarely seen elsewhere in cave art, such as lions and cave bears, the latter a species that became extinct between twenty and twenty-five thousand years ago. There is no clear depiction of a complete human figure in the Grotte Chauvet-Pont d'Arc, with the exceptions of the lower part of a female (the so-called Venus), adjacent to a man-bison composite drawing (the so-called Sorcerer).

The paintings fall into two main series, one group predominantly using red pigment; the other, mainly featuring black charcoal. Those rendered in red are located close to the present-day entrance to the cave. This phase also included simple images of animals, including cave bears, reindeer, and mammoth, in red and also black outline. These images are likely to date from the time when humans visited the cave around twenty-eight thousand years ago, although nothing directly indicates that humans ever lived in the cave. Evidence indicates that they used torches and a hearth, samples of which have been dated using AMS (accelerator mass spectrometry) and conventional radiocarbon dating. The cliff face where the modern-day entrance to the cave is situated apparently collapsed between twenty-two thousand and fifteen thousand years ago. Most of the images rendered in black charcoal, including horses, bison, and lions, date to this phase and are located in areas of the cave that are now perceived as deeper due to the relocation of the cave's entrance. Among the earliest may be a series of images of human hands, some rendered by the artist placing his or her hand against the cave wall as a stencil and blowing fluid pigment around the hand, with others being handprints. A fascinating discovery was a single track of footprints made by a child in what is today the deepest gallery of the cave.

Dordogne département

A particularly important group of rock shelters and caves in the Dordogne département are known as the Prehistoric Sites and Decorated Caves of the Vézère Valley, added to UNESCO's World Heritage List in 1979. The commune of Les Eyzies in the Vézère Valley is home to the Musée national de préhistoire, founded by Denis Peyrony in 1913 with the acquisition by the state of the ruined Château des Eyzies. A large new building was opened on the site in 2004, designed by the noted architects Buffi Associés.

The Abri Cro-Magnon in Les Eyzies is the rock shelter that gave its name to a group of early modern humans who lived around twenty-eight thousand years ago in the Upper Paleolithic period and who were first recognized at this site. The rock shelter was discovered in March 1868 during road building when the workmen had discovered fossilized human remains and stone tools. This led to a series of archaeological excavations, begun by Louis Lartet, son of the noted prehistorian Edouard Lartet, whose achievements are discussed in chapter 4. The work was completed in 1907 by Denis Peyrony. The rock shelter was found to have contained the fossilized remains of a total of five humans, four adults and a baby, as well as around three hundred perforated shells. It is generally believed that the humans had been buried deliberately in a single grave. The "type skeleton," named Cro-Magnon 1, is of a male aged under forty at death, and the other remains are fragmentary skeletons of two other adult males, a female, and a newborn baby. In addition, there are cranial fragments of another adult. In April 2014, a site museum opened at the Abri Cro-Magnon.

Another rock shelter in Les Eyzies is the Abri Pataud, which produced fossilized human remains in the course of excavations in the 1950s and 1960s by Hallam L. Movius of the Peabody Museum, Harvard University, in collaboration with the Muséum National d'Histoire Naturelle in Paris. The archaeologists found that the use of the rock shelter had changed over time. From about thirty-five thousand years ago to about twenty-eight thousand years ago, the rock shelter was used for short-term occupation by seminomadic hunter-gatherers. By twenty-eight thousand years ago, erosion had enlarged the rock shelter; by the end of the Gravettian period, about twenty-two thousand years ago, the roof had collapsed, leaving only a narrow passage. Archaeologists found the remains of six individuals who died at the end of the Gravettian period, a discovery that has shed light on funerary practices from this period. Excavations at the Abri Pataud recommenced in 2005, undertaken by the Muséum National d'Histoire Naturelle in Paris.

The Abri de la Madeleine, close to the small town of Tursac, is the "type site" for one of the later phases of the Upper Paleolithic in Western Europe, dating between 15,000 and 10,000 BC. The rock shelter produced many small carvings made from bone and antler, revealed during a series of excavations beginning in 1863 by Edouard Lartet. These excavations subsequently were continued by other archaeologists including Denis Peyrony, whose most spectacular find came to light in 1926. This was the burial of a small child, aged between two and four years, who died around 8,000 BC and now is popularly called "l'enfant de la Madeleine." The child was buried in the rock shelter accompanied by around fifteen hundred items of jewelry made from shells, bone, and teeth, and may have been wearing clothing decorated with beads made from shells. The burial of the child known as "l'enfant de la Madeleine" is now in the Musée national de préhistoire at Les Eyzies.

The Grotte de Lascaux, located two kilometers southeast of Montignac, undoubtedly is the most famous of the decorated caves. The cave is said to have been a chance discovery in September 1940 by four young boys who followed their dog into an opening that led to the cave. The importance of the paintings was recognized immediately by archaeologists Denis Peyrony, Jean Bouyssonie, André Cheynier, and Henri Breuil. It was fortunate that Breuil, who at that time was a professor in Paris, was staying at Brive, a little over thirty kilometers from Lascaux, at the time of the discovery.

The discovery of the Grotte de Lascaux initially was reported by Breuil in the journal *Nature* and in a preliminary report made to the Académie des Inscriptions et des Belles Lettres. It was more widely known in English-speaking countries through an article that appeared in the *Illustrated London News* in February 1942. Scientific excavation of Lascaux began in

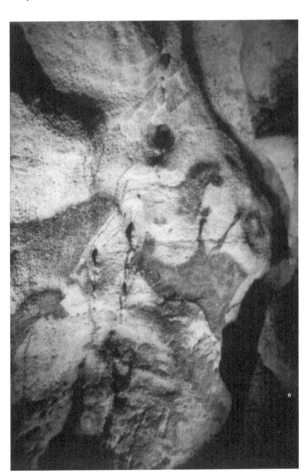

Figure 2.2. The "Falling Horse," La Grotte de Lascaux. Jean Vertut, P. Bahn collection

1947, when charcoal was recovered for radiocarbon dating, the first from a Paleolithic decorated cave. Between 1952 and 1963 an inventory of images was compiled by André Glory.

The Grotte de Lascaux's range of galleries have been given modern names: La Salle des Taureaux, Le Diverticule Axial, Le Passage, L'Abside, Le Puits, Le Nef, and Le Diverticule des Félins. They contain approximately fifteen hundred individual representations of animals, the majority engraved, some painted, together with "signs"—motifs that are either abstract or geometric in form. A wide range of animals are shown, particularly aurochs, horses, and deer, although more than half of the animal images are found in a single area, known as L'Abside, with a large number, albeit poorly preserved, in Le Passage.

The first large room in the cave, known as La Salle des Taureaux, is arguably the most spectacular of all the painted galleries at seventeen meters long, six meters wide, and seven meters high. The room is named from the images of a series of massive bull aurochs, more than five meters long. The aurochs were painted at a high level in black outline, often superimposed over older images. An intriguing image in the Salle des Taureaux is an indeterminate composite creature, misleadingly nicknamed "La Licorne" (unicorn) as it has two horns, with possible human characteristics. The series of animal images, which also include horses, stags, a few bison, and a single bear, are painted as though moving toward the Diverticule Axial, a narrow area that leads from the Salle des Taureaux.

The Diverticule Axial is decorated with aurochs, deer, wild goats, and horses, and includes the "Falling Horse" (figure 2.2), painted around a rock in a very skilfull manner. The paintings and engravings on the walls of Le Passage, which also leads from the Salle des Taureaux, of 286 animal figures—mostly of horses—that were recorded by André Glory are quite difficult to see. The number of animals in this gallery is exceeded only by L'Abside, which leads from it. The walls of L'Abside are covered with more than one thousand engravings and paintings, both animal figures and signs. The 250 recognizable animal figures include 125 horses, 70 deer, 38 cattle, and 17 ibex.

This leads to Le Nef, which contains some of the most famous images in the entire cave. Unlike other parts of the cave, where the lower part of the wall is distinguished from the ceiling by a high ledge or cornice, Le Nef has a deep recess at the back of the ledge. Nearly eighty animal figures have been recorded in this section, among which is a depiction of five deer, seemingly swimming with their heads above the water; a series of seven ibex; and a pair of bison facing in opposite directions with their crossed back legs giving the impression that one is closer than the other. Le Panneau de l'Empreinte has engraved and painted horses and bison, and a panel with a large black aurochs. These two latter sections include grid-like rectilinear symbols depicted below the animals. It is clear that all of the panels in Le Nef focus on several images of a particular species. The only section of the main galleries at Lascaux that apparently has no decoration is La galerie du Mondmilch, an extension of Le Nef, whose floor and lower walls are covered with a coating of friable white calcite popularly known as "mondmilch" (moon milk). Leading from Le Nef is a corridor known as Le Diverticule des Félins, which is decorated with engravings of lions. Also there are engravings and a few paintings of bison, horses, female deer, ibex, and signs, including some checkerboard designs.

La Grande Diaclase and Le Puits lead from L'Abside, although both would have been difficult to access. One wall of Le Puits is painted with figures of a human lying dead in front of a severely wounded bison, with a bird (or perhaps a sculpted spear thrower) and rhinoceros facing in the opposite direction. A horse's head is painted on the opposite wall. Analysis suggests that the pigment used for the rhinoceros, a species not depicted elsewhere in the cave, is sufficiently different to show that the scenes were not painted at the same time.

In addition to the wall paintings, around one thousand objects have been found in the cave, the most fascinating objects arguably being those used by the people who painted the cave, including lamps, grinding equipment for the minerals used to make pigments, hollowed stones still containing pigment, and around 160 fragments of the minerals themselves. Red and black, the dominant colors found in the paintings, were made from naturally occurring minerals, including red ochre, a form of hematite, and goethite to render red; and manganese oxide, as well as charcoal, to render black. Large areas of the walls, especially in the Salle des Taureaux and the Diverticule Axial, were covered with a thin layer of white calcite, which made the colored figures stand out.

The period of use of Lascaux has been very difficult to date, principally because the contents of the cave were cleared in 1948 without any archaeological investigation having been made. However, wood charcoal from the floor of Le Passage has been radiocarbon dated to 17,190 years ago, with another charcoal sample taken from Le Puits dated somewhat later, to 15,516 years ago. Although the conventional view is that the paintings and engravings at Lascaux were made in a single period of occupation, more recent thinking favors the view that it is likely that Lascaux was in use over a number of different periods.

Lascaux cave was opened to the public in 1948 and attracted large numbers of visitors. However, the decision was made to close the cave to the public in April 1963 due to the extreme deterioration of the paintings. To cater to public interest, a facsimile of the cave, known as Lascaux II, was begun in the early 1970s and opened to the public in 1983. In addition, an exhibition known as Lascaux III was devised; it primarily displays paintings not included in Lascaux II and has traveled to several destinations worldwide. Lascaux IV, more formally known as the Centre International d'Art Pariétal (CIAP), is a new facsimile of the cave that opened in winter 2016 and is discussed further in chapter 5.

Also in the Vézère Valley is the only decorated cave in France with polychrome paintings that remains open to the public: the Grotte de Font-de-Gaume, whose significance is discussed further in chapter 1.

Two of the caves in the Dordogne, Bernifal, close to Meyrals and Rouffignac, are noted for images of the now-extinct mammoth. In particular, the cave system at Rouffignac, more than eight kilometers long, contains at least 160 depictions of mammoths, approximately one-third of all known mammoth depictions in caves.

Lot département

Several decorated caves are located in the river valleys of the Lot and the Célé, but only two are open to the public: Les Grottes de Cougnac and La Grotte du Pech Merle.

Les Grottes de Cougnac, near Gourdon (Lot), was discovered in 1949 and 1952, although only one of the caves is decorated. The paintings were made using red ochre, almost always in outline, and depict mammoths, ibex, possible human figures, and, most striking, three megaloceros, a type of giant deer. It is notable that in many cases the ancient cave painters took advantage of the natural shapes of the cave wall, such as an image of an ibex whose legs were formed by natural fissures in the walls of the cave.

La Grotte du Pech Merle, near Cabrerets (Lot), southeast of Cougnac, is equally striking. The cave was discovered in 1914 by two students, who found the chamber later called the Salle Rouge. In 1922, the son of the owner of the land where the cave is located and his friend discovered the Salle Blanche and alerted the Abbé Amédée Lemozi, priest at Cabrerets, who had a great interest in prehistory. Later that year, further chambers were discovered. The cave, which extends for about two kilometers, has been open to the public since 1924, when an artificial entrance and walkway were created.

The decoration dates to two phases between twenty-eight thousand and twenty-two thousand years ago. The most renowned painting from the earlier phase of decoration is a scene about four meters long showing two horses, partly overlapping. Their coats are rendered by a series of black spots surrounded by images of stencils of human hands. The black charcoal pigment of one of the horses has been radiocarbon dated to more than twenty-four thousand years ago. The later phase of decoration included that found in the Chapelle des Mamouths, an alcove three meters high and seven meters long on the south side of the main chamber known as La Salle Préhistorique. The decoration includes the Frise Noire, a series of drawings of animal figures in black outline, predominantly mammoths, along with bison, aurochs, and horses. A small number of engravings are considered to be from the final phase of decoration and include the head of a bear. It appears that the Grotte du Pech Merle was never inhabited, the scant evidence of human presence indicated by the remains of twelve footprints of an adolescent or small adult, pointing in two directions, deep in the cave. The Musée Amédée Lemozi, named in honor of the Abbé Lemozi, is near the cave entrance. In 1934 he founded a prehistoric museum from his private collection, which provides an introduction to the prehistory of the Quercy region of southwest France, as well as the cave paintings.

Ariège département

One of the most accessible caves is the Grotte du Mas d'Azil (Ariège), a natural tunnel, 420 meters long and 50 meters wide, which was occupied from about 30,000 BC (figure 2.3). The D119 road from Carcassonne (Aude) to Lescure (Ariège) runs through the middle of the cave. The building of the road required embankments, whose construction revealed archaeological remains. The first scientifically organized excavations were conducted between 1887 and 1897 by Edouard Piette, who found stone tools and portable art, including examples of "galets peints" (so-called Azilian pebbles), discussed in chapter 5. In addition, Piette believed he had identified a new distinct culture, which he named the "Azilian era," which followed the Magdalenian. Further excavations by l'Abbé Henri Breuil in 1901 and 1902 revealed the first paintings and carvings in the cave. Joseph Mandement continued investigations between 1938 and 1958, discovering the human skull known as the "crâne de Magda" in 1949, which is now in the museum of Le Mas d'Azil. The results of new research at the Grotte du Mas d'Azil, announced in 2015, revealed that the cave was occupied from

Figure 2.3. Entrance to La Grotte du Mas d'Azil. Alamy

thirty-five thousand years ago, much earlier than previously known, in the Aurignacian period.

Access through the cave is facilitated by a series of staircases, where the galleries have been given modern names, some of which reflect natural or perceived features ("silex" [flint], "temple" [temple], "ours" [bear]), whereas others (Piette, Breuil, Dewoitine-Mandement) are named after archaeologists or, in the case of Dewoitine, an aircraft manufacturer who considered making planes in the cave in World War II. The areas of the cave with painted walls are not open to the public to limit their deterioration, although reproductions are on display in the museum in Le Mas d'Azil.

The majority of the finds from the Grotte du Mas d'Azil were collected by Edouard Piette and are now in the collection of the Musée National d'Archéologie nationale. Later finds were moved from the cave to the museum in the main square of town of Le Mas d'Azil, with a much smaller display in the interpretation center in the cave itself, which opened in 2013. However, the archaeologists have left a few objects in situ, such as the skull of a cave bear and mammoth teeth.

A small group of archaeological finds from the Grotte du Mas d'Azil were acquired by the town and initially exhibited in the Musée Ladeveze. The collection was expanded considerably in 1965 with the acquisition of the collection of objects excavated in the cave by Saint-Just Péquart between 1936 and 1944. In 1981 a new museum was opened on its present site in the main square of Le Mas d'Azil, now known as the Musée de la Préhistoire. The displays, which extend over three floors, include examples of the "galets peints" (so-called Azilian pebbles), whose simple designs painted in red ochre encouraged the widespread forgeries discussed in chapter 5. Other finds from the Grotte du Mas d'Azil include the "crâne de Magda," which are the only human remains found in the cave. The crâne de Magda is a human skull, without lower jaw or teeth, of a young woman aged between fifteen and twenty. A disc made from deer bone was found over her left eye, another near the skull. The woman was given the name Magda after the Magdalenian period when the cave was in use. The skull reportedly was found mixed with animal bones rather than given a separate burial. A decorated spear thrower, a type of hunting tool, is another renowned find from the cave. The spear thrower is carved from deer antler in the shape of a fawn turning its head toward two birds. The object is very similar to a spear thrower found in the Grotte de Bédeilhac, discussed later in this chapter. The top floor of the museum, in a display opened in 2011, gives the visitor the opportunity to see reproductions of the paintings and engravings in parts of the Grotte du Mas d'Azil that are not open to the public.

The Grotte de Niaux, in the Vicdessos valley, consists of a series of chambers and passageways, more than thirteen hundred meters long with the lateral galleries adding a further six hundred meters. The paintings at Niaux had been known since at least the nineteenth century, although their age and significance were not realized until study of the paintings in the gallery of the cave named the "Salon Noir," discovered in September 1906 by Commander Moland and his two teenage sons. The paintings came to the attention of Emile Cartailhac, a prehistorian from the University of Toulouse, who, together with Henri Breuil, published a partial survey in 1908. More recently, the images in the cave were recorded systematically by Jean Clottes and Denis Viatou between 1980 and 1981. The vast majority of animal figures in the cave, together with more than one-third of all of the abstract signs, are found in the Salon Noir, nine hundred meters from the entrance, and so called because of the color of the drawings using primarily charcoal. With one exception, all figures are rendered in black, with only a few signs in red. The animal images in the "Salon Noir" are dominated by bison, as well as deer, ibex, and horses. In addition to the walls, number of engravings are on the floor of this part of the cave. A full-size reproduction of the paintings in the Salon Noir is displayed at the nearby Parc de la Préhistoire at Tarascon-sur-Ariège.

The Grotte de la Vache, also in the Vicdessos valley, was opened to the public in 1979. Initially, it was excavated by Félix Garrigou in 1860 and more recently by Romain Robert, in excavations which took place over a period of twenty years, concluding in 1964. Robert's most spectacular find was the "Salle Monique," which he interpreted as a camp of prehistoric hunters. This room alone yielded more than 200,000 finds from the Magdalenian period, including around 143,000 animal teeth and bones. Other finds comprised about 36,000 stone tools, about 2,000 spear throwers, some 300 harpoons made from deer antler, and about 300 bone needles. Robert also found about 200 animal teeth and shells that had been pierced to act as jewelry, together with 220 pieces of portable art. There is no site museum at the Grotte de la Vache, and the finds are now in the Musée National d'Archéologie nationale-Domaine national.

The Grotte de Bédeilhac was first recorded by Marcorelle, who visited the cave in 1773 and in 1776 published his description of his "underground journey" in his book *Voyage souterrain, ou, Description des grottes de Lombrive et de Bédeilhac.* However, the first archaeological exploration did not take place until 1906, when l'Abbé Henri Breuil discovered in the "large gallery" a painting of a bison dating from the Magdalenian period, the first to be found in the Ariège département. This stimulated interest in the cave, and other archaeologists followed Breuil, discovering approximately one hundred images, mostly engraved. Unusually, some of the engravings were made on the soft floor of the cave. As mentioned above, one of the most notable discoveries in the Grotte de Bédeilhac is a spear thrower in the form of a fawn looking at a bird, which is very similar to a spear thrower from the Grotte du Mas d'Azil.

Apart from archaeology, the cave became famous in 1929 when it was the location of one of the first films made underground. In addition, this cave, as well as the Grotte du Mas d'Azil, was considered by Emile Dewoitine as the possible site for the manufacture of aircraft during World War II, although there is no substance in the rumor that the cave was used as a Nazi airbase in World War II. However, a small tourist plane was landed in the cave in 1972 by the test pilot Georges Bonnet. Bonnet repeated the feat in 1974 during filming of the dramatization of the novel *Le Passe Montagne* by Christian Bernadac. A replica of the plane is displayed close to the entrance of the cave. It is likely, however, that the leveling of the entrance to the cave led to the destruction of much archaeological evidence.

Sculpted Reliefs

An unusual type of Ice Age art are sculpted bas-reliefs, notable examples of which can be found at the rock shelters known as Le Roc-aux-Sorciers, the Abri du Cap Blanc, and the Abri du Poisson, the latter discussed further in chapter 5.

Le Roc-aux-Sorciers, near the commune of Angles-sur-l'Anglin (Vienne), was first investigated in 1927 by Lucien Rousseau, and the sculpted frieze excavated by Suzanne de Saint-Mathurin and Dorothy Garrod between 1950 and 1957. The exposed section of the frieze, which was cut into fine-grained limestone, is at least eighteen meters long and 2.5 meters high, and it has been suggested that it would originally have been in daylight. The decoration of the frieze consists of animal and human figures depicted at two levels. A facsimile of the frieze is displayed at the Centre d'Interprétation de la Frise Magdalénienne at Angles-sur-l'Anglin; some of the sculpted fragments, which apparently fell from the cave walls, are in the collection of the Musée d'Archéologie Nationale.

Another example of a sculpted frieze, although on a smaller scale than that at the Roc-aux-Sorciers, was found at the Abri du Cap Blanc, a rock shelter in the commune of Marquay (Dordogne). The relief frieze, which depicts a series of horses, bison, and deer, was discovered in 1909 by Dr. Gaston Lalanne, a medical doctor from Bordeaux. At the nearby rock shelter known as the Abri de Laussel, Lalanne also discovered the famous figure known as the "Venus of Laussel." The figure is around twenty-five thousand years old and was found carved in relief into a block of previously fallen limestone. The "Venus," which is forty-five centimeters high, is shown naked, holding a curved object. The figure originally was colored red with ochre, of which some traces remain. Other carvings from the same block as the Venus depicted additional female figures. All were removed to Bordeaux, where they entered the collections of the Musée d'Aquitaine in Bordeaux (Gironde). The museum also has in its collection a cast of the "Vénus déhanchée" ("Ungainly Venus"), the original of which was sold to a Berlin museum in 1912 and destroyed in World War II.

In 1911, further excavation at the Abri du Cap Blanc to install protection for the carved animal frieze revealed a human skeleton, which was lifted by Louis Capitan and Denis Peyrony. The skeleton was found two to three meters away from the frieze, lying on its left side, in a crouched position, immediately below a hearth from the Magdalenian period. In 1926 the skeleton was acquired in New York by Henry Field for display in the Field Museum in Chicago. For many years it was described as "Magdalenian

Figure 2.4.   Clay relief showing two bison from Le Tuc d'Audoubert. Jean Vertut, P. Bahn collection

Girl," although now it is considered to be the skeleton of an adult woman. A cast of the skeleton, including a cast of the rare, small ivory object found in the abdomen area of the skeleton, has been installed in its original findspot in the Abri du Cap Blanc.

Clay reliefs or figures from this period are exceptionally rare. Well-preserved clay reliefs were found by three brothers, Max, Jacques, and Louis Bégouën, in 1912 in the Tuc d'Audoubert cave in the commune of Montesquieu-Avantès (Ariège). They take the form of two bison, sixty-three centimeters and sixty-one centimeters long, sculpted in high relief, and probably date between 15,000 BC and 10,000 BC (figure 2.4). The only known example of a clay figure was found in the cave at Montespan-Ganties (Haute-Garonne), which is also noted for the clay reliefs decorating its walls. The figure, which was found in 1923, depicts a bear with no head. It is sixty centimeters high and one meter long, and it has been estimated to have been made from about seven hundred kilograms of clay.

Bouches-du-Rhône département: La Grotte Cosquer

Unlike the majority of decorated caves that are found in the southwest of France, the Grotte Cosquer is close to Marseille. The entrance to the cave, in the steep-walled inlet known as the Calanque de Morgiou, now is submerged thirty-seven meters below sea level, the only known painted cave with an entrance below modern-day sea level. The cave was discovered in 1985 by the diver Henri Cosquer, but the paintings were not reported until 1991. The main period of archaeological excavation of the cave was in 2002 and 2003, by a team led by Jean Courtin.

The part of the cave that is above the water line measures about seventy meters by fifty-five meters. Within the cave archaeologists found paintings, engravings, a few stone tools, and charcoal from fires. The images, probably executed between 19,500 and 18,000 years ago, consist of more than two hundred geometric signs, and almost 180 depictions of animals, with eleven separate species represented: horses, bison, aurochs, ibex, chamois, saiga antelope, red deer, megaloceros, felines, birds, and monk seal, the latter two reflecting the cave's location. Three figures, each about twenty-six centimeters long, are thought to represent great auks, the flightless birds that were once found off the Mediterranean coast of France. In addition, the cave has more than sixty stencils of human hands, made by both adults and children, some of which were made using red pigment. The majority of the animal figures were engraved, with a small proportion painted in black. More paintings undoubtedly existed originally, as much of the network of caves is now submerged, with the consequent destruction of any paintings.

Portable Art

Other artistic activity that has survived in the Ice Age archaeological record are examples of mobiliary, or portable art, the most famous of which are female figurines made from mammoth ivory.

The Dame de Brassempouy, sometimes called the Dame à la capuche, is one of the most famous works of portable art of the Upper Paleolithic period (figure 2.5). It is a rare depiction of human facial features and detailed hairstyle from the Ice Age. Traditionally interpreted as depicting a female, the object's name derives from its findspot, the Grotte du Pape at Brassempouy (Landes). Only 365 millimeters high, it was made in around 21,000 BC. Now part of the collections of the Musée d'Archéologie nationale, it was formerly in the collection of Edouard Piette, who bequeathed it to the museum in 1904. This collection consists of objects of prehistoric art discovered by Piette during the course of excavations undertaken from 1871. In addition, the Piette collection includes a group of figurines found in the Grimaldi caves on the Ligurian coast of Italy in around 1880 by an M. Julien and acquired by Piette in 1896. It should be noted, however, that some scholars have raised doubts about the authenticity of the "Venus"

Figure 2.5. "La Dame de Brassempouy." *Jean Vertut, P. Bahn collection*

figurines from the Grimaldi caves as well as the Dame de Brassempouy. The findspot of the Dame de Brassempouy was at a site where workers were rewarded for individual discoveries. This circumstance and the very unusual features of this object are the reasons why some have raised questions regarding its authenticity.

Another notable female figure is the "Venus of Lespugue," made between 24,000 BC and 22,000 BC. Standing 150 millimeters tall, the figure was found in 1922 in the Rideaux cave at Lespugue (Haute-Garonne). The archaeologist was René de Saint-Périer, who excavated the Grotte de Gouërris and the Abri des Harpons from 1924 until 1926. The figure is notable for the depiction of clothing in the form of a skirt supported by a belt present only at the back of the figure. It has been suggested that the corded appearance of the skirt indicates it was made from plant fibre. The many modern-day reproductions of this figure are testimony to its continuing appeal, and the artist Pablo Picasso owned two copies of the Venus of Lespugue, one in its present condition and one as it would have appeared when intact.

Other examples of portable art are personal ornaments fashioned from teeth, bone, or shell; or carved tools such as the decorated spear thrower in the shape of a fawn turning its head toward two birds found at the Grotte du Mas d'Azil, with a similar example with a single bird from the Grotte de Bédeilhac. Another example is the "bullroarer" from the Grotte de la Roche de Birol, near the commune of Lalinde (Dordogne). This is a flat piece of reindeer antler, eighteen centimeters long and four centimeters at its widest point, decorated with incised designs and colored with red ochre. It is likely that the perforation at one end allowed a cord to be attached. This would cause a whirring noise when the bullroarer was spun.

THE MESOLITHIC AND NEOLITHIC PERIODS IN FRANCE

The end of the Ice Age, which signals the beginning of the period known as the Mesolithic, is marked by a rise in temperature, which caused a change to the coastline of modern-day France, most notably the flooding of La Manche (the English Channel). In France, the Mesolithic period is considered to begin around 9600 BC and last until around 6000 BC.

More complex funerary customs are more visible in the archaeological record of the Mesolithic period. The sites of Téviec and Hoëdic (Morbihan), both now on small islands in the bay of Quiberon in the administrative region of Brittany, have produced evidence of elaborate burial practices.

Téviec and Hoëdic, which each occupy only two hundred square meters, were excavated in the late 1920s and early 1930s by Marthe and Saint-Just Péquart; they were in use toward the end of the Mesolithic period. One of the most notable burials was found at Téviec and contained the remains of two females aged between twenty-five and thirty-five, with deer antlers placed over their bodies. Offerings included jewelry made from shells and flint projectile points. The grave was excavated in a single piece and is now on display at the Muséum d'histoire naturelle de la ville de Toulouse (Haute-Garonne).

The Grotte des Perrats near the commune of Agris (Charente), also mentioned in chapter 3 as the findspot of an elaborate Iron Age helmet, produced evidence generally interpreted as indicating that cannibalism was practiced, at least at this site. Faunal remains in the cave included those of at least eight humans (five adults and three children) alongside other animals and birds apparently killed for food. The humans had been dismembered and probably eaten, their skulls and long bones opened for their contents.

An unexpected discovery from the Mesolithic period is a skeleton from the site of Combe Capelle, in the commune of Saint-Avit-Sénieur (Dordogne). Excavation at the site by Otto Hauser in 1909 revealed the skeleton of a man aged between forty and fifty, buried with grave goods including a necklace of pierced snail shells, and generally believed to have dated from the Ice Age. Hauser sold the skeleton to the Museum für Vor- und Frühgeschichte in Berlin, and at one time it was believed to have been lost in 1945. However, it is now apparent that the skull and necklace, together with the skull from the burial designated Le Moustier 1 (discussed further in chapter 1) had been removed to the Soviet Union in 1945 and returned to the German Democratic Republic in 1958, together with other art objects. The skull from Combe Capelle remained "lost" until parts of the skull were rediscovered in a museum store in Berlin in 2001, with further fragments identified in 2003, enabling the skull to be largely reassembled (Accession number Va 3798a). Dating of one of the teeth revealed the skull to date from around ninety-five hundred years ago, in the Mesolithic period and, accordingly, much more recent than previously considered.

The Neolithic period, considered to begin in France around 6000 BC and extend until around 2200 BC, is marked in the archaeological record by the abandonment of a nomadic way of life, the adoption of the use of pottery containers, and a change in stone tool technology, with the appearance of polished or ground stone axs.

The archaeology of Brittany is renowned for the large number of Neolithic monuments around the Gulf of Morbihan ("little sea" in the Breton language) in an area of around three hundred square kilometers, such as Gavrinis and the group of monuments around Carnac-Ville (both Morbihan). The monuments take the form of menhirs (standing stones, single or in a group, the latter in a linear alignment or circular arrangement), dolmens (burial chambers), tumuli (burial chambers covered by earth), and passage graves, consisting of a burial chamber accessed by a long, narrow passage.

The monuments are often termed "megalithic," from the Greek language and literally meaning "large stone": very appropriate, when one considers that the single stone known as the Grand Menhir Brisé (figure 2.6) is estimated to weigh three hundred tons. The visibility of the monuments in the landscape attracted antiquarian interest from the early eighteenth century, with the first extensive excavation of Carnac alignments taking place in the middle of the nineteenth century. The precise function of the monuments is unclear, although it seems likely that the standing stones marked ritual complexes, the locations of which were sometimes subsequently used as funerary monuments.

One of the earliest passage graves, which was constructed around 4400 BC, is the monument known as the Cairn de Barnenez, near Plouezoc'h (Finistère) on the Kernéléhen peninsula. It gained its name from the huge cairn made of small stones, some seventy-two meters long and up to eight meters high, which covered the entire tomb. The Cairn de Barnenez has eleven separate chambers, each of which is approached from the exterior via a separate passageway.

The most famous group of megalithic monuments are close to Carnac-Ville (Morbihan), with at least eleven "alignments" within eight kilometers of Carnac. The monuments, conventionally described as alignments, are rows of standing stones arranged in a series of parallel lines and often

Figure 2.6.   Le Grand Menhir Brisé, Locmariaquer. istock, 153535383

ending in an "enclosure" formed of upright stones marking out an oval or rectangular area. The alignments were constructed over a period of approximately five hundred years, beginning just before 3000 BC and ending around 2500 BC. The largest surviving alignment is at Kezerho, the most westerly of the Carnac alignments at Carnac-Plage, which is more than two thousand meters long and consists of a total of more than eleven hundred standing stones in ten rows. To the northeast of Kezerho is the alignment at Le Ménec, only a ten-minute walk from Carnac-Ville. The alignment is around twelve hundred meters long and has more than one thousand standing stones arranged in ten parallel rows measuring one hundred meters at its widest point. A single stone, much taller than its neighbors at around 3.5 meters high, is popularly known as the "Géant du Ménec" (the Giant of Ménec). The monument at Kermario (figure 1.3), to the east of Le Ménec, is about one thousand meters long, with more than one thousand stones in seven main rows and three partial rows. The alignment extends over the tertre (low burial mound) at Le Manio, strong evidence that the alignments at Kermario (and, indeed, elsewhere) were not built as a single event but evolved over time. Just to the south stands the Géant du Manio, a single standing stone more than six meters high, the tallest in the Carnac area. An information center is at Kermario, together with a footbridge that enables visitors to see the whole alignment, particularly informative now that access to the main alignments is restricted. East of Kermario are the alignments at Kerlescan, where a group of 594 standing stones in thirteen rows, 880 meters long and 139 meters wide, leads to a semicircular enclosure of thirty-nine stones. Further east is the small alignment of Petit Menée. An even smaller alignment is at Sainte-Barbe, near the commune of Plouharnel (Morbihan), formed of only four standing stones.

Other Neolithic monuments, both dolmens (burial chambers) and tumuli (burial chambers covered by earth), can be seen around Carnac-Ville and Carnac-Plage. Dolmens are found at Mané-Kerioned, with elaborate carvings; Rondossoc, comprising three underground chambers; Crucuno; and Mané-Croch. Tumuli in this area include the Tumulus Saint-Michel and Tumulus de Kercado. The Tumulus Saint-Michel, which contains two burial chambers, dates from the Early Neolithic period, about 4500 BC, and is more than one hundred meters long and about ten meters high. When excavated, the chamber was found to contain fine polished axs made of stone including jadeite, the latter considered prestige objects. Although the tumulus is no longer open to the public, it is worth climbing the tumulus not only to visit the Chapelle Saint-Michel but also to enjoy the view of the megaliths, together with the small islands in the Gulf of Morbihan.

The nearby Tumulus de Kercado also dates from the Early Neolithic period and is notable for the carvings on the stones that form the burial chamber inside the tumulus.

The village of Locmariaquer (Morbihan), east of Carnac at the entrance to the Gulf of Morbihan, is home to a group of megalithic monuments known as the "Ensemble mégalithique de Locmariaquer." The group consists of the tumulus of Er-Grah, the exceptionally large standing stone known as the Grand Menhir Brisé, and the Table des Marchands (figure 1.1), a Middle Neolithic passage grave. The tumulus of Er-Grah was originally two hundred meters long and is an example of the type of tumuli known as "Carnac Mounds," found at several sites around the Gulf of Morbihan. The Grand Menhir Brisé is the most spectacular of the Locmariaquer group. It is no exaggeration to say that it is one of the greatest prehistoric monuments in Europe. The Grand Menhir Brisé is a massive single stone, by far the largest known megalith from prehistoric Europe. Originally, it was more than twenty meters high and weighed more than 350 tons, but now is broken into four pieces. The menhir has an image of an ax carved on one of its sides. It is believed that the menhir was erected in the fifth or early fourth millennium BC. The type of granite from which the menhir was carved is from a quarry twelve kilometers away from Locmariaquer, and the transport of the stone to its present site would have involved many people. Although not as large as the Grand Menhir Brisé, other colossal standing stones are in the area around the Gulf of Morbihan. Furthermore, evidence is that further large standing stones, now no longer present, were close to the Grand Menhir Brisé, where empty footings have been found that once held similar menhirs. The evidence is that at least some of the dismantled menhirs were used in the fourth millennium BC in nearby passage graves, a good example being the menhir reused at the Table des Marchands and the passage grave at Gavrinis.

The name "Table des Marchands" has been used since the beginning of the nineteenth century, undoubtedly a reference to the tomb's original appearance; constructed from a large slab of stone resting on three supports, it looks like a table. It is unclear whether the "Marchands" was a reference to traders, or was a family name. The monument first was excavated from 1811, although any finds were either dispersed or lost, including the intriguing "peloton de fil d'or" (ball of golden thread). Further excavations took place in the second half of the nineteenth century and the beginning of the twentieth century, at which time the monument's structure was first stabilized. In 1937, Zacharie le Rouzic, best known for his work on the Carnac monuments, also attempted to strengthen the monument. Excavations resumed in 1986, under the direction of Jean L'Helgouac'h. The artificial cairn covering the tomb was added in 1993, offering protection to the structure and attempting to re-create its original appearance. Jean L'Helgouac'h was known not only as an eminent archaeologist, but also as a practitioner of traditional Breton music and composer of new works using traditional Breton instruments.

Another group of monuments a short distance from Locmariaquer are a dolmen tomb at Kerlud, a tumulus at Mané-er-Hroech, and the passage grave known as Les Pierres-Plates (figure 1.2). The entrance to Les Pierres-Plates, excavated in 1813, is marked by a standing stone. The walls of the passage leading to the burial chamber are decorated with carvings.

Figure 2.7. Engraving of axes, Gavrinis. Paul G. Bahn

To the east of Locmariaquer is the Gulf of Morbihan, which has several small islands. This picturesque area offers not only beautiful scenery, but also the opportunity to visit the small island of Gavrinis, which has a passage grave featuring decorated slabs, one of the most fascinating and unusual of all of the megalithic monuments in Brittany.

The tiny uninhabited island of Gavrinis, around 750 meters by 400 meters, is reached by boat from the town of Larmor-Baden. The passage grave was first excavated in 1835, continued by Zacharie le Rouzic in the 1920s, with further investigation in the later twentieth and early twenty-first centuries. The grave has a passage 14 meters long, which leads to a burial chamber around 2.5 meters square. The roof of the chamber is formed from a single stone slab made from a fragment of the same monument used in the construction of the Table des Marchands, four kilometers away, and, in all likelihood, the tumulus at Er-Grah. It was noted as early as 1834 that the decorated capstone of the Table des Marchands was broken at its eastern end, suggesting that originally it was longer. The adjoining part was located in 1983, almost 150 years later, during excavations at Gavrinis, with the decoration being an exact match. This raises intriguing questions regarding not only the possible connections between these monuments, but also the meaning of the standing stones. The Gavrinis tomb is the best-known example of passage grave art found in France, with twenty-three engraved and carved vertical stones, around two meters high, along both sides of the passage and around the burial chamber (figure 2.7). The recent survey project at Gavrinis, which suggests use of the tomb between 3900 BC and 3770 BC, is discussed in more detail in chapter 6.

To the southeast of Gavrinis is the tiny island of Er Lannic (Morbihan), now a bird sanctuary. On Er Lannic are two "circles" of standing stones, better described as a horseshoe shape. Excavation revealed that they were associated with large numbers of stone axs and a distinctively shaped pottery object known as a burner, typical of the Neolithic period in France. It has been suggested that the finds are the remains of a cemetery that preceded the stone circles. The northern monument today is partly submerged in the Gulf of Morbihan; however, the southern monument, perhaps slightly earlier in date, is totally submerged, appearing only at low tide. The presence of the bird reserve on Er Lannic means that it is not permissible to land on the island, although the boat to Gavrinis passes nearby, enabling visitors to see the northern circle.

South of the Gulf of Morbihan is the peninsula known as Presqu'île de Rhuys. The landscape can be viewed from the Tumiac tumulus (Morbihan), popularly known as the "Butte de César." This is a reference to the legend that from the tumulus Julius Caesar viewed the sea battle in 56 BC in which his forces were victorious over the Veneti, the indigenous people who lived around the Gulf of Morbihan in the first century BC. The Neolithic monument, which no longer is open to the public, was excavated in 1853, and produced stone axs and, most notably, three necklaces made from beads of the attractive green mineral variscite, popularly known as "callais," which are relatively rare finds elsewhere. The spacing of the variscite beads of the necklaces is very characteristic: smaller beads interspersed with larger oval pendants. Variscite occurs naturally in the area of Pannecé (Loire-Atlantique), to the southeast of Brittany, and undoubtedly was the source of raw material for the beads.

Objects found at the megalithic monuments in the Morbihan area are exhibited at two museums: the Musée de Préhistoire James Miln-Zacharie Le Rouzic at Carnac-Ville and the Musée archéologique de Morbihan in the town of Vannes (Morbihan), situated at the head of the Gulf of Morbihan. The name of the museum at Carnac honors the first excavators of the sites in the area: the Scotsman James Miln and Zacharie Le Rouzic, who was from Carnac and whose early excavations are discussed in chapter 1. On display in the museum are several aspects of the area's prehistory: Paleolithic stone tools from the site of Saint-Colomban and objects from Mesolithic burials at Téviec and Hoëdic as well as a significant amount of material from the Neolithic period. The galleries cover the development of megalithic architecture in the Neolithic period, as well as displays of carvings, stone tools, jewelry, and pottery. Also included are sections on objects from the Bronze Age and Iron Age, as well as objects from the luxurious Gallo-Roman villa at Bosseno, near Carnac-Ville. The villa, which was excavated by James Miln in 1874, was built in the second century AD overlooking the bay of Quiberon. The decoration included lavish frescoes, dating to the third century AD, which had the unusual addition of seashells. Objects found at early excavations of megalithic monuments, including the Tumulus Saint-Michel in the Carnac area, Locmariaquer, and Presqu'île de Rhuys, are exhibited in the Musée archéologique de Morbihan in Vannes. The main types of objects on display are polished stone axs made from a variety of stones including jadeite, and bracelets and necklaces made of variscite.

There are also notable megalithic monuments in Brittany outside the south Morbihan region. One of the finest of all megalithic monuments is the very well preserved passage grave known as La Roche-aux-Fées (Fairy Rock) in Essé (Ille-et-Vilaine), in the east of Brittany (figure 2.8). Dating from the Middle Neolithic period (fourth millennium BC), this is the larg-

Figure 2.8.   Tomb known as La Roche-aux-Fées, Essé. istock, 835390424

est known megalithic tomb in Brittany at twenty meters long, six meters wide, and four meters high. It is built from forty-two stones of purple schist, the source of which is in the forest at Theil-de-Bretagne, four kilometers south of Essé. The monument's modern name is derived from the weight of the stones, as it was said that only the legendary Viviane (the "Lady of the Lake"), with her fairy helpers, could carry such heavy stones.

South of the Brittany peninsula, at Saint-Nazaire (Loire-Atlantique), is the Tumulus of Dissignac. Built between 4700 BC and 4500 BC, it is the oldest of the megalithic monuments in the Loire-Atlantique département and was designated a historic monument in 1889. The tumulus was excavated in 1873, but no objects were recovered. Further excavations between 1970 and 1980 directed by Jean L'Helgouac'h produced pottery dating from the fourth millennium BC and stone tools, including ground stone axs made from jadeite, considered to be prestige objects.

Elsewhere in western France, the necropolis at Bougon (Poitou-Charentes), consisting of five tumuli, was discovered in 1840 and re-excavated in the 1960s. A museum opened on the site in 1993 and, as well as material excavated from the site, including jewelry, houses a replica of part of the passage grave at Gavrinis, discussed earlier. An outdoor display includes reconstruction of how megalithic monuments were built. In 1979, an experiment at Bougon succeeded in erecting a Neolithic stone block weighing thirty-two tons by using three large wooden levers, each using the force of twenty people.

In addition to megalithic monuments, France has a series of other sites from the Neolithic period, such as the Middle Neolithic site at Saint-Michel-du-Touch in Toulouse (Haute-Garonne), occupied between 4500 BC and 3400 BC. The site, which initially was excavated by G. Simonnet between 1964 and 1973, is situated on a promontory at the confluence of the rivers Garonne and Touch. The site consisted of an enclosure, protected on the landward side by a series of palisades, which gradually increased the area within the palisades from five hectares to more than thirty hectares. Other sites of this type have been found in the area around Toulouse, at the commune of Villeneuve-Tolosane and Château Percin at the commune of Seilh. Inside the palisades, Simonnet discovered wells; large storage pits; more than three hundred rectangular or circular hearths that used heated pebbles; and burials, which provided valuable evidence of funerary practices in this period. One of the burials was of a male whose skeleton was well preserved, aged between sixteen and eighteen. He was 1.6 meters tall and had been buried in a crouched position on his left side. Two ceramic vessels had been placed near his skull.

Simonnet also discovered a double burial, of an adult and a child, accompanied by a lavish range of grave goods. The burials had been disturbed in antiquity and, in particular, the adult had been given a form of secondary burial. The bones had been rearranged, with two humeri placed end-to-end as if it were the bone from a single limb. The offerings included a wide range of pottery, including vase supports, and beads made from the green mineral variscite, popularly called "callais." As mentioned earlier in this section, variscite occurs naturally in France in the area of Pannecé (Loire-Atlantique), to the southeast of Brittany, and accordingly it is possible that the beads, or the material from which they were made, were imported to the site. Similarly, some tools accompanying the burials were made from flint of a nonlocal type, also indicating contact with communities outside the settlement. It was noticeable, however, that the deceased were placed in pits or ditches whose original function was not funerary, as was usually the case in the Middle Neolithic period. A rare exception was discovered in 2008 at Sauzas, in the commune of Blagnac (Haute-Garonne). A dedicated burial area was found consisting of six distinct graves, each in a pit covered with a mound of pebbles.

On the island of Corsica, La Dame de Bonifacio is the name given to the well-preserved skeleton of a woman discovered in 1972 in the Grotte de l'Aragvina, close to Bonifacio (Corse-du-Sud). The woman, who was 1.55 meters tall, was aged around thirty-five when she died between 7000 BC and 6500 BC. La Dame de Bonifacio is now in the Musée départemental de l'Alta Rocca at Levie (Corse-du-Sud).

NEOLITHIC AND BRONZE AGE "LAKE VILLAGES"

The banks of the lakes close to the boundary between modern-day France and Switzerland have provided evidence of settlements traditionally called "lake villages." The original theory was proposed by the Zurich-based archaeologist Ferdinand Keller, who reported the discovery of the first "lake dwellings" in the middle of the nineteenth century. Keller believed that the structures were not built on dry land, but on piles or stilts in the water close to the shore. Although it was subsequently suggested that the majority of "lake villages" were built on dry land at the edge of the water, archaeological excavation has revealed a more complex situation: some houses with floors raised above flood level as well as houses built on packed earth in shallow waters or peat bogs. In France, a group of lake settlements is on the shores of Lake Annecy (Haute-Savoie) and Lac du Bourget (Savoie), as well as in the département of Jura, particularly on the shores of Lake Chalain and the larger lake at Clairvaux.

The first Neolithic site in France recognized where remains were preserved due to wet conditions is La Motte-aux-Magnins on a peninsula with peaty soil on the shore of Lake Clairvaux. The site first was identified in 1869, with further excavations conducted between 1970 and 1983, and indicates that La Motte-aux-Magnins was occupied from the early fourth millennium BC until the middle of the second millennium BC. Finds from the site include organic objects, preserved as a result of the waterlogged environment, including weights for fishing nets made from pieces of limestone wrapped in birch bark and a box made from linden bark. Archaeological work began in 1970 on the shores of two small lakes, Lake Chalain and Lake Clairvaux, about twelve kilometers apart. These initial investigations revealed fifteen settlement sites at Chalain and nine at Clairvaux, ranging in date from about 5000 BC to 700 BC, a remarkable density of sites from the Neolithic and Bronze Age periods. Further archaeological evaluation in 2000 and 2001 indicated that the number of known sites on the western shore at Chalain is now almost thirty, with twenty sites at Clairvaux. The main periods of occupation were between around 3800 BC and 1400 BC, and it appears that from around 3800 BC to around 2500 BC, there was regular movement between the two lakes. One of the largest settlements on Lake Chalain is designated Chalain 19. Archaeological investigation between 1995 and 2001 indicated the presence of two successive villages. The second phase, which produced radiocarbon dates from 3173 BC to 2916 BC, revealed a village occupying an area of almost two thousand square meters enclosed by a curved oak palisade. A wooden trackway, around one hundred meters long and two meters wide, was used for transport, suggested by the discovery of a yoke and a large triangular sledge of the type possibly shown on petroglyphs in the Vallée des Merveilles, discussed below. The site of Clairvaux II, which was discovered and partly excavated between 1972 and 1974, was found to have been occupied between around 3470 BC and 3445 BC. The excavation was significant in demonstrating that houses were built in more than one fashion: with raised floors on pilings in flood zones and on packed earth in damp areas. The houses with raised floors were used as the model for an experimental archaeology project undertaken in 1988 at Lake Chalain, where two Neolithic houses were constructed, with part of the work being done using Neolithic technology. The houses no longer exist, having collapsed in 2000. Although the archaeological zones at Lake Chalain and Lake Clairvaux cannot be visited, the areas of Neolithic and Bronze Age habitation can be seen from several viewpoints. Finds from the excavations at Lake Chalain and Lake Clairvaux are housed at the Musée d'Archéologie de Lons-le-Saunier (Jura), including a log boat made from an oak tree trunk, radiocarbon dated to 959 BC. The log boat, which is 9.35 meters long, was found in 1904.

Further south, the site of Les Baigneurs close to Charavines, on the southern shore of Lake Paladru near Grenoble (Isère), was occupied about five thousand years ago during the Neolithic period. Although the first Neolithic remains were identified by Hyppolyte Müller in 1921 during a fall in water levels in the lake, excavation of Neolithic Charavines did not begin until 1972, by Aimé Bocquet and his colleagues from the Centre de Documentation de la Préhistoire Alpine (Alpine Prehistory Documentation Centre). Bocquet discovered that the site was occupied during two distinct phases, each lasting about thirty years. The environmental conditions enabled the preservation of wood and other organic material that normally would not survive. The first settlement at Charavines was established around 2740 BC and consisted of six or seven rectangular houses, built of wood from the European silver fir. Dendrochronological dating, based on tree ring sequences, indicated that the houses were repaired after nine years and abandoned at the end of twenty years. It is not clear why the first settlement of Charavines fell out of use, but it was clear that it was superseded some fifty-seven years later by a second settlement, consisting of a large house, again constructed from European silver fir with other buildings made from elm, ash, willow, and alder. The second settlement was occupied for a further twenty years before finally being abandoned. The many diverse finds from the site include handles made from coiled willow still attached to finely worked flint daggers. Other wooden objects included spoons, combs, and needles, as well as many ceramic vessels of various types. There were also indications of foodstuffs, including barley, wheat, and peas, which were grown and eaten by the inhabitants of Chara-vines. Evidence of other trees, most notably apples, hazel, and beech, also was found.

THE BRONZE AGE IN FRANCE

The Bronze Age in France is considered to extend from the earliest evidence of copper technology, around 2200 BC, lasting until around 800 BC. Some of the most significant archaeological discoveries are a series of petroglyphs in the French Alps, megalithic monuments on the island of Corsica, and deposits of bronze weapons and jewelry in deposits or hoards.

Petroglyphs in the French Alps

The area of Mont Bego (Alpes-Maritimes) in the Mercantour National Park is noted for a large number of petroglyphs, incised and carved images, found in two valleys, Meroviglie/Les Merveilles and Fontanalba, at a height of between two thousand and twenty-six hundred meters. Although the petroglyphs were noted as long ago as the fifth century, neither their age nor significance was realized, and they were first recognized as prehistoric in 1877 by the French prehistorian Emile Rivière. In 1897, Clarence Bicknell, Anglican vicar in Bordighera, Italy, who also was an amateur botanist and antiquarian, recorded almost thirteen thousand of the petroglyphs by taking rubbings. Research on the petroglyphs, of which almost thirty-seven thousand have been recorded, continues, most recently by Henry de Lumley and his team. The motifs depicted are somewhat limited in range, comprising tools and weapons; horns (sometimes interpreted as plows drawn by oxen); human forms, including the famous "Sorcerer," a schematic figure with upraised hands; geometric motifs; and dots (figure 2.9). Comparison between archaeological examples and the weapons depicted, which are axs, halberds (combined spears and axs), and daggers with archaeological ex-

Figure 2.9.   Engraving known as the "Sorcerer," Monte Bego. Paul G. Bahn

amples, may indicate that the petroglyphs were made between around 2500 BC and 1800 BC. Many are shown slanted, as though pointing in a particular direction, which has led to the suggestion that they were way markers used by herdsmen. Further research of the images, using microscopy and experimentation, has indicated that the engravings of some of the images of daggers may have been made by incising around a real dagger.

The petroglyphs are one of the themes of the Musée des Merveilles at Tende (Alpes-Maritimes). Their displays include a few original petroglyphs, such as the "Chef de Tribu," removed as it was considered to be under threat; and the "Echelles du Paradis," which had been partly destroyed and the fragments retrieved, together with casts of some of the other petroglyphs.

Corsica in the Bronze Age

On the island of Corsica, the period is characterized by the megalithic monuments, many of which take the form of "statue-menhirs," with the stones being carved with human faces, human torsos, and weapons, to represent warriors.

Filitosa in the Taravu Valley (Corse-du-Sud) was discovered in 1946. Excavations by Roger Grosjean, a noted specialist in Corsican prehistory, began in 1955 and lasted for eighteen years. Arrowheads and pottery date the earliest occupation of Filitosa to the Neolithic period, from around 3300 BC. Somewhat later, in around 1500 BC, an impressive group of "statue-menhirs," between two and three meters high, were erected (figure 2.10). About fifteen kilometers from the commune of Sartène (Corse-du-Sud) is a group of megalithic monuments on the plateau of Cauria. The alignments of Stantari and Rinaghju include both simple, uncarved menhirs and statue-menhirs, and the well-preserved dolmen tomb of Funtanaccia (figure 2.11).

However, the most impressive megalithic structure on Corsica is at Palaggiu, southeast of Sartène. The alignments consist of 258 menhirs, in seven groups, including statue-menhirs, although the majority are no longer standing and are concealed by the scrub vegetation. The site was recorded in the late nineteenth century by Etienne Michon, who later became chief curator at the Musée du Louvre. It was excavated by Roger Grosjean between 1964 and 1968 and was classified as an ancient monument in 1974. Grosjean also conducted excavations at the site of Casteddu di Cucuruzzu in the commune of Levie (Corse-du-Sud) in 1963 and 1964. The site, which

Figure 2.10.   Statue-menhirs at Filitosa, Corsica. istock, 522621641

Figure 2.11. Dolmen tomb at Funtanaccia, Corsica. istock, 525076327

was designated an ancient monument in 1982, was a fortified village, occupied from around 1400 BC. The visible remains largely consist of a circular stone tower surrounded by a high wall.

Two sites in the commune of Serra-di-Ferro (Corse-du-Sud) are the dolmen tomb made from pink granite known as the Tola di U Turmentu and the single statue-menhir known as U Paladinu (Le Paladin). U Paladinu is 2.91 meters tall, and although it possesses human characteristics, does not apparently carry weapons.

Archaeological finds from excavations conducted throughout Corsica are housed in Le Musée départemental de préhistoire corse et d'archéologie in Sartène (Corse-du-Sud). The museum was refurbished in the 2000s; a new building was opened in 2009, including a room dedicated to the statue-menhirs of Corsica.

Bronze Age Hoards

Outside Corsica, the most characteristic discoveries of the Middle and Late Bronze Age in northern and central France have been deposits, or hoards, of metal objects, dating between 1600 BC and 800 BC. In many cases, it is not clear why the hoards were deposited; perhaps they could have been hidden for safekeeping or made as a religious offering.

One of the earliest is the hoard found in 1910 at Villeneuve-Saint-Vistre (Marne), which can be dated to between 1600 BC and 1300 BC, containing the earliest gold objects found in France. The hoard, which is in the collection of the Musée d'Archéologie nationale-Domaine national, consisted of two small gold cups, twelve centimeters high; and jewelry, mostly bracelets and rings.

The deposition of weapons continued in the Late Bronze Age, with a spectacular discovery at Marmesse (Haute-Marne) during excavations between 1974 and 1980 of seven bronze cuirasses. The cuirasses are believed to have been a votive deposit. All of the cuirasses, now in the collection of the Musée d'Archéologie nationale, are elaborately ornamented with stamped decoration on front and back, emphasizing the anatomy of the wearer. The hoard known as the "Dépôt de Feuilly" was found during excavations undertaken in 2000 by Inrap (Institut national de recherches archéologiques préventives) at Saint-Priest in Lyon. The hoard contained bronze weapons, tools, and items of jewelry, mostly bracelets, which could be dated between 1100 BC and 900 BC. In 1985 a discovery was made in Meschers (Charente-Maritime) of a group of objects deposited toward the end of the Bronze Age. The deposit comprised fifty-five bronze objects, including bracelets, swords, and axs. A distinctive object was an element of a tintinnabulum, a large bronze disc with two smaller discs, designed to strike together as the horse moved, either part of the horse trappings or the equipment of a chariot. Better-preserved examples of Late Bronze Age tintinnabula have been found elsewhere in France, such as those from Bouzonville (Moselle) and Frouard (Meurthe-et-Moselle).

France is one of the most significant sources for Paleolithic art in Europe. Likewise, it is apparent that other phases of prehistory are well represented in France, particularly the Neolithic period monuments in Brittany and the Neolithic and Early Bronze Age lakeside settlements in eastern France, as well as intriguing evidence of early human activity throughout the region that constitutes modern-day France.

3

FROM COLONIZATION TO KINGSHIP

Iron Age, Gallo-Roman, and Early Medieval France

Iron Age, Gallo-Roman, and Early Medieval France, the chronological period from the seventh century BC until the seventh century AD, saw many political and social changes that are reflected in the archaeological remains. For much of the period between 600 BC and the Frankish victory over the Romans in AD 486, the region of modern-day France was considered by ancient writers as "Gaul," the term used in this chapter. Discoveries made recently through ongoing archaeological research, both new sites and reinterpretations of existing discoveries, are considered in chapter 6.

This chapter focuses on five topics, beginning with evidence of contact between Gaul and the Mediterranean world during the seventh century BC, including the foundation of the Greek colony of Massalia. Second, there is consideration of the evidence of indigenous settlement during the Iron Age, followed by consideration of the changes that were brought about by the Roman conquest of Gaul. A further theme is information regarding maritime trade shown by the discovery of Etruscan and Roman shipwrecks and, finally, archaeological evidence of the influx of non-Gallic people and the establishment of the Merovingian dynasty.

GREEK SETTLEMENT IN GAUL AND LINKS WITH THE MEDITERRANEAN WORLD

The earliest contact point between Gaul and the ancient Mediterranean world was at the mouth of the Rhône, with late seventh-century BC Etruscan and Greek pottery found at the indigenous settlements of Saint-Blaise and La Couronne (both Bouches-du-Rhône), both to the northwest of Marseille. At this time, the majority of Greek pottery found at Saint-Blaise and La Couronne was from "East Greece" (modern-day Turkey); some was produced in Corinth on the Greek mainland.

Shortly after, in about 600 BC, the ancient Greek colony of Massalia was founded on the site of the modern-day city of Marseille (Bouches-du-Rhône), on the mouth of the river Rhône. It was established by the inhabitants of the East Greek city of Phokaia (modern-day Foça on the coast of western Turkey). The presence of Massalia facilitated trade to inland France as well as the development of local societies, including the introduction of cultivation of the vine. Pottery kilns have been found during excavation on the hill of Les Carmes, on the outskirts of Marseille, and examples of their output have been found outside the city, in the lower Rhône valley. The pottery includes a distinctive type of amphora, used for the transportation of wine, discovered at the modern-day town of Arles (Bouches-du-Rhône). The objects discovered in the area of the port of Marseille include both Etruscan and Greek pottery, although the foundation of Massalia led to a rise in the number of Greek imports at the expense of those from the Italian mainland. Archaeological evidence for the mechanisms of maritime trade between Gaul and the Etruscans is found on the shipwrecks off Cap d'Antibes (Alpes-Maritimes) and Grand Ribaud (Var), discussed later in this chapter.

The development of the modern city of Marseille means, however, that very little of Greek Massalia is visible today. Massalia was located on a hill to the north of modern-day Marseille's Vieux Port (Old Harbor). However, excavations in 1977 in the area of the Bourse (Stock Exchange) building in advance of the construction of a shopping center indicated that occupation of Massalia extended along the northern side of the harbor. Excavations were undertaken in 2009 in the area known as the Panier, immediately to the north of the Vieux Port, in advance of the renovation of the Collège Vieux Port. The archaeologists discovered that the area was inhabited between 600 and 480 BC.

Massalia was a very prosperous city, minting its own coins in large numbers, marked ΜΑΣΣΑ or ΜΑ, indicating "Massalia." In addition, the city was sufficiently wealthy in the late sixth century BC to make a lavish offering in the panhellenic sanctuary at Delphi in Greece in the form of an elaborately decorated marble building conventionally called a "treasury." By the second century BC, Massalia had acquired a city wall with stone foundations; one of its gateways with projecting towers, overlooking the inner harbor, was discovered in the excavations on the Bourse site.

Massalia founded its own colonies, one of which was Olbia, which was located at l'Almanarre on the Mediterranean coast, east of Marseille, and very close to the town of Hyères (Var). Olbia has been extensively excavated, initially from 1947 to 1951 and again from 1956 to 1971. Excavations recommenced from 1982 to 1989, and again between 2002 and 2008. According to ancient authors, along with Tauroention (sometimes identified with modern Saint-Cyr-sur-Mer), Antipolis (modern Antibes), and Nikaia (modern Nice), Olbia was founded as a colony by Massalia in the fourth century BC to help protect Massalia from maritime raiding. However, offshore excavations conducted by DRASSM between 1996 and 2000, which revealed the presence of sherds of Massaliot and Etruscan amphorae, indicate earlier occupation of the area, well before the foundation of the colony at Olbia in about 330 BC. Although now more than 150 meters from the sea, archaeology suggests that Olbia also served as a small trading port, with black-glazed pottery from Italy found in the settlement. Most apparent to the modern visitor are the walls with square towers, which had been strengthened in the second century BC. The single gateway into the town led to the ancient port, which is now silted up. In common with many other ancient Greek colonies, Olbia was built on a grid plan dividing the settlement into four blocks separated by wide streets, with a communal well in the center of the town. Olbia may have fallen under Roman domination in 49 BC, when Julius Caesar and his armies conquered the area. It is possible that at this time Olbia can be identified as Pomponiana, a settlement that is named in ancient accounts but has not been identified with certainty. Archaeologists have found evidence, however, that Olbia thrived during the Roman period, at which time three bath complexes were built, one of which was constructed in the first century BC inside the walls of the settlement. A new quay was built in the Roman period, remains of which are visible on the beach at modern-day l'Almanarre, seemingly to replace the earlier quay that had silted up.

Trade flourished elsewhere along the Mediterranean coast of pre-Roman Gaul, examples being at the coastal oppida (indigenous fortified settlements) of Saint-Blaise (Bouches-du-Rhône) and Pech Maho (Aude).

The ancient name of the settlement at the mouth of the river Rhône now known as Saint-Blaise is unknown, although it may be identified with the town called Mastrabala by the Roman author Avienus, writing in the fourth century AD. The Early Medieval settlement on the site, founded in the fifth century AD, was known as Ugium, and subsequently as Castelveyre from about AD 1200. The name Saint-Blaise was adopted in the sixteenth century AD.

The oppidum at Saint-Blaise was first excavated in 1935 by Henri Rolland, whose career is considered in chapter 4. Pottery finds from Saint-Blaise show contact with the Etruscan and Greek worlds. The archaeology indicates how the pattern of trade changed in the sixth century BC. Etruscan objects predominate between 600 and 550 BC, facilitated by the location of Saint-Blaise, including many amphorae used for the transport of commodities such as wine. However, from the middle of the sixth century BC, there is more evidence of Greek objects, both amphorae and pottery made in Athens, linked to the expansion of Massalia. The walls constructed in the Hellenistic period, in the second century BC, are the most impressive ancient remains that can be seen today at the site.

Pech Maho (Aude) was occupied continuously from the middle of the sixth century BC until the end of the third century BC. A particularly significant discovery that sheds light on the relationship between Pech Maho and other communities is a thin lead sheet, inscribed on both sides, found in an archaeological context dating to the fifth century BC. The piece of lead has been unrolled by specialist conservators and found to be 115 millimeters wide, 52 millimeters high, yet only 1.1 millimeters thick. The inscription on the outer side of the lead sheet is written in Etruscan, whereas that on the inner side is in Greek. The Etruscan inscription, which is incomplete, mentions Matalia, interpreted as Massalia. The more complete Greek inscription documents the purchase of a boat from the people of Emporion. This coastal town is known today as Empúries in the region of Catalonia in northeast Spain and famous in antiquity as a trading center founded by Massalia in the early sixth century BC. The text records that the purchaser also bought additional boats from elsewhere and passed over half a share of the boats to the writer of the inscription. The inclusion of the names of two witnesses to the transaction suggests that the document was not purely commercial in nature, but that the text also has formal legal aspects. It has been suggested that the document may have been written at Emporion and brought to Pech Maho by an itinerant merchant. The significance of the inscribed lead sheet lies in the light it sheds on trade along this part of the Mediterranean coast during the fifth century BC.

Further archaeological evidence of the expansion of the influence of Massalia along the Mediterranean coast from the late sixth century BC until the arrival of the Romans can be found at the coastal settlement of Lattes (Hérault), west of Marseille. Lattes originally was an indigenous community with links to the Etruscan world and became a trading outpost of Massalia from about 500 BC. Stone architectural remains have been found dating from the late fourth to the late third centuries BC.

In the period of Greek colonization, it is believed that Arles (Bouches-du-Rhône) was known to the Greeks as Theline. Although the later development of Arles has restricted our knowledge of this period of the town's history, evidence of occupation during this era are finds of Greek pottery and amphorae from Massalia and of Phoenician origin, which would have been transported to the town by ship up the river Rhône, as well as fragments of a pre-Roman building in use from the sixth to the second centuries BC.

Agde (Hérault), on the coast west of Marseille, is believed to have been a colony of Massalia, founded in the late sixth century BC. Archaeologists have found circuit walls dating from the second century BC, built on foundations from the fourth to the third centuries BC. The Musée de l'Ephèbe, which opened in 1987, houses finds from underwater excavations from the coastal lagoons of the delta of the river Hérault and the Mediterranean Sea. The most famous exhibit is the bronze statue of a young man, 1.3 meters tall, after which the museum is named. It has been suggested that the statue, which was made during the Hellenistic period, may represent Alexander the Great. It was found in September 1964 on the bed of the river Hérault, opposite the cathedral at Agde. The statue probably was lost from a ship in the Roman period rather than having been displayed in ancient Agde. It was found in a very fragile condition with the forearms and feet no longer present. The left leg was not found until six months after the original excavation; the left arm was not attached until 2010.

IRON AGE GAUL

Away from the Mediterranean coast, indigenous sites in Gaul continued to flourish, a notable example being the settlement on the hill of Mont-Lassois, which dominates the commune of Vix (Côte-d'Or) on the river Seine, about 195 kilometers from Paris. The settlement, which was inhabited from the Neolithic to the Merovingian period, was at its height during the sixth and fifth centuries BC. The settlement was excavated between 1929 and 1939, revealing not only locally produced objects, but also evidence of contacts with societies outside Gaul from the sixth century BC onward. In particular, archaeologists found amber and Athenian pottery decorated in the black-figure style.

The most spectacular discovery from the excavations that recommenced in 1947 was an elite female burial from the sixth century BC, found in 1953 at the foot of Mont-Lassois. At the time of excavation, it was the richest of all Iron Age tombs to have been found in France.

Close to the river Seine, the excavators investigated a large tumulus, some forty meters in diameter and between five and six meters high, in the center of which was a burial chamber. In one corner of the chamber was a large vessel of the type known as a volute krater, 1.64 meters high and weighing 208 kilograms, its style suggesting that it was made in one of the Greek colonies in southern Italy (figure 3.1). The vessel is made from bronze and able to be dismantled for transportation; some of the pieces were lettered to facilitate reassembly. The neck is decorated with a chariot procession, and the cast volute handles are decorated with gorgon's heads. The vessel had a lid with a statuette of a woman, nineteen centimeters high, to serve as a handle, and the krater had been covered with matting made of organic fibers that has been partly preserved because of the wet conditions in the tomb, the result of its proximity to the river Seine. Other finds in the tomb were two Athenian pottery cups, one decorated in the black-figure technique that dates it to between 530 and 520 BC, and three Etruscan bronze vessels, imported from Italy.

A chariot originally had been placed in the center of the tomb, indicated by the remains of iron and bronze fittings. The wheels of the chariot had been carefully removed before burial and stored in the tomb, with some of the wood from the hubs still preserved. Inside the chariot was a skeleton, which had deteriorated; only the skull was well preserved. The deceased was a woman aged about thirty, buried in an extended position, with more than twenty-five pieces of jewelry. She wore anklets and bracelets, one made of amber beads, and a gold torc-style necklace weighing 480 grams. Her clothes apparently had been held together with iron and bronze fibulas, a type of brooch. In particular, four of the bronze fibulas were very lavish, decorated with coral and red amber. The discoveries from the tumulus are on display in the Musée du Pays Châtillonais in nearby Châtillon-sur-Seine (Côte-d'Or).

Later excavations at Mont-Lassois have revealed more of the settlement. In particular, excavations in 2006 revealed a group of up to three buildings constructed in the late sixth century BC. The central building, thirty-five meters by twenty-one meters, had an apsidal end. Finds in the area include amphorae from Massalia and Athenian pottery. It is not surprising, perhaps,

Figure 3.1. "Vix krater" from the female burial found at Mont-Lassois. Alamy

that the building has been associated in the popular press with the woman buried in the large tumulus and has led to the structure's nickname of the "Palais de la Princesse" (palace of the princess).

Another tumulus at La Garenne, two kilometers from the lavish tomb at Vix, was excavated in the 1860s. It held a bronze cauldron, made in the artistic style known as "Greek Orientalizing," dating to the middle of the sixth century BC. The cauldron, which stood on a tripod, is thirty-two centimeters high and seventy centimeters in diameter. Below the rim of the cauldron are four decorative projections known as protomai, in the form of griffins, one of which is slightly different in style and may have been replaced in antiquity. Another example of a griffin protome came to light in 1897 at Port-Thibault on the bank of the river Loire at Angers (Maine-et-Loire). Unfortunately, the protome has no archaeological context, as it was a chance find by a farmer.

Funerary practices in the Iron Age were diverse, reflecting not only changes in burial customs, but also the status of the deceased.

Excavations at the commune of Eterville (Calvados) have revealed an unusually large cemetery of around 150 burials. The cemetery was in use for inhumation burials from the sixth century BC until the start of the third century BC, and it is believed that it fell out of use because of a general change in funerary customs from inhumation to cremation, which by the second century BC had become the preferred practice.

A characteristic type of Iron Age funerary practice attested in northeastern and central France from the sixth century BC are a series of elite burials where the deceased, either male or female, was laid in a chariot. Around 140 burials of this type are known, although very few have been discovered undisturbed. One of these was found in 1873 in the commune of Somme-Bionne (Marne). The burial, dated to between 450 and 300 BC from the style of its finds, was re-excavated and recorded by Léon Morel. Morel, an amateur archaeologist who undertook many excavations of Iron Age, Gallo-Roman, and Merovingian sites in the Marne département, had been able to talk to the original excavators of the chariot burial at Somme-Bionne. The grave was 2.85 meters long, 1.8 meters wide, and 1.15 meters deep and lay at the center of a circle sixteen meters in diameter, surrounded by a ditch. Metal parts of the chariot survived, together with decorated harness fittings. The skeleton was in an extended position and was buried wearing a sword, knife, and gold ring. The grave offerings also included imported goods: an Athenian two-handled pottery drinking cup decorated on the inside in the red-figure technique and a bronze flagon of the characteristic Etruscan shape known as a "Schnabelkanne," alongside a locally made pedestal vase, its surface red-slipped. Many of the finds, including the vessels, are now in the collection of the British Museum in London, acquired in 1901. The fifth century BC chariot burial from Lavau (Aube) will be discussed in chapter 6.

An extremely unusual type of burial from the late Iron Age was discovered in 2002 at the oppidum site of Gondole in the commune of Le Cendre (Puy-de-Dôme) during construction of a bypass south of the city of Clermont-Ferrand (Puy-de-Dôme). Around three hundred meters outside the wall of the oppidum, a communal burial of eight males, of whom seven were adult and one was an adolescent, accompanied by their horses, was discovered, their bodies arranged in two rows of four. No weapons, harness elements, or personal objects were found in the burial. The horses were small, measuring only 1.2 meters at the shoulder, which suggests they were local animals. The project to excavate Gondole, which was much less known than the neighboring oppida of Gergovie and Corent (both Puy-de-Dôme), took place from 2002 until 2005. It was discovered that Gondole, which occupied a strategic position at the confluence of the rivers Allier and Auzon, extended over an area of seventy hectares, both inside and outside its walls. Excavation of an area outside the walls of Gondole revealed that it was occupied by artisans, with evidence of pottery kilns and forges.

Some elements of Iron Age material culture are particularly distinctive, and of note are discoveries of three helmets dating to the fourth century BC. The most elaborate was found in the Grotte des Perrats in the commune of Agris (Charente). It consisted of an iron cap covered with bronze bands, above which was a thin layer of gold, decorated with coral. The first fragments of the helmet were found in 1981 with further discoveries in 1983 and 1986, although the helmet still is incomplete. Now restored, it is in the Musée d'Angoulême (Charente). Less elaborately decorated is a helmet found in 1876 by Paul du Chatellier at the oppidum of Tronoën, in the commune of Saint-Jean-Trolimon (Finistère). The fragmentary helmet, in the collections of the Musée d'Archéologie nationale, was made using a similar technique of an iron cap, covered with a thin layer of bronze, decorated with coral on the top of the helmet and on the surviving cheek piece. Perhaps slightly later in date is the helmet found in 1841 at the commune of Amfreville-sous-les-Monts (Eure). Now in the Musée d'Archéologie nationale, it was restored between 1981 and 1982. The helmet is decorated with a wide, single band of gold foil and red enamel inlay.

A typical pre-Roman archaeological site is the oppidum of Ensérune (Hérault), in the commune of Nissan-lez-Ensérune. The site was discovered in 1915, initially producing remains from the fourth and third centuries BC. Additional excavation showed that the site initially was occupied earlier, from the sixth century BC. The hill fort was destroyed at the end of the third century BC, rebuilt and regained prosperity after the arrival of the Romans and the foundation of a colony in Narbonne in 118 BC, but its population declined from the first century AD onward. The site museum houses finds from the sixth century BC onward, including pottery that was imported as well as produced locally. Inscriptions in an ancient language sometimes described as "Iberian" have been found at Ensérune, indicating links with the area, which is now modern-day Spain. A significant discovery was a drinking cup, made in Athens between 425 BC and 400 BC and decorated in the red-figure technique with a scene of the myth of Kephalos and Procris painted inside the cup. Some of the original remains at Ensérune were left in situ, including dolia (large storage vessels sunk into the ground), the remains of columns, and wall foundations.

Other elements of indigenous Gallic society, however, show no evidence of Greco-Roman influence, most notably ritual practices. Enclosures associated with Gallic ritual activity have been found at several locations in France, with the best-studied being at Gournay-sur-Aronde (Oise) and Ribemont-sur-Ancre (Somme), both in northern France. At Gournay-sur-Aronde, archaeologists found a rectangular enclosure built around 300 BC and in use during the following three hundred years. Pits in the enclosure contained animal bones, which are believed to have been from sacrifices. In addition, about two thousand iron weapons were deposited in the ditch surrounding the enclosure. Ribemont-sur-Ancre, approximately seventeen kilometers east of Amiens (Somme), produced deposits of human skeletal remains from somewhere between 200 and 250 individuals. The deceased mostly were young men, some of whom exhibited injuries caused by bladed weapons. No skulls, ribs, or spines were found among the skeletal remains, and cut marks on the neck vertebrae suggest that the deceased were decapitated. Large amounts of iron weapons, some of which are displayed in the Musée de Picardie in Amiens, were also found at Ribemont-sur-Ancre, which is believed to date from the third century BC. The ossuary was covered in the Roman period by a sanctuary, discussed later in the chapter.

ROMAN GAUL

The second century BC saw major political and social changes, as the conquest by the Romans began, and the area became part of the Roman provinces that comprised Gaul. These encompassed not only modern-day France, but also northern Italy, Belgium, Luxembourg, western Switzerland, and the parts of the Netherlands and Germany that lie west of the river Rhine. Roman armies first entered southeastern Gaul in 154 BC to help with the defense of Massalia against invaders. The Romans conquered this area from 125 BC; in 121 BC they annexed the coastal area from modern-day Montpellier (Hérault) to the Pyrenees. The Romans gradually took over the area that is now modern-day France, governing the area for the next five hundred years. This section will consider archaeological evidence from the Roman provinces of Gallia Narbonensis, Aquitania, and Gallia Lugdunensis.

The first province north of the Alps was named by the Romans Provincia Nostra, meaning "Our Province." The term Provincia Nostra has survived in the name "Provence," the eastern part of Provincia Nostra, the western part being located in what is now the modern region of Languedoc, both southern France. The province was renamed Gallia Narbonensis by the emperor Augustus in 27 BC after its capital Colonia Narbo Martius, the modern-day town of Narbonne (Aude), which had been a Roman colony founded in 118 BC. Colonia Narbo Martius was located in a strategic position; the settlement had access to the sea as well as to the interior via the river Aude and was at the junction of two important Roman roads. The Via Domitia, built in the second century BC, linked Italy to Spain; and the Via Aquitania started in Narbonne and ran west to the Atlantic coast through Toulouse (Haute-Garonne) to Bordeaux (Gironde), known to the Romans as Tolosa and Burdigala respectively.

Subsequent development means that very little of Roman Narbonne is visible today, although part of an underground warehouse, known as a horreum, dating to the late first century BC, can be visited (figure 3.2).

Figure 3.2.   Horreum (underground warehouse), Narbonne. istock, 467276787

Other remains from Roman Narbonne can be seen at the site known as the Clos de la Lombarde, just north of the town. Excavations from 1973 have revealed houses, workshops, and baths from the Roman period, as well as an early Christian church. The area was a large residential quarter during the Roman period, with some streets lined with porticos undoubtedly once housing small shops. Several of the houses have produced wall paintings from the first and second centuries AD, particularly House IV, including a depiction of Phaeton driving the chariot of his father, Helios, the sun god. Other paintings were found in the "House with the Large Triclinium" and, most notably, the "House of the Genius." The House of the Genius was built in the first century AD and expanded in the third century AD with the addition of a second story. The house had several mosaic floors made from black and white tesserae, and wall paintings showing Winged Victory, Apollo, and the Genius, carrying a cornucopia and pouring a libation, which gives the villa its modern name. The houses were abandoned in the third century AD and a church built over their remains in the fourth century AD. A baptistery has been found, together with several burials, including an amphora containing the burial of a child. A large number of objects from Roman Narbonne, including the wall paintings from the houses at Clos de la Lombarde, are in the collection of the Musée archéologique at Narbonne, housed in the eleventh- to twelfth-century AD archbishop's palace.

Part of the Via Domitia in the center of the old town of Narbonne, close to the Town Hall, was revealed in 1997 and is on display in situ. A longer section of the Via Domitia can be seen at Ambrussum, in the commune of Villetelle (Hérault), where it passed through the settlement (figure 3.3). Ambrussum originally was founded as an oppidum, although occupation continued after the Romans arrived in the area and the settlement was remodeled. Ambrussum was recorded as a trading post on the Antonine Itinerary, a list of distances along various Roman roads that was compiled around the third century AD.

There is little physical evidence of the military campaigns that led to the final conquest of Gaul by Gaius Julius Caesar, known as the "Gallic Wars." These took place between 58 and 52 BC and are recorded by Caesar in his *Commentarii de Bello Gallico* (Commentaries on the Gallic War). Caesar documented his final struggle against Vercingetorix, who by 52 BC had become the leader of all of the indigenous tribes from the river Seine in the north to the river Garonne in the southwest. Caesar wrote that the struggle against Vercingetorix culminated in the final battle at Alésia, the capital of the Mandubii tribe, a hill fort where Vercingetorix and his warriors had taken refuge. The site of Alésia was not known and, as discussed in chapter

Figure 3.3. Roman road known as the Via Domitia at Ambrussum. Alamy

1, in 1864 the French Emperor Napoleon III issued an official decree that Alésia was located on Mont-Auxois, in the commune of Alise-Sainte-Reine (Côte-d'Or). Indeed, the presumed site of the battle is overlooked today by a colossal statue of Vercingetorix, commissioned in 1864 by Napoleon III from the sculptor Aimé Millet. Standing on a stone base 7 meters high, designed by the architect Eugène Viollet-le-Duc, the statue, covered in sheet copper, stands 6.6 meters high and, accordingly, dominates the landscape.

More recently, survey and excavations were conducted at Alise-Sainte-Reine between 1991 and 1997 by a Franco-German team led by Michel Reddé and Sigman von Schnurbein, their objective being to confirm that Alésia and Mont-Auxois were the same place. Their excavations revealed the traces of a Gallo-Roman town, which prospered largely as a result of the activities of bronze workers, before being abandoned in the fifth century AD. Buildings at Alise-Sainte-Reine include a monument to Ucuestis, a Gallic deity linked with metallurgy; and a bronze vase inscribed with the names of Ucuestis and his consort, Bergusia, had been found during excavation of the monument in 1908. Controversy still surrounds the identification of Mont-Auxois as Alésia, which will be discussed more fully in chapter 5.

A section of the Roman fortifications that would have surrounded the hill fort have been reconstructed at the Muséoparc Alésia in Alise-Sainte-Reine. These reconstructions are based on the account by Julius Caesar and the excavations undertaken by Napoleon III, and give the visitor an impression of the work necessary to conduct a siege in the Roman period.

Other evidence from the period of the Gallic Wars can be found close to the oppidum of Liercourt-Erondelle (Somme). Aerial photography has suggested an enclosure with a ditch near the oppidum, and the area also has produced Iron Age pottery and coins. It is unclear whether the enclosure housed a garrison consisting of Roman or Gallic mercenaries guarding the hill fort, or whether the occupants were a group protecting the hill fort after expelling the local Gauls. Although other enclosures in the Somme département, identified as "camps," sometimes are associated with Caesar's Gallic Wars, they are likely to be later in date.

Bibracte, twenty-five kilometers from the modern-day town of Autun (Saône-et-Loire), was an oppidum on Mont Beauvray. Bibracte was capital of the Aedui tribe from the end of the second century BC and, at its height, had an estimated population between five thousand and ten thousand inhabitants. The Aedui were treated favorably by the Romans and, accordingly, had contact with the Roman world before the conquest of this part of Gaul in 52 BC, undoubtedly aided by its strategic position on an important trading route along the rivers Loire and Saône. This is apparent from the discovery of amphorae imported from Italy that would have contained wine. Despite being the place where Vercingetorix was made leader of the indigenous Gallic tribes, the status of Bibracte meant that it was left unscathed after the Roman victory at Alésia; and, indeed, Julius Caesar wrote his *Commentarii de Bello Gallico* (Commentaries on the Gallic War) at Bibracte. The foundation of Augustodunum (modern-day Autun) in about 15 BC led to the gradual abandonment of Bibracte, as the need for the protection given by its location on Mont Beauvray became unnecessary.

The first excavations at Bibracte were funded by Napoleon III and conducted by Jacques-Gabriel Bulliot from 1867; they were continued by his nephew Joseph Déchelette from 1897 until 1901 and again in 1907. On Déchelette's death in 1914, archaeological work ceased at Bibracte. However, a major research project began in 1984 involving a multinational team. Modern-day visitors to the archaeological park at Bibracte can see public buildings, houses, workshops, and fortification walls from the Gallo-Roman town, extending over an area of two hundred hectares. The reconstructed fortifications extend 5.2 kilometers around the Gallo-Roman site and, with their main gateway, were constructed in the first century AD. An earlier fortification, still covered, was built in the second century BC when Bibracte was founded and extends seven kilometers around the site.

Once Gaul was finally under Roman administration as a consequence of Julius Caesar's victory in the Gallic War, "romanization" began. Romanization was the gradual adoption by at least the upper echelons of the indigenous Gallic society of the customs, types of artistic and architectural expression, technology, style of dress, Latin language, and religious beliefs that are referred to as "Gallo-Roman." Although the Gallo-Roman people retained their cultural and social identities by remaining members of their local indigenous tribe, they could become citizens of the Roman Empire, including serving in the Roman army. Indeed, by the second century AD, many of those serving in the Roman army were from Gaul.

Striking evidence of the fusion of Roman and indigenous Gallic culture can be seen on a statue known as the Vachères Warrior, named from its findspot in the commune of Vachères (Alpes-de-Haute-Provence). This is now in the Musée Lapidaire, the archaeological collection of the Musée Calvet, in the town of Avignon (Vaucluse). Dating to the later first century BC, the warrior is identifiable as an indigenous Gaul by the torc around his neck; he wears the dress and equipment of a Roman soldier. Accordingly, this demonstrates that the Gallic elite had the chance to advance in Roman society, yet retain their status in the local community.

The first Roman emperor to have been born in a province was Claudius, who was born on 1 August 10 BC in Lugdunum (modern-day Lyon) and reigned from AD 41 until his death in AD 54. It was during the reign of Claudius that members of the Gallo-Roman elite were first admitted to the Senate in Rome, a trend that continued throughout the second century AD.

A wealth of sites that have visible archaeological remains from the Roman period are in the south of France, in particular in the modern-day départements of Gard, Vaucluse, and Bouches-du-Rhône. The most notable are the towns Nîmes (Gard) and its nearby aqueduct bridge of Pont-du-Gard, Arles, Glanum/St. Rémy (both Bouches-du-Rhône), and Orange (Vaucluse).

The town of Nîmes (Gard), known in antiquity as Nemausus, was the capital of the Volcae Arecomici tribe before its conquest by the Romans and incorporation into the province of Gallia Narbonensis in the second century BC. The town further developed in the reign of the emperor Augustus (27 BC to AD 14), and was honored with the name Colonia Augusta Nemausus.

The Maison Carrée (translated as Square House), a name first applied to the building in 1560, stood in what originally would have been the Roman forum in Nîmes, of which no other buildings remain (figure 3.4). The Maison Carrée, which dates to the Augustan era, was a temple whose exceptional preservation is the result of subsequent reuse for a variety of functions.

The temple is typically Roman in architectural form, with a staircase at the front and the whole building on a high podium. Built from local limestone, originally it would have had porticos on three sides; they are no longer present. Temples in this style are relatively rare in Roman Gaul, another example being the well-preserved temple dedicated to Augustus and Livia in Vienne (Isère). The columns of the Maison Carrée are in the Corinthian order, the most elaborate of the Greco-Roman architectural orders, decorated with stylized acanthus leaves and scrolls. There is a combination of freestanding columns at the front of the temple and engaged columns part way down the sides and back. The Corinthian column capitals are carved in three different styles, suggesting that three separate teams of artisans were employed. Two lines of small holes on the facade of the Maison Carrée indicate the position of the dedicatory inscription made in individual letters, probably made from bronze, but now no longer present. This indicated that the temple was an example of the imperial cult, dedicated to Gaius Caesar and Lucius Caesar, who Augustus had intended to be his heirs. They were the sons of Marcus Vipsanius Agrippa, appointed governor of Transalpine

Figure 3.4. "Maison Carrée," Nîmes. istock, 628563362

Gaul in 39 or 38 BC by Octavian before he took the name of Augustus. The titles of Gaius Caesar and Lucius Caesar in the inscription establish a date of around AD 1 for the construction of the temple. The Maison Carrée was much admired by the U.S. president Thomas Jefferson and influenced the design by Jefferson and Charles-Louis Clérisseau of the State Capitol building in Richmond, Virginia.

The amphitheater at Nîmes, dating to the later first century AD, was built of locally quarried stone and would have held twenty-four thousand spectators (figure 3.5). It is also extremely well preserved due to its later reuse. After the ban on gladiatorial games in AD 404, the arena was not used until the twelfth century, when a chateau was built inside and occupied by the Chevaliers des Arènes. The chateau was occupied until the fourteenth century, when the inhabitants moved to a new building on the site of the town gate known as the Porte d'Auguste. A village, including two churches, subsequently developed inside the amphitheater, which by the eighteenth century had approximately seven hundred inhabitants living in fifteen hundred houses. It was not until the early nineteenth century that the last remaining houses were demolished and the amphitheater restored to its appearance in the Roman era.

Figure 3.5. Roman amphitheater, Nîmes. istock, 521208624

The town was fortified in the reign of the emperor Augustus, although the only remains are the Porte d'Auguste, which was one of the main gates to the town; and the Tour Magne, which stands on Mont Cavalier, the highest point of the city (figure 3.6). Although the construction of the Tour Magne dates from the Roman period, it incorporates the remains of an earlier Iron Age monumental tower.

An essential element of Roman towns was the provision of a good water supply. Roman Nîmes was served by an aqueduct whose remains are well preserved. Built in the first century BC, it carried water from the town of Uzès (Gard) at the source of the river Eure, a distance of fifty kilometers, to Nîmes. The route of the aqueduct involved a combination of masonry structures, channels, and tunnels to maintain a gradual falling gradient. The most famous structure is the aqueduct bridge now known as the Pont-du-Gard, which spans a gorge above the river Gardon (figure 3.7). At its highest point it is forty-nine meters above the river, making the Pont-du-Gard the highest surviving bridge in the Roman world. The Pont-du-Gard was constructed with three tiers of arches, comprising six spans on its lowest level, eleven on its middle level, and thirty-five (originally forty-seven) on its upper level. A well-preserved example of the way the water was distributed throughout a Roman town is found at Nîmes, where the "castellum divisorium" is preserved. This is a circular reservoir at the end of the aqueduct that enabled

Figure 3.6.   Tour Magne at Nîmes. istock, 175964858

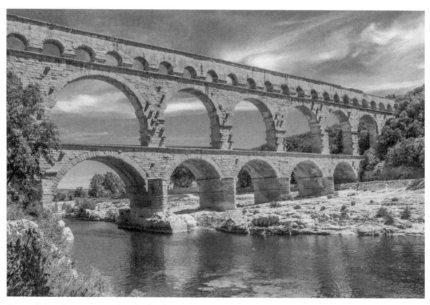

Figure 3.7.   Roman aqueduct-bridge known as Le Pont-du-Gard. istock, 159314951

the water flow to be regulated as it was distributed through lead pipes to the bathhouses, fountains, and lavish private houses in Nîmes. The Pont-du-Gard was also a landmark in later periods, and engravings of initials and tools were made by the "compagnons," the traveling stonemasons who were apprenticed to master artisans, to signal the symbolic end of their travels. These engravings, the earliest of which is dated 1631, can still be seen on the east side of the Pont-du-Gard.

The town of Arles (Bouches-du-Rhône), known in the Roman period as Arelate, is situated on the river Rhône and was at the end of the Via Julia Augusta that ran from Placentia, modern-day Piacenza in Italy. The coastline has altered since Roman times, and modern day Arles is further from the sea than its Roman counterpart. Impressive surviving Early Roman monuments include a theater, forum, and, most notably, a cryptoporticus and a very well preserved amphitheater. The cryptoporticus was built in the first century BC and is a series of subterranean galleries in the form of three double parallel tunnels that form the substructure of the Roman forum. Although the usual suggestion for the use of a cryptoporticus is for the storage of grain, the galleries at Arles are too damp for this purpose, and the possibility exists that they were used as barracks for public slaves. The amphitheater was built in the first century AD and was capable of holding twenty thousand spectators. Its good preservation is a result of later use; in the post-Roman era the amphitheater was used as a fortress, with the addition of towers in the medieval period. The area became residential, which continued until the late eighteenth century. Restoration of the amphitheater began in 1825 at the instigation of Prosper Merimée, the author of the novella *Carmen*, then Inspecteur général des monuments historiques. It remains in use today for the performance of plays, concerts, and bullfighting.

Evidence of food production in the Arles region in the Roman period is found at the watermill complex at Barbegal, twelve kilometers north of Arles. The remains are of a multiple mill with sixteen overshot waterwheels arranged as two parallel sets of eight, and of an aqueduct that provided water from the Alpilles hills to Arles. The waterwheels were used as the source of power for a flour mill, which may have been employed as a sawmill when it was not grinding corn. The mill was in use from the end of the first century AD until the end of the third century AD, and estimates are that it was capable of producing 4.5 tons of flour per day, enough to provide bread for ten thousand people. The Musée de l'Arles et de la Provence antiques displays a reconstructed model of the Barbegal water mill.

In AD 395 Arles became the seat of the Praefectura praetorio Galliarum (Praetorian Prefecture of the Gauls), which was the catalyst for a new phase of building, particularly the Baths of Constantine. This was a large bath complex, of which only the northern area has been excavated.

The necropolis of Alyscamps is situated a short distance outside the old town of Arles, where the Via Julia Augusta entered the town. By the fourth century AD the necropolis had several thousand tombs and was used not only by the elite families of Arles, but also by those in the surrounding area. Some of the sarcophagi from the necropolis are now on display in the Musée de l'Arles et de la Provence antiques. The artists Vincent van Gogh and Paul Gauguin visited Alyscamps in October 1888, and both painted the same view of the cemetery to compare their work.

The remains of Glanum, originally a Gallo-Greek and then Roman town set in the Alpilles hills close to the modern town of St. Rémy (Bouches-du-Rhône), were excavated by Henri Rolland between 1928 and 1933, and again in 1942. The excellent preservation of the town is due in part to Glanum's abandonment in the third century AD in favor of St. Rémy. Originally founded in the sixth century BC, contact between Glanum and the Greek colony of Massalia is reflected in the civic architecture, particularly a building resembling a Greek bouleuterion (council chamber), an agora (marketplace), and stone-built houses with peristyle colonnades. The romanization of Glanum is visible in its monuments, particularly its triumphal arch and the mausoleum of the Julii (figure 3.8). The triumphal arch is one of the earliest known examples in France, dating to the latter part of the reign of the emperor Augustus. The upper part of the arch, including its inscription, is no longer present. The surviving part of the arch is a Roman propaganda statement, its sculpture showing images of defeated Gallic prisoners. The mausoleum of the Julii is technically a cenotaph, as it has no burial chamber. It is a very imposing structure, being eighteen meters high and built in three stories, with scenes of mythical combat sculpted on its lowest section. The mausoleum was erected between 30 and 20 BC by three brothers of a Gallic family who had been granted Roman citizenship by Julius Caesar and built in honor of the brothers' father and grandfather. The monument, which stands close to the triumphal arch alongside what was then the main road into Glanum, would have proclaimed the status of the deceased and was an indication of the wealth of the town.

The town of Orange (Vaucluse) is noted for its Roman remains, particularly the well-preserved theater and triumphal arch (figure 3.9). Roman Orange was founded in 36 BC on the site of an earlier Gallic settlement. Known to the Romans as the Colonia Julia Firma secundanorum Arausio, it was home to veterans of the second Legion. The theater was built in the first century AD during the reign of the emperor Augustus. The theater's

Figure 3.8.   Roman arch and Mausoleum of the Julii, Glanum. istock, 458250481

most notable architectural feature is its scaenae frons (rear wall), which survives to a height of thirty-seven meters. King Louis XIV (reigned 1643–1715) was reported to have said during a visit to Orange, "C'est la plus belle muraille de mon royaume" (It is the finest wall in my kingdom). The Edict of Thessaloniki in AD 380 established Nicene Christianity as the official religion of the Roman Empire. Accordingly, in AD 391 the emperor Theodosius closed the theater, in common with those elsewhere, and Orange became a bishopric. As at Arles, restoration of the theater began in 1825 at the instigation of Prosper Merimée. The first Roman Festival was held at the theater in 1869, renamed the Chorégies from 1902, and continues today, primarily as a festival of opera. The Roman triumphal arch at Orange is more than nineteen meters high, has three spans, and is decorated lavishly with military themes of battle and the spoils of victory. The date of the arch has been the subject of much debate. Its initial construction traditionally is dated to the reign of Augustus to honor both those who fought in the Gallic Wars and the second Legion. The arch seemingly was reconstructed in AD 27 by the emperor Tiberius, as evidenced by an inscription, to celebrate the victories of Germanicus over the local tribes in the Rhineland. However, another opinion is that the triple arch would indicate a later date, perhaps in the late second century or early third century AD. The arch was incorporated into the city walls of Orange in the medieval period and restored as a freestanding monument in the middle of the nineteenth century.

Figure 3.9. Roman arch at Orange. istock, 479520446

Away from the major towns in southern France are a number of Roman archaeological sites.

The Trophée des Alpes, also known as the Tropaeum Alpium, is a prominent Roman monument, located at La Turbie (Alpes-Maritimes), above modern-day Monaco (figure 3.10). It is situated at the highest point on the Via Julia Augusta, the main Roman coastal road from Italy to Gaul. The Trophée des Alpes was erected by the emperor Augustus between 7 and 6 BC. It celebrates the conquest in 15 BC by Tiberius and Drusus, the stepsons of Augustus, of forty-five tribes described on the monument's inscription as "Alpine." The Trophée des Alpes, which dominates the landscape and is visible from the sea, serves as a tangible statement of the power of the Roman Empire.

Figure 3.10.   Le Trophée des Alpes, La Turbie. istock, 144956354

An unusual reminder of the Gallo-Roman era is found at the coastal settlement of Saint-Cyr-sur-Mer (Var), east of Marseille, where a villa was built in the first century AD in a very picturesque location. The villa site is now incorporated in the Gallo-Roman Museum of Tauroentum, although no clear evidence links the modern-day Saint-Cyr-sur-Mer with the ancient city of Tauroention (Roman Taurontum). Tauroention is recorded historically as a Greek trading post active from the fifth century BC and the site of a decisive naval battle between Caesar and Pompey for the control of Massalia. The location of the villa was known during the reign of King Louis XIV (1643–1715), who commissioned a survey of the site, but excavation only was begun in the 1920s, under the direction of Antoine Charras. The importance of the site was recognized in 1926, when it was classified as a historic monument. The site museum, constructed on top of the villa, opened in 1966. The highlight is the villa itself, although the museum also displays objects found on site, including amphorae, glass, and coins. A group of graves of different types includes a rare "house tomb." A Roman villa on the coast, such as this, similar to the type known from the Bay of Naples, is a very unusual discovery in France, the more usual villa being inland. The villa at Saint-Cyr-sur-Mer had a long open colonnade consisting of eighty granite columns, facing the sea, and three of its rooms had mosaic floors. It has been suggested that the abandonment of the villa was hastened by an earthquake in the third century AD.

Evidence of Gallo-Roman religion comes from the important rural healing sanctuary at Source-Seine (Côte-d'Or) in a small, enclosed valley in the Châtillon plateau to the northwest of the town of Dijon. Plausibly, it originated as an indigenous sanctuary that further developed in the Roman period, from the first century AD until the end of the fourth century AD. The first Gallo-Roman objects were found on the site in the eighteenth century, and excavations were conducted between 1836 and 1843 under the direction of Henri Baudot. Baudot's excavations uncovered the foundations of the sanctuary, which consisted of baths and a temple adjacent to the spring that is the source of the river Seine, as well as votive offerings. A find in one of the rooms of the baths was a pot inscribed with the name of the goddess Dea Sequana, the goddess of the river Seine, containing 120 anatomical votive offerings in the forms of eyes, breasts, and sexual organs made from bronze coated with gold or silver. In addition, wooden votive offerings have been preserved through the waterlogged environmental conditions. These consisted of a group of anatomical votives and complete human figures, likely to have represented worshippers. A statuette, thirty centimeters tall, of a female standing in a boat, is likely to be a representation of the goddess Sequana. The statuette now is housed in the Musée archéologique in Dijon (Côte'd'Or).

Another significant rural Gallo-Roman sanctuary was located at Ribemont-sur-Ancre (Somme), whose pre-Roman ossuary was discussed earlier in the chapter. The sanctuary is located on the slope of the valley of the river Ancre. At the highest point of the site was a large temple, with other buildings at a lower level, including a bath complex and theater seating three thousand spectators. Some of the stone sculpture from the temple is on display at the Musée de Picardie in Amiens (Somme).

Modern-day La Graufesenque (Aveyron) and Lezoux (Puy-de-Dôme) in southern and central France were the most important pottery production centers in the Roman Empire. They were known for the type of pottery technically called terra sigillata, colloquially referred to as "Samian ware." East Gaulish terra sigillata was made in what is now Germany. The earliest type of terra sigillata was made at Condatomagus (literally "the market where the rivers meet"), today known as La Graufesenque, on the outskirts of the town of Millau, on the small plain at the confluence of the rivers Tarn and Dourbie. Condatomagus was ideal for the production of pottery on a large scale, having access to good-quality clay, plentiful water, and large quantities of wood from the forests on the Causses, the series of limestone plateaus situated to the east of Millau.

Excavations at La Graufesenque took place in 1950, again from 1972 until 1982, and have provided useful evidence of the practicalities of the production of terra sigillata. The kilns at the site were in use between 10 BC and AD 150, with the major period of pottery export being between AD 40 and AD 100. It has been calculated that approximately six hundred potters would have worked at Condatomagus during its period of pottery production, about two hundred at any given time. Condatomagus is estimated to have had about fifty kilns in an area of ten hectares, although apart from the "grand four" (large kiln), few are visible today as only 2 percent to 3 percent of the site has been excavated. The Musée de Millau et des Grands Causses in the eighteenth-century Hôtel de Pégarolles houses displays that include a reconstructed kiln, examples of the different shapes of pottery vessels, and large quantities of "wasters," which are defective vessels that had been discarded. Interestingly, the "wasters" include pottery vessels stamped by different makers but fired in the same kiln.

The other major production center in France of terra sigillata was Lutosus, in the modern-day commune of Lezoux, near the city of Clermont Ferrand (Puy-de-Dôme). Many years of excavation have revealed hundreds of kilns whose output was exported widely in the Roman Empire. The names of about twelve hundred potters have been recorded, the most prolific of whom were Cinnamus and Paternus. Production at Lutosus began in the early first century AD, with the main phase of production being between AD 120 and the end of the second century AD.

In northern France, Paris has its origins in the pre-Roman period. The oppidum of the Parisii tribe was on the Ile de la Cité, in the heart of modern-day Paris, which they occupied from the mid-third century BC until the first century BC. Little is visible of Roman Lutetia, which developed on the left bank of the Seine from the mid-first century BC, exceptions being an arena, sometimes called an "amphitheater," and part of the Roman baths. The Arènes de Lutèce (figure 3.11), which dates between the late first century AD and second century AD, was discovered in the mid-nineteenth century in advance of the construction of a tram depot. Additional excavation and restoration took place in the early twentieth century, and the area now is used as a public recreation area. The Arènes de Lutèce was not a conventional amphitheater as it had a stage building, significant remains of which are preserved, including nine niches that seemingly were present to aid the acoustics in the arena. The preserved remains include small rooms, believed to be animal cages, which opened onto the arena. The frigidarium

Figure 3.11. Remains of the Arènes de Lutèce, Paris. istock, 462346127

(cold room) and caldarium (hot room) of a third-century AD Roman bath-house now form part of the Musée national du Moyen Age-Thermes et hotel de Cluny. The frigidarium also houses carved blocks from the altar known as the Pilier des Nautes, found under the Cathedral of Notre-Dame de Paris in the early eighteenth century. Dating to the first century AD, the altar was dedicated to Jupiter and other Roman and Gallic deities. The "Archaeological Crypt," now attached to the Musée Carnavalet, opened in 1980 under the square in front of the Cathedral of Notre-Dame and displays finds from excavations conducted there from 1965 to 1972. Visitors can see architectural remains of the early settlement, including a section of the quay on the river Seine and fourth-century AD baths, together with the foundations of the defensive wall built around the Ile de la Cité in AD 308. More recently, in 2006, excavations on the campus of the Université Pierre-et-Marie Curie in Paris revealed a Roman road and private houses with baths and a hypocaust.

Lutetia was connected to other Gallo-Roman settlements, including Diodorum, which lies close to the communes of Jouars-Pontchartrain and Tremblay-sur-Mauldre (both Yvelines). First identified in the mid-twentieth century, excavation of the site was in advance of the construction of the N12 road, which bypasses Jouars-Pontchartrain. Founded in the first century BC, Diadorum was on a strategic location at the crossroads of several long-distance routes. The settlement developed into a large Gallo-Roman administrative and trading center, extending over forty hectares, with sanctuaries and a theater. Evidence of daily life at Diadorum also was found, including pottery kilns, granaries, and a structure in one of the houses used for either drying cereals or smoking meat or fish. Information about the diet of Diadorum's inhabitants came from middens of shells and the bones of butchered animals.

The acquisition of the northern coast of Gaul aided the Roman conquest of Britannia. In AD 43 the emperor Claudius is reported to have assembled four legions close to Gesoriacum, the modern-day town of Boulogne-sur-Mer (Pas-de-Calais) in readiness for the invasion across the Channel. Following the invasion, Gesoriacum became the headquarters of the Classis Britannica, part of the Roman imperial navy, which protected both sides of the Channel. Archaeological evidence of the Classis Britannica is indicated by large numbers of ceramic tiles stamped CL.BR as well as inscriptions erected by naval officers. The naval base was on a hill overlooking the harbor, below the modern town. Built in the early second century AD, it had stone-built walls with rectangular towers surrounded by a ditch. Excavation in the northeastern section of the fort's interior revealed a large barracks, able to accommodate up to at least four thousand men. The writer Cassius Dio recorded the presence of a triumphal arch in celebration of Claudius, but this, together with the location of the first century AD naval base, has not yet been located. A first century AD lighthouse, known as the Tour d'Ordre, previously was located a couple of kilometers northwest of the fort. It disappeared in the seventeenth century as a result of the erosion of the cliff on which it stood and is known only from literary accounts and drawings.

On the island of Corsica, the commune of Aléria (Haute-Corse) on the east coast has archaeological remains from the pre-Roman and Roman periods. The settlement was founded as Alelie, a colony of the East Greek city of Phokaia (modern-day Foça in western Turkey), in the mid-sixth century BC before becoming an Etruscan colony. Archaeological evidence from the Etruscan period includes finds from burials in the Casabianda necropolis, to the south of Alelie, which was excavated in the 1960s by Jean Jehasse. The Etruscan-type tombs, more than two hundred in number, contained grave offerings from Etruria, Greece, and the Greek colonies in southern Italy, dating from the early fifth century BC until the third century BC. The city fell under Roman administration in 259 BC and subsequently was given the Roman name Aléria when the area became part of the Roman province of Sardinia and Corsica in 238 BC. By about 80 BC the Etang de Diane, a saltwater lagoon to the north of Aléria, become a major naval base. The remains of the Roman city of Aléria first were noted in 1839 by Prosper Merimée but not excavated until the 1950s. Among the prominent buildings discovered were the remains of baths, the forum, and a triumphal arch. However, in AD 410 the city of Aléria was devastated by fire and did not recover for several centuries. Finds from the site are displayed in the Musée Archéologique Jérôme Carcopino in Aléria, which is housed in a fourteenth-century Genoese fortress.

Elsewhere on Corsica, the now abandoned site of Mariana, in the modern-day commune of Lucciana (Haute-Corse), has produced evidence of the adoption of Christianity on Corsica and important new information regarding the cult of Mithras on the island during the Roman period. According to the Roman writers Seneca and Pliny, Mariana was founded as a colony by Gaius Marius in the early first century BC. Although the site was recognized in the nineteenth century, the first excavations did not take place until 1930. Further excavation was undertaken in the 1960s and 1970s, when cemeteries east and west of the settlement were located. In addition, excavations in the area of La Canonica, the medieval cathedral of Mariana, revealed the remains of an early Christian basilica and baptistery, constructed around AD 400, considered the first archaeological evidence of Christianity on Corsica. Research recommenced in 2000 by a team drawn from universities in France, Italy, and Belgium, who, in particular, discovered several structures dating from the first to the third centuries AD. The most recent excavations at Mariana have been conducted by Inrap, with the discovery announced in early 2017 of a Mithraeum, a sanctuary of Mithras, found on the outskirts of the Roman settlement. This discovery, and how it relates to other evidence of the cult of Mithras in Roman Gaul, is discussed in chapter 6. In 2012, an announcement was made that a new museum and archaeological park were being planned for Mariana, showcasing its history from the Roman period until its decline through malaria in the early thirteenth century and, finally, abandonment in the early sixteenth century when the Episcopal seat was transferred to Bastia (Haute-Corse).

The Late Roman Empire in France

The political crisis that affected the Roman Empire in the later third century AD led to the formation of the "Gallic Empire," which in practice was a separate state from the rest of the Roman Empire. Established by Postumus in AD 260, at its peak the Gallic Empire included the provinces of Germania, Gaul, Britannia, and, for a time, Hispania. It declined from AD 268, and returned to Roman rule under the emperor Aurelian in AD 274. In AD 286, Carausius, the Roman naval commander of the Classis Britannica, tried to usurp the emperor Maximian. Carausius established a regional empire, sometimes called the "Britannic Empire," declaring himself emperor over Roman Britain and much of northern Gaul, where a mint issuing coins with his name operated at Rouen (Seine-Maritime). In AD 293, Constantius Chlorus successfully besieged Gesoriacum, modern-day Boulogne-sur-Mer (Pas-de-Calais), and defeated Carausius, who was murdered by Allectus, his own official. Archaeological evidence of the uncertain political situation may be reflected in the modification of the fort at Boulogne-sur-Mer. Large towers were added to the front of the defensive walls of the fort, with a completely new wall built using the ditch of the earlier walls as its foundation trench. A find from this period from Arras (Pas-de-Calais) is a gold medallion depicting Constantius Chlorus's triumphal entrance into Londinium (London) in AD 296 after the defeat of Allectus.

In the late fourth century AD, the Roman Empire was divided into eastern and western administrative areas, within which were two prefectures in each part. The former Gallic provinces, together with modern-day England, Wales, Spain, Portugal, and northern Morocco, became the Praefectura praetorio Galliarum. Archaeological evidence of these political changes may be found in Arles, which became the seat of administration of the Praefectura praetorio Galliarum, as discussed earlier in this chapter. In addition, the archaeology of late Roman Gaul is characterized by evidence of the spread of Christianity.

Prior to these changes, archaeological evidence of early Christianity in Gaul is found at Lugdunum, the modern-day city of Lyon, whose amphitheater of the Three Gauls (figure 3.12) is considered to have been the site of the persecution of Christians, in particular Blandina and Pothinus, who died in AD 177 and later were canonized. The building of churches was encouraged following the Edict of Toleration for Christian worship of AD 313. Lyon has good evidence of Christian architecture of the late fourth century AD, in the late Roman town on the banks of the river Saône, where the remains of the churches of Sainte-Croix and Saint-Etienne are displayed in the "archaeological garden" adjacent to the present-day cathedral.

Earlier buildings occasionally were converted into Christian use. For example, at Cimiez (Roman Cemenelenum), a northern suburb of Nice (Alpes-Maritimes), a Christian basilica was built on part of the East Baths in the fourth century AD.

Figure 3.12.   Roman amphitheater of the Three Gauls, Lyon. istock, 600371110

France also shows archaeological evidence of early monasticism. The monastic community at Ligugé, near Poitiers (Vienne), the present-day Abbaye Saint-Martin de Ligugé, was established by Martin of Tours around AD 360. It was founded on the site of a Roman villa, and excavation suggests that some of the villa's rooms were adopted for use as a church. The fourth century AD church had a nave and apse eighteen meters long, to which a martyrium in the form of a cross was added in the early fifth century AD.

Maritime Trade: Shipwrecks from the Etruscan and Roman Periods

France has played a leading role in the development of underwater archaeology, discussed further in chapter 4. This section focuses on shipwrecks found off the southern coast of France from two discrete periods: the sixth and fifth centuries BC and first century BC to the first century AD. These shipwrecks provide invaluable evidence of trade in these periods.

The shipwrecks from the sixth and fifth centuries BC date from the period following the establishment of the Greek colony of Massalia. Two shipwrecks from this period are discussed in detail, the Cap d'Antibes and the Grand Ribaud F wrecks.

The wreck off Cap d'Antibes (Alpes-Maritimes) was excavated between 1955 and 1969 and found to have been partly looted by sport divers. The main cargo of the ship, which was wrecked in the middle of the sixth century BC, was at least 180 Etruscan amphorae. It also included Greek amphorae together with more than sixty examples of the characteristic Etruscan pottery known as bucchero and a few vessels decorated in the Etrusco-Corinthian style.

Slightly later in date is the shipwreck discovered in 1999 west of the island of Grand Ribaud, one of the Hyères Islands (Var), at a depth of around sixty meters. The particular wreck designated Grand Ribaud F was excavated in 2000 and 2001. The cargo suggests that the ship was wrecked at the end of the sixth century BC or beginning of the fifth century BC. Much of the hull of the ship, which was around twenty-five meters long, was preserved thanks to protection by its cargo of amphorae. Up to one thousand Etruscan amphorae from Cerveteri in modern-day central Italy, some of which carried inscriptions, were discovered together with fine-ware and coarse-ware ceramics and small bronze dishes.

Other shipwrecks from this period have been found off the coast of southern France, most notably Bon Porte, near Saint-Tropez (Var); Pointe Lequin, on the north side of Porquerolle island (Var); and Dattier, west of Cap Cavalaire (Var). The Bon Porte I wreck, found in 1971, was a small vessel carrying Etruscan and Greek amphorae. The Pointe Lequin IA wreck carried a much larger cargo, predominantly amphorae from diverse areas of the Mediterranean together with a large number of Greek fine wares. The small wreck found off the coast at Dattier in 1971 had already been looted, although fifteen amphorae were noted. Sadly, the majority of these were looted during the course of excavation before they could be raised to the surface.

Many Roman shipwrecks have been found off the southern coast of France. This section concentrates on the important wreck at Madrague de Giens (Var), with some discussion of wrecks found close to the lighthouse at La Chrétienne, near Saint-Raphaël (Var); and at Port Vendres (Pyrénées-Orientales), close to the border between modern-day France and Spain.

The Madrague de Giens wreck was discovered in 1967 by French naval divers in the harbor at Madrague de Giens, on the northwest tip of the Giens peninsula, lying at a depth of between nineteen and twenty-two meters. The ship came to rest on the seabed leaning to one side, covered by sediment, which aided the excellent preservation of the upper part of the ship's hull. The excavation by a team led by André Tchernia began in 1972 and continued for eleven seasons. The ship was found to have been wrecked in the first century BC, between about 75 and 60 BC, while exporting wine from central Italy, probably destined for Massalia and the cities of southern Gaul.

The Madrague de Giens wreck was fully excavated. It was a large ship, forty meters long, and is estimated to have carried between fifty-eight hundred and seventy-eight hundred amphorae, stacked up to three or four levels, making it one of the larger Roman merchant vessels. The amphorae and silt covering helped preserve some of the hull, with the major timbers made from oak and the lesser timbers from pine or elm. The presence of large ballast stones, foreign to the area, seemingly were used as diving aids by salvage divers in the Roman period. The salvage divers appeared to have cleared valuable commodities, including many amphorae, meaning that large parts of the cargo had been raised in antiquity. It is not known how common salvage would have been in the past, but it is clear that the loss of a valuable cargo would have been considered catastrophic. The ship that sank at Madrague de Giens was clearly large, undoubtedly with a correspondingly rich cargo, and its owners may have ordered salvage.

The majority of the amphorae found on the Madrague de Giens wreck were of the Dressel 1B type, elongated in form. Many carry the stamps of Publius Veveius Papus, an estate owner, from Terracina, south of Rome. Few such seals survive on land sites, as the seals would have been broken to release the wine. The placement of the amphorae in the hold of the ship can be reconstructed. Analysis of the sediments in the amphorae indicates that the wine from the Madrague de Giens shipwreck was a red wine. The cargo also included defrutum, made from boiling down must, the freshly pressed grape juice. A secondary cargo was pottery, mainly black slipware produced both in Campania and other parts of Italy, which was widely exported. It also included some amphorae from East Greece, modern-day Turkey. Rather than being part of the cargo to be sold, this type of amphora probably either contained stores for the crew or were older amphorae carrying water or other produce.

More than one hundred other Roman shipwrecks are found along the coast of southern France. Although some sank before the second century BC, the majority sank in the second and first centuries BC, decreasing in number after the reign of Augustus (first century AD and later). The majority of the second and first century BC ships found wrecked off the coast of modern-day France sailed from ports on the Italian peninsula, carrying locally produced goods.

One of these shipwrecks is designated the Chrétienne C, discovered close to the lighthouse of La Chrétienne and investigated by Jean-Pierre

Joncheray in the early 1970s. The ship, which sank between 175 BC and 150 BC, represents the early stage of the wine trade between Italy and France. The ship, which was only fifteen meters long, carried about five hundred Greco-Italian amphorae, possibly the produce from a single estate. Shipboard materials included tools and three sounding weights.

The shipwreck designated Port Vendres II was found off the Mediterranean coast, close to the border between France and Spain, and excavations took place between1974 and 1984. The wreck, which can be dated to the mid-first century AD, carried a cargo primarily consisting of amphorae carrying Spanish olive oil, wine, and salted fish. The cargo also included ingots of copper, lead, and tin, some of the latter marked with inscriptions giving dates between AD 41 and AD 48. Some of the other objects found on the ship, including spoons, a strigil, a comb, lamps, and a ceramic inkwell, may have belonged to the crew. The Port Vendres II wreck is particularly useful for its insight into trade from the area of modern-day Spain in the Early Roman Imperial period.

The rivers of France were used extensively to transport goods in the Roman period. Good evidence of this came to light in 2004 with the discovery by Luc Long and his team of the remains of a barge in the river Rhône at Arles (Bouches-du-Rhône), known as Arles Rhône 3. The barge dated to the first century AD, the time of the monumentalization of Roman Arelate. It was a trading vessel, thirty-one meters long, carrying a cargo of building stone quarried some fifteen kilometers north of Arles. The archaeologists, who excavated the barge between 2008 and 2010, also found the vessel's galley, identified by the presence of cooking utensils. The oak timbers of the hull were well preserved, and the decision was taken to cut the vessel into ten sections and raise it in 2011. The barge has been on display in the Musée de l'Arles et de la Provence antiques since 2013.

A similar vessel was found during excavations that took place in 1989 and 1990 in the Place Tolozan in Lyon, close to the river Rhône. The barge, which dates between AD 30 and AD 40, was excavated in advance of the installation of an underground cable. It was lifted in three parts and conserved between 1990 and 2003 at l'Atelier Régional de Conservation Nucléart (ARC-Nucléart) in Grenoble (Isère). The barge was found to be 7 meters long and 2.4 meters wide and had apparently been abandoned. It is now in the collection of the Musée Gallo-Romain du Lyon-Fourvière.

The group of six Gallo-Roman ships discovered in the river Saône at Lyon is discussed further in chapter 6.

EARLY MEDIEVAL FRANCE

Although Roman Gaul did not formally come to an end until AD 486 with the victory of the Franks at the Battle of Soissons, it had been preceded by a period of decline. The fifth century AD in Western Europe was character-ized by the movement of non-Gallic people into Gaul. Vandals, Alans, and Suevi entered Gaul from Germania, crossing into modern-day Spain in AD 407. From the south, following their sack of Rome in AD 410, the Visigoths entered Gaul in AD 412. The Visigoths subsequently invaded modern-day Spain in AD 415, but in AD 418 they withdrew back into Gaul and estab-lished a capital at Tolosa, modern-day Toulouse (Haute-Garonne). Other groups of non-Gallic people were the Burgundians, who settled in the areas around the rivers Saône and Rhône; and the Alamanni, who moved into Alsace. The Franks settled in northern France, in the modern-day Ile-de-France region.

There is little archaeological evidence for the presence of any Visigoths in southwest Gaul in the fifth century AD. An exception is the series of carved stone sarcophagi often given the names "Visigothic," "Aquitanian," or "southwest Gallic," found in the area known as Septimania, which was regarded as part of Gaul in the fifth century AD. The borders of Septima-nia were defined by the Massif Central to the north, the Pyrenees to the west and south, and the Camargue marshes to the east. The "Visigothic sarcophagi" were usually made from marble quarried in the commune of Saint-Béat (Haute-Garonne). Carved in very low relief, the earlier sar-cophagi are fairly plain, with typical decoration being apostles under a row of arches, whereas the later type are more ornate and feature vine decora-tion. The main centers of production were Narbonne (Aude) and Béziers (Hérault), although sarcophagi have also been found in Toulouse (Haute-Garonne), Agen (Lot-et-Garonne), and Bordeaux (Gironde). It seems clear that Narbonne-based artisans specialized in sarcophagi with ivy-branch decoration, made from local marble quarried at the nearby commune of Saint-Pons-de-Thomières (Hérault), as opposed to the Saint-Béat marble used elsewhere. Five examples of this type of sarcophagus are in the Musée Lapidaire at Narbonne.

Another characteristic object were the "Aquitanian buckles," large bronze buckles with a tinned surface, decorated with incised geometric and animal motifs. A particular type of buckle had a beak-like projection, and the distribution of finds suggests they may have been worn by locally re-cruited troops who defended Toulouse and the Garonne valley from attacks from the Visigoths of Septimania. The distribution of Visigothic objects in southern Gaul suggests that production of rectangular cloisonné belt buckles was divided between modern-day Spain and Septimania. Simpler buckles and radiate-headed brooches may well have been made locally. The buckles are found along the coast from Perpignan (Pyrénées-Orientales) to Montpellier (Hérault), with others around Carcassonne (Aude) and Albi (Tarn). Finds from excavations at the commune of Giroussens (Tarn) suggest that it was probably a Visigothic cemetery, a rare Visigothic site found in Frankish territory. Few Visigothic objects are found elsewhere in Aquitaine, two fine exceptions being a fibula in the shape of an eagle, decorated in the cloisonné technique, said to be from the commune of Valence d'Agen (Tarn-et-Garonne); and a buckle with an eagle-headed terminal from the fourth-century AD Gallo-Roman "Villa de Nymfius" in the commune of Valentine (Haute-Garonne). Visigothic coins, minted with the names of their kings, have been found in Septimania and southern Gascony but nowhere else in Gaul apart from occasional examples in hoards.

The characteristic pottery from southern Gaul made between AD 350 and AD 600 were gray and orange stamped wares. It has been classified into three main groups distinguished by the fabric and decoration: Languedoc, Provencal, and Atlantic, the latter probably based in Bordeaux (Gironde). The pottery has been useful in determining trade patterns during this period. Languedoc wares were barely exported, in contrast to the Provencal pottery, exported to the east coast of Spain, Italy, and the eastern Mediterranean, including Athens. The Atlantic pottery was exported to the English Channel ports, Wales, and Switzerland. The inward-looking aspect of Septimania also is suggested by the lack of evidence of use between the fifth and eighth centuries AD of the once-flourishing Roman road known as the Via Aquitania, which linked Narbonne (Aude), Toulouse (Haute-Garonne), and Bordeaux (Gironde).

The Rise of the Franks

Clovis, who was leader of the Franks from AD 480 to AD 511, became the dominant ruler in what had been Gaul and the first king of the Merovingian dynasty. The Frankish kingdom expanded; the Burgundians and Alemanni were conquered by Clovis, and the Visigoths withdrew from Aquitania into modern-day Spain. Even though the Franks gave their name to the modern-day country of France, their kingdom extended beyond present-day boundaries into what is now Belgium, the Netherlands, and northern Germany. Although some architectural remains survive from this period, most of the archaeological evidence comes from tombs.

Interaction between the recently arrived Franks and the existing inhabitants is evident from excavations at the cemetery in the commune of Frénouville (Calvados), near the town of Caen. The cemetery began to be used for burials in the fourth century AD and was in continuous use until the seventh century AD. However, the orientation of the graves changed in the early fifth century AD, and it is apparent from excavation that those aligned north to south are Late Roman whereas those aligned east to west are Frankish.

Other evidence of the transition from the Late Roman to the Early Medieval period has been found elsewhere in Normandy at the commune of Mondeville (Calvados), where a Merovingian cemetery was excavated by Capitaine G. Caillaud between 1913 and 1917. Subsequent excavations at the cemetery at Mondeville revealed eighth-century AD wooden buildings in the form of "grave houses" over burials, either singly or in groups.

The few architectural remains from this era are overwhelmingly Christian, most notably the Baptistère Saint-Jean at Poitiers (Vienne) and Merovingian crypts at Jouarre (Seine-et-Marne) and Grenoble (Isère).

The Baptistère Saint-Jean, adjacent to the cathedral at Poitiers, is considered to be one of the most notable examples of Merovingian architecture. It was founded traditionally in AD 360 on the instructions of Saint-Hilaire, the first bishop of Poitiers, although the structure visible today is Merovingian and Carolingian in date. The initial archaeological research at the baptistery was undertaken by Etienne-Marie Siauve in 1803. Siauve was an interesting character; initially a priest, he later became a soldier, including serving as military commissioner from 1800 until his death during the retreat of the French Grande Armée from Russia in 1812. Siauve was also the author of several archaeological publications and a member of the Académie celtique, which became the Societé nationals des antiquaires de France. At the baptistery in Poitiers, Siauve discovered an octagonal basin below floor level alongside a channel that connected it to the disused Roman aqueduct. Damage to the baptistery undoubtedly led to the building's acquisition by the French government in 1834, with extensive renovations between 1852 and 1859. Elsewhere in Poitiers, in 1878 preparations for the building of artillery defenses uncovered part of a Gallo-Roman cemetery. The site was excavated by Camille de la Croix, a Jesuit priest from Belgium. He reported that he had found an Early Medieval subterranean mausoleum, which has been given the name the Hypogée des Dunes. Unusually for the time, la Croix reburied the monument, which has been dated to the seventh century AD, until there was a way in the future to protect it, although he retrieved finds from the excavation. Restoration of the Hypogée des Dunes has begun, and visitors are able to visit the monument a few days each year.

The two crypts at Jouarre (Seine-et-Marne), the Crypt of Saint-Paul and the adjoining Crypt of Saint-Ebrégisile, are part of the Abbaye Notre Dame de Jouarre. In particular, the Crypt of Saint-Paul, which was built surrounding two colonnades of Gallo-Roman columns topped by capitals carved in the Merovingian style, is noted for a series of burials in sarcophagi, most notably of Agilbert. Agilbert, who died in AD 681, was the brother of Abbess Theodochilde, who founded the abbey around AD 630. The carvings on Agilbert's sarcophagus show scenes of the Last Judgment and Christ in Majesty and are considered to be among the best surviving examples of pre-Romanesque sculpture in France.

Another stunning example of Merovingian architecture exists in Grenoble (Isère), where the Musée archéologique Grenoble-Saint-Laurent houses the crypt of Saint-Oyand. The site of the museum has a long history, incorporating the deconsecrated twelfth-century church of Saint-Laurent. This was built on a Carolingian church, itself built on a church associated with burials and crypt dating to the sixth century AD. It was in this latter period that the cult of Saint-Oyand, usually called "Eugendus" in English, was introduced following his death in AD 510. The sixth-century AD church was built on a cruciform plan, with the north and south arms forming the exterior of the twelfth-century AD church. The crypt under the east arm is preserved under the choir of the later church. The roof of the crypt is supported by a colonnade of twenty columns, of which sixteen are original. These are surmounted by richly carved capitals, typical of the pre-Romanesque era.

The crypt of Saint-Oyand was brought to scholarly attention in 1803 through an article by Jacques-Joseph Champollion-Figeac, the elder brother of the renowned Egyptologist Jean-François Champollion. The crypt also attracted the attention of Prosper Merimée, Inspecteur général des monuments historiques, who was alerted to damage to the building in 1846. The crypt was categorized as a historic monument in 1850, one of the earliest to be designated in France.

The most characteristic Merovingian archaeological remains are grave goods from elite burials excavated throughout France. Collections of these grave goods were formed mainly between 1870 and 1914.

A major collector was John Evans, who purchased Merovingian objects, most notably grave offerings found at Picquigny (Somme) dating to the sixth century AD. Rather than from a single burial, as originally believed, the "group" comprises a combination of objects associated with both male and female burials. On Evans's death in 1908, much of his collection, including the objects from Picquigny, was presented to the Ashmolean Museum in Oxford, England, by his son, the noted archaeologist Arthur Evans. Finds from Picquigny include objects made from gold and silver gilt, decorated in the cloisonné technique with garnets and glass. These include radiate-headed bow brooches, earrings, and a finger ring. A particularly interesting object was a rock crystal amulet, thought to have been worn at the waist.

An early excavation of a Merovingian cemetery was the result of a chance find in 1886 by Philippe Delamain from the commune of Jarnac (Charente), a member of the local family famous for its production of cognac. The cemetery was found at Herpès, in the commune of Courbillac (Charente), and was excavated by Delamain between 1889 and 1893. Most of Delamain's finds were bought by the collector Edouard Guilhou in 1901 and sold in 1905. Many of the objects were purchased by the British Museum in London; others, the Metropolitan Museum of Art in New York. The objects are typical of Merovingian production in the sixth century AD, and comprise brooches of different types, made from silver gilt and garnets, belt mounts, buckles, and weaponry. Bowls there were made of both glass and pottery. Delamain also excavated a Merovingian cemetery in the commune of Biron (Charente-Maritime).

A group of Merovingian tombs came to light in the early twentieth century while quarrying for chalk at Rosay, now part of the commune of Val-de-Vière (Marne). The grave goods, which date between AD 500 and AD 550, include six pieces of jewelry now in the Metropolitan Museum of Art in New York. They are all decorated in the cloisonné technique with garnets and glass, and comprise a pair of silver gilt radiate-headed bow brooches and a pair of gold earrings, both very similar to objects from Picquigny mentioned previously, together with a pair of silver gilt disc brooches.

The most lavish known Merovingian burial is of Queen Arégonde, who died in AD 580 or 581, excavated at the Basilica of Saint-Denis (Seine-Saint-Denis). The basilica was built on a Gallo-Roman cemetery, the reputed burial place of Saint Denis, who was martyred in about AD 250. The first king to be buried in the basilica was Dagobert in AD 639. However, the area below the present basilica was used as a necropolis for the Merovingian elite from the late fifth century AD, which led to the flourishing of this location. In addition, excavations below the present basilica suggest that many women in particular were buried there, seemingly a desire for their remains to be as close as possible to Saint Denis.

In 1959 a stone sarcophagus was found containing the burial of a woman, who was identified from a ring inscribed with her name as Queen Arégonde and giving her the title of queen (figure 3.13). The grave goods were appropriate for Arégonde, who was the daughter of a king (Clovis I), wife of a king (Clotaire I), and mother of another (Chilperic). Jewelry, in the collection of the Musée d'Archéologie nationale, included gold filigree earrings; a gold belt buckle with garnet and glass fittings; and pins, including a large and elaborate pin inlaid with garnets and glass. Arégonde's clothing was unusually well preserved. It was made from very high-quality textiles, some of which had been imported from outside the Frankish kingdom. The cuffs of her long garment were made of samite, a heavy silk fabric incorporating thread of precious metal, which would have been imported from Persia. Her head and shoulders had been covered with a veil made from a similar fabric. Above Arégonde's long garment, dyed with purple dye made from murex shells, and below her burial shroud was a lavish textile made from a mixture of very fine wool and beaver hair. Fragments of leather were found from Arégonde's shoes, together with metal fragments, which have enabled the reconstruction of her shoes and leg bindings. This burial has been especially helpful to archaeologists in the reconstruction of the clothing of an elite Merovingian woman.

The Abbaye-Saint-Victor in Marseille (Bouches-du-Rhône) includes a fifth-century AD crypt, notable for excavations of burials, particularly that of a woman that included well-preserved textiles and plant remains. The woman, who died in the late fifth century AD aged in her late twenties, was buried in a stone-built tomb. She was wrapped in linen wearing a decorated silk damask tunic and fringed cloak. The woman, whose head rested on a cushion of flowers, was buried with a gold cross on her forehead.

Important Merovingian discoveries continue to be made. A group of five rich burials, dating from the fifth to sixth centuries AD, was excavated in 1987 in the commune of Louvres (Val-d'Oise), close to Paris-Charles-de-Gaulle airport. The burials were found around the Tour Saint-Rieul, the remains of a twelfth-century AD church. Four of the burials were of females; the fifth, a man, was accompanied by his iron sword. All burials included grave goods of high-quality cloisonné jewelry; the women were buried with pendants, bracelets, buckles, and brooches of different shapes. In the case of the man, the scabbard of his sword was ornamented with cloisonné decoration.

France has provided a major contribution to the current understanding of ancient maritime trade in the western Mediterranean through exploration of shipwrecks found off its Mediterranean coast and along its major

Figure 3.13.   Sarcophagus of Queen Arégonde, Basilica of Saint-Denis. Alamy

rivers. Likewise, discoveries from the Iron Age and the period of Roman occupation in France have shed light on the effects of Greek colonization and the conquest by Rome. The arrival of non-Gallic people into Late Roman and Early Medieval France, culminating in the establishment of the Merovingian dynasty of kings, is also a main feature of French archaeology in this period.

4

FRENCH ARCHAEOLOGY
AND ARCHAEOLOGISTS

The influence of French archaeologists spreads beyond the borders of France, throughout Europe and beyond. The first part of the chapter considers the archaeologists, not all of them French, whose archaeological work in France has made a significant contribution to our knowledge of the past. The second part of the chapter discusses innovations of French archaeology, the case studies being the naming of type sites for phases of the Paleolithic period in Western Europe and beyond from sites in France, the development of underwater archaeology, the use of aerial photography in archaeology, and the application of archaeological science in France.

EARLY ARCHAEOLOGISTS

As discussed in chapter 1, interest in France's past began in the early sixteenth century, when certain learned individuals assembled collections of Gallo-Roman antiquities. However, it was not until the work of Bernard de Montfaucon (1655–1741) that objects were considered as historic documents in the same way as texts.

Bernard de Montfaucon, perhaps best known as the individual who first used the term paléographie to describe the study of ancient handwriting, also was interested in the material remains found in France. In 1719, he published an account of the megalithic tomb found at Cocherel (Eure), discussed in chapter 1, in which he deduced that it must have been from the "stone age" because of the absence of metal. Montfaucon was drawing on the work *De rerum natura* written in the first century BC by the Roman poet and philosopher Lucretius. Lucretius proposed the concept of a "three-age system," which demonstrated the cultural development of humankind by their use of available materials, namely, stone, followed by copper, then iron. In addition, in 1734 Montfaucon showed his interest in ancient indigenous artifacts through his presentation *Anciennes Armes des Gaulois* in a communication to the Académie des inscriptions et belles-lettres.

Jacques Boucher de Perthes (1788–1868) became a key figure in the knowledge of the antiquity of humans. In 1825, Boucher de Perthes became director of the customs office at Abbeville (Somme). As discussed in chapter 1, it was not until the 1840s that his application of the method of stratigraphy, borrowed from geology, to prehistory indicated the presence of humans in the area much earlier in time than previously believed.

In 1863, Boucher de Perthes was awarded the Légion d'Honneur by the emperor Napoleon III and was invited by the emperor to deposit the outstanding pieces from his archaeological collection in the museum founded in 1867 in Saint-Germain-en-Laye (Yvelines), today the Musée d'Archéologie nationale. The same year, these objects were exhibited at the Exposition Universelle in Paris.

PREHISTORIANS

Among the many outstanding figures who pioneered the discovery of the Paleolithic period in France were Edouard Lartet, Emile Cartailhac, Denis Peyrony, and, the most renowned, Henri Breuil.

Edouard Lartet (1801–1871) initially was a lawyer, but he developed an interest in fossils from 1833, when he was shown a mastodon tooth. A few years later he discovered the first of a series of fossilized animal remains at his family's property at Sansan (Gers) and subsequently published reports on his discoveries. Lartet joined in the scholarly debate on the age of early humans and their coexistence with extinct animals such as mammoths. Accordingly, in 1860 he began archaeological exploration of La Grotte du Ker de Massat (Ariège) and L'Abri d'Aurignac (Haute-Garonne), whose significant finds are discussed later in this chapter. Lartet's excavations in the Dordogne in 1863 and 1864 were crucial in determining the age of human antiquity. The excavations were funded by the English banker and businessman Henry Christy (1810–1865), whose name perhaps is best known for providing the idea of the "Turkish towel," the type widely used today, which was based on samples he brought home from his Eastern Mediterranean travels in 1849 and 1850. The type was popularized when Christy demonstrated a sample of "Turkish toweling" to Queen Victoria and Prince Albert at the 1851 Great Exhibition in London.

In 1852, Christy largely withdrew from business. He already had an interest in social issues such as the rights of indigenous people and traveled widely in Europe, North Africa, and North and Central America, most notably in Mexico. Christy also wished to contribute to the current debate on human evolution, and in 1860 he visited the Somme Valley, where Jacques Boucher de Perthes had proved the association of humans and long-extinct animals. Lartet's work in the Dordogne, funded by Christy, revealed evidence of human occupation that was more recent, and of a different type, than that previously found in the gravels of the Somme. In particular, Lartet's excavation of l'Abri de la Madeleine, discussed further in chapter 2 and later in this chapter, is considered to provide definite evidence of human antiquity, as well as providing the basis for the subdivision of the late Ice Age into discrete periods. In 1864, Lartet and Christy published in the *Revue archéologique* what may be the first general article on Paleolithic art titled "Sur les figures d'animaux gravées ou sculptées et autres produits d'art et d'industrie imputables aux temps primordiaux de la période humaine" (On the engraved or sculpted animal figures and other pieces of art and artifacts ascribed to the primordial times of the human period). Lartet and Christy worked together on many sites in the Vézère Valley (Dordogne), including the Abri Lartet in the Gorge d'Enfer, L'Abri de Laugerie-Haute, and L'Abri de Laugerie-Basse, all in Les Eyzies; L'Abri de la Madeleine in Tursac; Le Moustier in Peyzac-le-Moustier; and Le Pech-de-l'Azé I in Carsac-Aillac. In Paris, Lartet, collaborating with Emile Cartailhac and Gabriel de Mortillet, discussed later in this chapter, was responsible for the prehistoric displays at the Exposition Universelle in Paris in 1867. In 1868, Lartet was appointed professor of palaeontology at the Muséum d'Histoire Naturelle in Paris. His son, Louis, was also a paleontologist and geologist, and he excavated the site of l'Abri Cro-Magnon, discussed in chapter 2.

Like Lartet, Emile Cartailhac (1845–1921) trained as a lawyer but showed no interest in pursuing this career and devoted his life to the study of the prehistory of France and the Iberian Peninsula. Cartailhac was introduced to prehistory by his uncle, the naturalist Jean Louis Armand de Quatrefages de Bréau, and in 1863 excavated many dolmen tombs in the Causse de Larzac, a plateau in the south of the elevated region known as the Massif Central in central France. Cartailhac always was aware of the need to disseminate knowledge through museums and gave finds from his early excavations to museums in Toulouse and London. Furthermore, between 1882 and 1884 Cartailhac ran a free course in archaeology at the Faculty of Sciences at the University of Toulouse. From 1888 until his death in 1921, Cartailhac was professor of prehistoric archaeology at the Faculté des Lettres at the University of Toulouse.

Denis Peyrony (1869–1954) is another archaeologist who made a significant contribution to our knowledge of French prehistory, excavating at a range of important sites in the Dordogne département, such as La Ferrassie, Laugerie-Haute, le Moustier, and la Madeleine. In particular, the authenticity of Paleolithic cave art was established by Peyrony's discoveries in 1901 at a further two caves close to Les Eyzies (Dordogne): namely, la Grotte de Font-de-Gaume and Les Combarelles I, the latter with Henri Breuil and Louis Capitan. In addition, in 1913 Peyrony founded the Musée des Eyzies, now the Musée national de préhistoire, at the ruined Château des Eyzies at Les Eyzies (Dordogne). In 1940, toward the end of his career, Peyrony, along with Jean Bouyssonie, André Cheynier, and Henri Breuil, recognized the importance of the paintings that had been discovered in the Grotte de Lascaux, discussed in chapter 2.

Henri Edouard Prosper Breuil (1877–1961) is considered the leading authority on Paleolithic art of his generation (figure 4.1). Breuil often is known by the title "Abbé" as he had trained as a priest, although he also had a strong interest in natural science, and one of his teachers at the seminary where he trained encouraged this interest. Indeed, Breuil was allowed to concentrate on the study of prehistory and undertook few religious duties. In summer 1897, Breuil and Jean Bouyssonie visited several important archaeological sites and made the acquaintance of many of France's most eminent prehistorians, including Edouard Piette and Emile Cartailhac. As he had a talent for drawing animals, Piette and Cartailhac enlisted his help with the illustration of Paleolithic portable and cave art. Breuil discovered many decorated caves and galleries himself, and his work is important as his drawings are sometimes the only record of images that no longer exist. At the start of his career, Breuil undertook a few small-scale excavations in Le Mas d'Azil cave (Ariège) and the rock shelter Abri Dufaure (Landes). However, his later career was wider in scope and concentrated on other aspects of prehistoric archaeology, also working on the megalithic art of France. Outside France, he turned his attention to the Iberian Peninsula and in the 1940s began a project copying rock art in southern Africa. Although now superceded, Breuil's view, based on ethnographical analogies, was that the

Figure 4.1. Henri Breuil.
Paul G. Bahn

main function of Paleolithic images was primarily as hunting magic. In addition, he considered the images in caves as single images arranged in groups.

André Leroi-Gourhan (1911–1986) generally is considered to be the most influential figure in the study of Paleolithic cave art and settlements in the 1960s and 1970s. After his studies, Leroi-Gourhan worked in various museums initially at the Musée d'ethnographie du Trocadéro in Paris. Between 1940 and 1943, Leroi-Gourhan was a curator at the Musée Guimet and subsequently at the CNRS (Centre national de la recherche scientifique). From 1944, Leroi-Gourhan was a lecturer at the University of Lyon, until his appointment in 1956 as chair of ethnology at the Sorbonne University in Paris, where he specialized in prehistoric art. During this time, he additionally served as deputy director of the Musée de l'Homme, part of the Muséum national d'Histoire naturelle. In 1969, Leroi-Gourhan was elected to the Collège de France, a long-established higher education and research establishment in Paris.

Leroi-Gourhan's view was that students should be encouraged to undertake archaeological fieldwork. He conducted field schools at the Grotte des Furtins, in the commune of Berzé-la-Ville (Saône-et-Loire) between 1945 and 1948, and from 1946 at the complex of nine caves that form les Grottes d'Arcy-sur-Cure (Yonne), including the Grotte du Renne, discussed in chapter 2. At the field school at Arcy-sur-Cure, Leroi-Gourhan taught archaeological methods that were very different from those that had gone before. He laid great emphasis on meticulous excavation, paying particular attention to the different floor levels.

In 1964, a team from the CNRS, led by Leroi-Gourhan, began work at the open-air site of Pincevent in the commune of la Grande-Paroisse (Seine-et-Marne), a project which is still ongoing. The site was found accidentally, during commercial quarrying of sand. Leroi-Gourhan could use his then pioneering technique of horizontal excavation on a large-scale Paleolithic site, encouraging students to adopt these techniques. Leroi-Gourhan also pioneered the use of new archaeological techniques, including recording floors by making latex moulds. The Pincevent site had fifteen separate levels of occupation from the Late Magdalenian period, around 10,000 BC; and excavation revealed more than one hundred living areas, likely to have been covered with tents, and twenty large hearths. The animal remains, almost entirely reindeer bones, indicate that the site was occupied from early summer to early winter. It is considered that Leroi-Gourhan's article "L'habitation magdalénienne no. 1 de Pincevent," which was published in 1966 in the journal *Gallia préhistoire*, revolutionized the discipline of Paleolithic settlement archaeology.

Leroi-Gourhan's research in Paleolithic art highlighted what he perceived as a dualism of male and female. Accordingly, he interpreted the horses and bison, whose images dominated the decoration of caves, as male and female, respectively. In addition, he believed that nonfigurative motifs should be interpreted as either male (phallus) or female (vulva). Furthermore, unlike Henri Breuil, whose view was that cave decorations were assemblages of individual images, Leroi-Gourhan believed that the decoration of caves were homogenous compositions that had been planned in their entirety and set out in a preconceived format. He studied the animal depictions in each cave, noting their location and associations with other animals, observing that 60 percent of all of the animals were horse or bison, in general depicted on the central areas of the caves. Other species, such as ibex, mammoth, and deer, were in more peripheral locations. Some species—rhinoceros, large cats, and bears—were rarely drawn, with any examples being shown deep in the caves. Accordingly, Leroi-Gourhan thought this model was a blueprint for cave paintings of animals. It is now believed that this theory is rather too general and that the pattern of depiction in each cave is different. Nevertheless, it is still recognized that the animal figures are placed on the cave walls in a deliberate manner.

In addition, Leroi-Gourhan devised a chronological sequence of four different successive styles of cave art, a theory now considered to be flawed. The approach of trying to identify groups of images that are similar stylistically and technically, and thus the work of a single artist or group, was rejected by Leroi-Gourhan. His belief was that Ice Age art remained essentially unchanged for twenty thousand years, a view that is now challenged. Since Leroi-Gourhan's death, the consensus is that the decoration of caves is an accumulation of different compositions through time.

Discoveries of the earliest humans in France began in the 1960s at La Caune de l'Arago, also known as la Grotte de Tautavel (Pyrénées-Orientales), discussed further in chapter 2. Excavations began at the site in 1964 by a team of archaeologists led by Henry de Lumley (b. 1934), who, with his wife Marie-Antoinette de Lumley, also undertook excavations at two other French sites that have produced early evidence of humans, Terra Amata and la Grotte du Lazaret. Previously, from 1957 to 1968, he had excavated la Grotte de la Baume Bonne at Quinson (Alpes-de-Haute-Provence), a site with evidence of occupation from around four hundred thousand years ago. Henry de Lumley was also instrumental in the creation of Le Musée de Préhistoire des Gorges du Verdon at Quinson to house archaeological finds from the many sites in the area. The museum has a second site on the bank of the river Verdon, the "Village préhistorique de Quinson," discussed further in chapter 1.

Jean-Paul Demoule (born 1947) is noted for his research on the Neolithic and the Iron Age in Europe, together with the history of archaeology and its social role. In addition he is prominent in the field of preventive archaeology, being instrumental in the development of French law in this area. Demoule served as president of Inrap (Institut national de recherches archéologiques préventives) between 2001 and 2008 and is emeritus professor of protohistory at the Sorbonne university in Paris. Along with other archaeologists, he conducted excavations within the framework of the Programme de sauvetage regional de la Vallée de l'Aisne (Aisne and Pas-de-Calais), which took place between 1971 and 1992. Demoule was also involved in projects outside France, most notably in Bulgaria and northern Greece.

IRON AGE AND GALLO-ROMAN ARCHAEOLOGISTS

Henri Rolland (1886–1970) is a leading figure in the archaeology of the Iron Age in France. Rolland's interest in archaeology began with numismatics, a field in which he published discoveries from Nîmes (Gard), the oppidum of Entremont and the Gallo-Roman site of Glanum (both Bouches-du-Rhône). In addition, Rolland directed a number of excavations, a significant discovery being the oppidum at Saint-Blaise (Bouches-du-Rhône), which he excavated from 1935 at his own expense. From 1928 until 1933, Rolland worked on a sanctuary to the south of Glanum, taking charge of the site from 1942 until 1969. From 1945, Rolland ran what then was the only field school specializing in classical archaeology. In addition, he was appointed director of the Circonscription archéologique for Provence-Nord from 1956 to 1964. On the death of Fernand Benoit in 1969, Rolland became vice president for France of l'Institut international d'études ligures (International Institute of Ligurian Studies). Along with Benoit, Rolland was one of the first scholars to recognize the presence of Etruscan bucchero ware in southern France and to associate this with commercial links between the Etruscans and southern France.

Rolland also was prominent in finding a suitable setting for finds from excavations from the Glanum site at the late fifteenth-century mansion known as the Hôtel de Sade in Saint-Rémy-de-Provence (Bouches-du-Rhône). The building was acquired and classified as a historic monument by the French state in 1929 at the behest of Jules Formigé (1879–1960), architect of historic monuments, and Pierre de Brun (1874–1941), who founded the Musée des Alpilles in Saint-Rémy-de-Provence, both of whom had excavated at Glanum since 1921. From 1954, Henri Rolland was instrumental in ensuring that the Hôtel de Sade became the archaeological repository of excavation finds from the Glanum site, whose collection opened to the public in 1968.

Another major figure in the Gallo-Roman archaeology of southern France was Fernand Benoit (1892–1969). In 1922, Benoit had attended the Ecole française in Rome; on his return to France, he became an archivist in Arles (Bouches-du-Rhône) and later a curator, then director, of the Arles archaeological museum. At this time Benoit conducted excavations in the Arles area, including cemeteries at Trinquetaille and Alyscamps, as well as the water mill complex at Barbegal, discussed in chapter 3. In 1943 Benoit had been appointed director of historic antiquities of Provence and Corsica, and since 1946 had been director of the Musée Borély in Marseille (Bouches-du-Rhône). Archaeological work conducted by Benoit in the area around Marseille included the Gallo-Roman site of Cemenelenum in Cimiez, a suburb of Nice (Alpes-Maritimes); the crypt at Saint-Victor in Marseille; and the Vieux-Port of Marseille, the latter leading to his interest in shipwrecks, which he considered to be as important as land sites. However, as discussed in chapter 5, Benoit's inability to dive led to the misinterpretation of the Roman shipwreck discovered at the rock of Grand Congloué, south of Marseille. Benoit was also a pioneer in working with archaeologists from other European countries, an unusual practice in the early twentieth century. With the Italian archaeologist Nino Lambroglio, Benoit founded "l'Institut international d'études ligures" and worked with other Italian and Spanish archaeologists.

FRENCH ARCHAEOLOGISTS OUTSIDE FRANCE

Other French archaeologists have made significant contributions to archaeology outside France.

One such individual was Charles Ernest Beulé, who had studied at the prestigious Ecole normale supérieure in Paris and the Ecole française d'Athènes, where he excavated on the Acropolis. His best-known discovery is the gate that bears his name, the Beulé Gate, which was built in the late third century AD to protect the sanctuary on the Acropolis, which was discovered during Beulé's excavations in this area in 1852 and 1853. In 1859 he undertook excavations at Carthage at his own expense and was the first to reach the archaeological layer that revealed evidence of the destruction of the city in 146 BC. In addition, a Roman building at Carthage consisting of a series of vaulted rooms, known as "les Absides de Beulé," is named after Beulé, While still holding the post of professor of archaeology at the Bibliothèque impériale in Paris, Beulé became a politician, was elected to the Assemblée Nationale in 1871, and served as minister of the interior in the Broglie government of 1873.

The vast majority of early French archaeologists were men, reflecting the social conventions of the nineteenth and early twentieth centuries. An exception was Jane Dieulafoy (figure 4.2), considered to be the first female French field archaeologist, noted for her work in Persia and Morocco. She was born Jane Magre in Toulouse in 1851, and, showing early academic promise, was sent to Paris to be educated. In 1870 she married Marcel Dieulafoy, who shared her interest in art and archaeology. The extraordinary nature of Jane Dieulafoy's life is reflected by her decision to accompany her husband when he served in the Army of the Loire in 1870; she dressed in male uniform and joined her husband at the front. In 1874, Marcel Dieulafoy became architect of historic monuments under Eugène Viollet-le-Duc, architect to the emperor Napoleon III. It is believed that his discussions with Viollet-le-Duc on the origins of Western architecture inspired the Dieulafoys to travel during the 1870s to Egypt, where the

Figure 4.2.   Jane
Dieulafoy. Alamy

French scholar Auguste Mariette was conducting excavations; Morocco; and several European countries. In the 1880s the Dieulafoys traveled to Persia (modern-day Iran), visiting several cities, and obtained permission to excavate the remains of the ancient city of Susa in 1885 and 1886, the first French excavations on the site, which followed the work by the British archaeologist William Kennett Loftus in 1851. Among the discoveries Jane and Marcel Dieulafoy made were friezes of glazed bricks showing archers and lions from the palace of the Achaemenid King Darius I, who reigned between 522 and 486 BC. Four hundred crates of archaeological finds that had been excavated by the Dieulafoys in 1885 and 1886 were sent to Paris, where they were received at the Musée du Louvre by Léon Heuzey, who had been appointed as the Louvre's first curator of the department of Oriental antiquities. On her return to France in 1886, Jane decided to continue to wear male dress, and photographs taken of her at this time made her famous. In the same year, she was honored by the French government with the award of Chevalier of the Légion d'Honneur.

Jane Dieulafoy published an account of her work in Susa in the review *Le Tour du Monde*, as well as writing fiction, including *Parysatis*, whose action takes place in Susa, set to music by Camille Saint-Saëns in 1902. She was one of those who initiated the literary prize known as the Prix de la Vie Heureuse, first awarded in 1904, which became the Prix Femina, still in existence today.

From the 1880s, the Dieulafoys ran a "salon," where men and women could engage in intellectual conversation, at their home on the rue Chardin in the Passy district of Paris. This became one of the most fashionable events in Paris, attended by scholars, poets, artists, and musicians, most of whom were members of l'Institut de France, discussed in chapter 1.

At the same time, the Dieulafoys visited Spain and Portugal, making twenty-three trips between 1888 and 1914. During World War I, Jane accompanied her husband to Morocco, where she directed the excavation of the Hassan Mosque at Rabat. Jane Dieulafoy died in Toulouse in 1916 following an illness contracted in Morocco. She is justly famous, as it was extremely unusual for a French woman to be a field archaeologist in the late nineteenth and early twentieth centuries.

Although the Dieulafoys did not return to what then was known as Persia (modern-day Iran), excavations there were dominated by French archaeologists from the late nineteenth century onward. The main site was Susa, where excavations had resumed in 1897, conducted by Jacques de Morgan. However, in general, the focus tended to be on the nature of finds rather than their context. A more methodical approach to excavation in Persia was adopted by Roman Ghirshman (1895–1979), who was born in Kharkov in Ukraine and arrived in Paris in 1923. Ghirshman not only excavated at Begram, an Indo-Greek and Kushan city in Afghanistan, but also in Persia, known as Iran from 1935, and was unusual in conducting archaeological work outside Susa, for so long the focus of French excavations. Most notably, his work at Tepe Sialk in Kashan established the first chronology of Iranian prehistory. In 1946, Ghirshman was appointed director of the Mission Archéologique en Iran, and archaeological work recommenced at Susa, where, under Ghirshman's direction, entire architectural complexes were being discovered for the first time.

Bohumil Soudský (1922–1976) was an influential figure in Neolithic archaeology. Although born in what is now the Czech Republic, Soudský studied at the Sorbonne University in Paris between 1946 and 1948, and from 1971 until his death in 1976 he returned to Paris to lecture in European protohistory at the Sorbonnne. Soudský's excavation at the large Neolithic site of Bylany in the Czech Republic in the 1950s and 1960s led him to propose the idea of "cyclical agriculture," which developed from the earlier hypothesis of "primary Neolithic shifting agriculture." Soudský suggested that the development of pottery styles at Bylany was not a continuous process, which may have been caused by periodic abandonment of the site. Soudský believed he had located other sites in the immediate area around Bylany, where pottery finds corresponded to gaps in the record at the main site. Accordingly, he proposed that the inhabitants of Bylany moved from one settlement to another on a regular basis as part of their agricultural system, to allow vegetation and the fertility of the soil to regenerate, with each cycle lasting on average sixty years. Soudský's view was very influential at the time, although his hypothesis has been overtaken by more recent ideas.

Although Jean Guilaine (born 1936) has been involved in Neolithic and Iron Age archaeological projects in France, he is also noted for his excavations at the Neolithic site of Shillourokambos on Cyprus. The site achieved popular renown in 2004, with the discovery of the complete skeleton of a cat which accompanied a human burial dating between 7500 BC and 7000 BC. The deceased was aged around thirty at death, and was buried with offerings that included stone tools and ochre pigment. As no local feline species had been found, it was suggested that the remains represented the oldest known evidence for the domestication of cats. Jean Guilaine has had a distinguished academic and research career, serving as director of studies at the CNRS (Centre national de la recherche scientifique) and Ecole des Hautes Etudes en Sciences Sociales (EHESS), as well as being an honorary professor of the Collège de France. He founded, with Daniel Fabre, the body now known as the Centre d'anthropologie de Toulouse. Guilaine is perhaps best known for the introduction of "agrarian archaeology," using both environmental and archaeological data.

Not all archaeological work in France has been conducted by French archaeologists. For example, the English archaeologist Sir Mortimer Wheeler undertook a survey of oppida in the regions of western Normandy and Brittany during the winter of 1936–1937. In 1938 he undertook excavations at several sites, most notably the oppidum popularly known as Le Camp d'Artus (Arthur's Camp), close to the commune of Huelgoat (Finistère).

THE CHRONOLOGY OF THE PALEOLITHIC PERIOD

The valuable contribution of French archaeology to the study of Paleolithic stone tools is recognized by the large number of type sites for phases of the Paleolithic period in Western Europe and beyond. The names, derived from sites in France, first were used by Gabriel de Mortillet (1821–1898).

Previously, Edouard Lartet had also suggested a chronology for phases of the Paleolithic period. Lartet adopted the geological principles of stratigraphy to his study of l'Abri d'Aurignac, establishing a relationship between the type of animal and the geological layer in which its remains was found. At l'Abri d'Aurignac, Lartet distinguished four periods, defined by animal remains— namely, cave bear, mammoth and rhinoceros, reindeer, and aurochs or bison, with cave bear being the oldest. Lartet presented this research to l'Académie des Sciences at their meeting in September 1859, where he made a case for the great age of mankind. Félix Garrigou subsequently added the period "hippopotamus," which he believed preceded the cave bear period.

Gabriel de Mortillet had published pamphlets in 1848 strongly criticizing king Louis-Philippe and the politician François Guizot and accordingly went into exile in the Duchy of Savoie, at that time not part of France. He became director of the Musée d'Annecy (Haute-Savoie); during his travels in Switzerland and Italy, he became interested in the Neolithic and Bronze Age "lake villages," retaining his interest in Italian archaeology after his return to France. In 1867, Mortillet was appointed secretary of the Commission for Prehistoric Archaeology at the Exposition Universelle in Paris and the following year was appointed by the newly founded museum in Saint-Germain-en-Laye (Yvelines) to organize the collection of Edouard Lartet and the display of the prehistoric galleries.

In 1869, Mortillet published an essay in which he formulated the first version of his chronology of prehistory founded on the classification of lithic industries. He proposed a new method of archaeological terminology, by attributing objects that are different by reference to names derived from selected sites. Rather than the Three Age System of Thomsen and Worsaae and the modified chronology proposed by Lartet, Mortillet chose technological evolution to determine prehistoric chronology. The names of four phases, namely, Acheulian, Mousterian, Solutrean, and Magdalenian, still are in use. Chellean, which was the name given to the period identified by Garrigou as "hippopotamus" and named from the type site of Chelles (Somme), is outdated, and biface tools from this phase now are classified as Early Acheulian.

Gabriel de Mortillet used the term "Acheulian" to designate the oldest stone tools known in the mid-nineteenth century. In the 1840s, shortly after the discoveries of Boucher de Perthes at Abbeville, a large number of stone tools were found in gravel quarries at Saint-Acheul, a suburb of Amiens (Somme). They were distinguished by a large number of tools made as bifaces—that is, worked on both sides. The site of Saint-Acheul

Figure 4.3.   The Roc de Solutré. istock, 184450168

is now presented as an "archaeological garden," le Jardin archéologique de Saint-Acheul.

The lower of the two rock shelters at Peyzac-le-Moustier (Dordogne), first excavated in 1863 by Edouard Lartet and Henry Christy, is the type site for stone tools of the Mousterian phase. Use of the term was extended outside France, and Mousterian has a wide geographical distribution across Europe, Asia, and North Africa.

The Solutrean type site is the Roc de Solutré (figure 4.3), also known as the Crot du Charnier, which overlooks the commune of Solutré-Pouilly (Saône-et-Loire). The site was found at the base of the rock by Adrien Arcelin, who, with Henry Testot-Ferry, conducted excavations there between 1866 and 1869. Finds suggested that Solutré was a hunting camp, in use for more than twenty-five thousand years, between 35,000 BC and 10,000 BC. Arcelin's son, Fabien Arcelin, also conducted excavations at Solutré in the 1920s and gave his finds to the Labotatoire de Géologie at Lyon. The most recent excavations at Solutré were conducted by Jean Combier, then director of prehistoric antiquities for the Rhône-Alpes region, between 1967 and 1978. Both Testot-Ferry and Arcelin assembled large collections, particularly Testot-Ferry, whose collection at his death contained more than five thousand objects, many of which were sold by his grandson to the Musée des Ursulines at Mâcon (Saône-et-Loire) and the British Museum in London. Much of Adrien Arcelin's collection is now in the Muséum National d'Histoire Naturelle in Paris, although Arcelin may be best known for his "prehistoric novel" *Solutré ou les chasseurs de rennes de la France centrale* (Solutré, or the reindeer hunters of central France), published in 1872 under the pseudonym Adrien Cranile, which is an anagram of Arcelin. The novel tells of the legend of horses falling from the top of the Crot du Charnier, pursued by hunters, a story contradicted by analysis of the archaeological remains.

Solutrean stone tools were made using by a distinct technology known as lithic reduction percussion and pressure flaking. These techniques enabled the production of very fine tools from thin pieces of flint. The lithic material from the Crot du Charnier was examined in 1869 by Gabriel de Mortillet, who assigned the name "Solutrean" to this type of technology.

"Magdalenian," dating between 15,000 and 10,000 BC, is named from the Abri de la Madeleine in the commune of Tursac (Dordogne) and is the "type site" for one of the later phases of the Upper Paleolithic in Western Europe. As discussed in chapter 2, the rock shelter was excavated from 1863 by Edouard Lartet, and subsequently by other archaeologists including Denis Peyrony.

The chronology was further subdivided, with the addition of Aurignacian and Gravettian technologies.

In 1852, Jean-Baptiste Bonnemaison, a quarry worker from Aurignac (Haute-Garonne), made a chance discovery of a rock shelter during road making. Inserting his arm into a small opening in the hillside, he found the fossilized remains of animals. Edouard Lartet was alerted to this discovery, and in 1860 he undertook the excavation of the rock shelter. He retrieved much archaeological material, notably worked tools made from stone and deer bone, the remains of a hearth, and the skeletons of animals that are extinct. Lartet presented his finds at the Exposition Universelle in Paris in 1867. In 1906, Henri Breuil first used the term "Aurignacien" and, accordingly, l'Abri d'Aurignac became the eponymous type site of the Aurignacian period, characterized by the material culture from around thirty-eight thousand to twenty-eight thousand years ago. The site became a historic monument in 1921. Further excavations in front of the Abri d'Aurignac were conducted by Fernand Lacorre in 1938 and 1939. Two periods of use of the rock shelter were revealed: one Aurignacian and the other more recent, in the Neolithic period. Today there is a museum in Aurignac, le Musée Forum de l'Aurignacien, which opened in 2014, to replace a much smaller museum of prehistory that opened in 1969.

The term "Gravettian" was used for the first time in 1938 by the English prehistorian Dorothy Garrod in discussing the lithic technology found on the site of La Gravette in the commune of Bayac (Dordogne) between twenty-eight thousand and twenty-two thousand years ago. The stone tools characteristic of Gravettian technology are blades, scrapers, and distinctive points. The site was discovered in 1880, and several excavations took place at the end of the nineteenth century, with the finds dispersed in various museums. The last excavations on the site were undertaken by Fernand Lacorre between 1930 and 1954. The site currently is very overgrown, as it was donated by Lacorre to the French state on the condition that it not be excavated for at least another fifty years.

The study of worked stone tools advanced as a result of the research of the French archaeologist François Bordes (1919–1981). Bordes developed systematic typologies of Paleolithic tools and was the initiator of the method of statistical analysis in the study of ancient lithic industries. Bordes conducted excavations at the well-stratified sites of le Pech-de-l'Azé in the commune of Carsac-Aillac (Dordogne) for two seasons from 1948, and at Combe-Grenal, in the commune of Domme (Dordogne), between 1953 and 1965; it produced fifty-five distinct Mousterian levels. His study of the stone tool industries led him to propose a new way of studying them, founded on statistical analysis, by consideration of percentages of different types of tool. Bordes published his first article on the use of statistical analysis in the study of stone tools in 1950, and his proposal quickly was adopted by researchers in this field.

UNDERWATER ARCHAEOLOGY OFF THE COASTS OF FRANCE

In the twentieth century, France has led the way in the development of the technology necessary for archaeological excavations to be conducted under water. This archaeological discipline did not progress until the commercial development of a system that used a high-pressure cylinder and a demand valve, which delivers air only when the diver is breathing in. The Aqua-Lung was developed by Jacques-Yves Cousteau, a French naval officer, and the engineer Emile Gagnan. The term "scuba" (originally capitalized as SCUBA), an acronym standing for self-contained underwater breathing apparatus, first was used in 1962 by Major Christian Lambertsen, formerly a physician in the U.S. Army Medical Corps. The SCUBA specifically described the closed circuit rebreather apparatus Lambertsen had developed, although in modern usage the term "scuba" is now extended to include the Aqua-Lung.

The use of the Aqua-Lung by sport divers in the 1940s and 1950s had led to chance finds of ancient shipwrecks and their cargo in the Mediterranean, including dozens of wrecks found off the coast of southern France. However, these were primarily salvage operations, whose aim was the retrieval of antiquities such as Roman amphorae. It was not until it became normal practice for archaeologists to learn to dive that modern archaeological techniques were employed on underwater excavations.

One of the pioneers of underwater archaeology was Philippe Tailliez (1905–2002), an officer in the French navy who had helped Jacques-Yves Cousteau in testing the AquaLung. In 1945, Tailliez was appointed director of the GRS: Groupe de recherche sous-marine (Group for underwater research), from 1950 known as the GERS: Groupe d'études et de recherche sous-marine (Group for underwater study and research); and, in addition, was involved in archaeological investigations off the Tunisian coast at Mahdia. Alongside his naval career, Tailliez is most renowned for his work on the wreck of the Roman vessel known as the *Titan*. The wreck was found in 1948 at a depth of between twenty-seven and twenty-nine meters off the northeastern tip of l'Ile du Levant, one of the Iles d'Hyères (Var). The wreck initially was surveyed in 1954, but, as discussed further in chapter 5, subsequently it was looted. The wreck was excavated by Tailliez in 1957 and 1958, using underwater recording techniques including plotting finds in relation to a grid system on the seabed. The cargo consisted of around seven hundred amphorae, mostly of the Dressel 12 type, containing fish sauce from Hispania (modern-day Spain). Other finds included some bronze vessels, pottery lamps, Campanian ceramics, and a few coins. The coins, ceramics, and lamps enabled the wreck to be dated to the middle of the first century BC. The wreck also had an example of the tradition of placing a coin inside the socket of the ship's mast step. Although Tailliez undoubtedly was constrained by his lack of familiarity with archaeological techniques, the excavation of the *Titan* is notable for the early use of scientific methods.

As discussed in chapter 1, France was the first country with a dedicated government department for underwater archaeology. In 1966, André Malraux, then French minister of culture, created Le Département des Recherches Archéologiques Subaquatiques et Sous-marines (usually abbreviated to DRASSM), based in Marseille. Its original survey ship *L'Archéonaute*, which had mapped almost a thousand archaeological sites, was replaced in 2012 by a new ship named the *André Malraux*.

AERIAL PHOTOGRAPHY IN ARCHAEOLOGY

The use of aerial photography in archaeology was pioneered by French archaeologists.

Antoine Poidebard (1878–1955) was one of the first people to use aerial photography to research terrestrial and underwater archaeological sites. Born in Lyon, Poidebard was ordained as a Jesuit priest and in 1924 traveled to Beirut to take part in the rescue of Armenian refugees. In 1925, Poidebard was commissioned by the Société de géographie de Paris to fly over the region to find sources of water and underground water courses. During these flights, Poidebard noticed that the raking evening light revealed the remains of structures, and accordingly he devised a method of using aerial photography to record the ancient remains in the Syrian desert. With the logistical support of "l'Aéronautique Militaire," which in 1934 became l'Armée de l'Air française (French air force), Poidebard subsequently made the first systematic documentation using aerial photography of the ancient roman frontiers of Syria (1925–1932), the port of Tyre (1934–1936), the Byzantine frontiers of Chalcis (1934–1942), and the port of Sidon (1946–1950), in collaboration with René Mouterde, a Jesuit priest and archaeologist, and Jean Lauffray, architect and archaeologist. Poidebard also undertook similar aerial photographic research in Tunisia and Algeria.

René Goguey (1923–2015) first became acquainted with aerial photography while a pilot in the French air force. In 1958, he surveyed the Gallo-Roman sanctuary in the commune of Essarois (Côte-d'Or) and later made plans of the large sites at Alésia, Vix, Mirebeau-sur-Bèze, and les Bolards (all Côte-d'Or). He also discovered several Gallo-Roman villas. In 1968, while still serving with the French air force, Goguey was awarded a doctorate by l'Ecole pratique des hautes etudes in Paris, where his thesis focused on the techniques of aerial archaeology that he had used on the archaeological sites in the Bourgogne region. On his retirement from the French air force in 1973, Goguey continued to conduct aerial surveys, funded by the Direction régionale des affaires culturelles (DRAC) of Bourgogne. In 1976, favorable dry climatic conditions led to numerous discoveries by Goguey, especially a previously unknown Gallo-Roman theater at Autun (Saône-et-Loire). He also conducted aerial surveys in Eastern Europe, as well as directing the excavation of several terrestrial sites. It is estimated that during his career Goguey took around one hundred thousand aerial photographs and recorded four thousand archaeological sites.

Roger Agache (1926–2011), formerly director of prehistoric antiquities for Nord-Picardie, was another pioneer of aerial archaeology, particularly in northern France. Agache began his career working on terrestrial archaeological sites, but from the late 1950s turned his attention to aerial archaeology. One of his earliest, and most important, discoveries was the entrance to a Roman camp on Mont Câtelet in the commune of Vendeuil-Caply (Oise), identified in 1962. Agache was also instrumental in the use of aerial photography during the winter months, when frost can aid the identification of archaeological sites. Among his many publications is the *Atlas d'archéologie aérienne de Picardie. La Somme Protohistorique et Romaine*, a two-volume work coauthored with Bruno Bréart, which documents numerous sites.

ARCHAEOLOGICAL SCIENCE

Valuable contributions to the study of individual classes of object have been made following the development of more sophisticated analytical techniques. The study of ancient metals in France has been facilitated by the establishment in 2005 of LEACA, Laboratoire d'Etude des alliages cuivreux anciens (Laboratory for the study of ancient copper alloys), directed by Anne Lehoërff, professor of European protohistory at the université Charles-de-Gaulle-Lille-3. Lehoërff's national responsibilities include acting as vice president of CNRA: Conseil national de la recherche archéologique (National Council for Archaeological Research), a government body that is part of the Ministry of Culture and Communication and deals with matters relating to archaeological research in France.

The Atelier Régional de Conservation Nucléart (ARC-Nucléart), based in Grenoble (Isère), was founded in 1967. It specializes in the conservation and restoration of organic materials and conducts research to develop new methods of treating organic remains. In addition to carrying out projects in their laboratories at Grenoble, staff from ARC-Nucléart work on archaeological sites. Among the archaeological discoveries conserved at ARC-Nucléart are three Gallo-Roman barges: two found at Lyon, the other at

Arles. One of the more unusual commissions undertaken by ARC-Nucléart was the treatment of a baby mammoth, found in Siberia in 2009 and given the name Khroma, prior to a temporary exhibition at the Musée Criozatier in the town of le-Puy-en-Velay (Haute-Loire).

The work of French archaeologists has shaped our knowledge of the archaeology of the region, particularly the Paleolithic period in France, including the naming of type sites for phases of that period. In addition, the discipline of underwater archaeology developed thanks to innovations pioneered in France, particularly the AquaLung, which revolutionized the ability of archaeologists to work under water.

5

DEBATES, CONTROVERSIES, AND SCANDALS

French archaeology has not been without its share of debates, controversies, and even scandals. Some of these have led to changes in practice or interpretation, whereas others continue to be debated.

THE "MISSION HÉLIOGRAPHIQUE"

In 1851, the Commission des Monuments Historiques, directed by Prosper Merimée, instigated a project now known as the "Mission Héliographique" to document the monuments of France. The Commission proposed the use of the new medium of photography, which had been invented in the 1830s. The monuments selected to be recorded were not necessarily the most important, but rather those that were in the course of, or awaiting, restoration. Although the majority of sites to be recorded were ecclesiastical buildings, the survey was to include Gallo-Roman structures and a few prehistoric monuments. At the time, it was one of the largest photographic projects and also one of the first to be commissioned by a government agency.

The five photographers selected were all members of the Société Héliographique, considered to be the first known photographic society in the world. Edouard Baldus was chosen to document southern France, and among the Gallo-Roman monuments he photographed were the aqueduct bridge known as the Pont-du-Gard, the arch at Orange, the Maison Carrée in Nîmes, and the amphitheaters at Arles and Nîmes, discussed in chapter 3. One of the few prehistoric monuments to be recorded was the Dolmen de Bagneux in the commune of Saumur (Maine-et-Loire), photographed by Gustave le Gray and Auguste Mestral. It is not clear, however, whether all five photographers submitted their photographs to the Commission; indeed, only a handful of examples by Hippolyte Bayard, who documented the monuments of Brittany and Normandy, survive.

However, the Commission never published or exhibited the photographs, although they were discussed in the photographic press. Indeed, the photographs remained largely unknown until 1980, when Philippe Néagu, then curator of the Archives photographiques des Monuments Historiques (Historical Monuments Photographic Archives), published around one hundred negatives that had been housed in the collection. This led to the recognition and discovery of more than 180 original photographic prints, which mostly had been kept in public collections. The rediscovery in the archives of the photographs led to an exhibition in spring 2002 at the Maison européenne de la Photographie, Ville de Paris.

It is not recorded why the Commission des Monuments Historiques chose not to make the photographs accessible to the public, but rather kept them in its archives. Néagu's publication of the negatives led to speculation in the 1980s as to why such an important group of photographs had remained unrecognized for more than a century. One suggestion is that the photographs, many of which are highly accomplished in terms of their composition and lighting, were unsuitable as a record of the poor, unrestored condition of the buildings, but rather created some of the first photographic impressions of "romantic ruins."

As well as being of interest from an archaeological point of view, in recording buildings in their pre-restored condition, the photographs are of particular importance in the study of the history of photography, as one of the earliest examples of a collection of images made for a specific purpose. The surviving negatives from the "Mission Héliographique" are now housed in the collection of the Musée d'Orsay in Paris.

ALÉSIA AND GERGOVIA

The locations of Alésia and Gergovia, the sites of important battles in 52 BC during in the Roman conquest of Gaul by Julius Caesar, have been the subject of much debate.

Archaeologists disagree on the location of Alésia, the site of the final battle between Julius Caesar and Vercingetorix. These discussions have been parodied in the Astérix comic book story *Astérix and the Chieftain's Shield*, published in 1967. The chief Abraracourcix (whose name in English is "Vitalstatistix") says to Astérix, "What do you mean, Alésia? I don't even know where Alésia is! Nobody knows where Alésia is!"

The excavations initiated in 1861 by the French emperor Napoleon III at Mont-Auxois, near Alise-Sainte-Reine (Côte-d'Or), which he believed could be identified as Alésia, were discussed in chapters 1 and 3. As a result of these excavations, Napoleon III issued an imperial decree in 1864 that modern-day Alise-Sainte-Reine should be identified as Alésia. The association between Alise-Sainte-Reine and Alésia was made as long ago as the ninth century AD by Heiric d'Auxerre, a monk at the Benedictine monastery of Saint-Germain d'Auxerre (Yonne). Even before Napoleon III's decree, excavation in 1784 by Pierre Laureau, an officer in the household of the Count of Artois, revealed coins and inscriptions. The discovery of an inscription in the Gaulish language naming "Alisiia" (CIL XIII, 2880) during further excavation in 1839 on Mont-Auxois, added extra weight to its identification as Alésia.

Alternative suggestions concerning the location of Alésia have been made. As early as 1696, Louis des Ours de Mandajors claimed that Alésia was situated at Alès (Gard), although this was given little credence. Alphonse Delacroix, an architect at Besançon (Doubs), suggested in 1855 that Alésia was located at Alaise, now in the commune of Eternoz (Doubs). More recently, the association of Alésia and Alise-Sainte-Reine was challenged in the 1960s by André Berthier, who studied the text of Caesar's *Commentarii de Bello Gallico* (Commentaries on the Gallic War) and believed that Caesar's description of the battle site did not match the topography of Alise-Sainte-Reine. Berthier considered around two hundred potential sites and in 1962 announced that he had found a match between the literary description of Alésia and the commune of Chaux-des-Crotenay (Jura). After Berthier's death in 2000, his work was continued by Danielle Porte.

However, the views of Berthier and Porte have not been accepted by the majority of scholars; and, in particular, the Franco-German survey and excavations on Mont-Auxois between 1991 and 1997 support the original identification as Alésia.

Similarly, debate regards the location of Gergovia, which is recorded by Julius Caesar in his *Commentarii de Bello Gallico* as the site of the battle in 52 BC in which Vercingetorix successfully repulsed him. Possibilities for the site of the battle usually have been identified as three oppida of the Averni tribe: namely, Corent, Gondole, and Gergovie, all of which are around seven kilometers apart.

Corent, the indigenous settlement of forty-five hectares that is named after the nearby village and plateau, is situated on a naturally defended hilltop. However, discoveries of coins and broken amphorae during excavations conducted by a team led by John Collis of the University of Sheffield, England, and Vincent Guichard, director of the Centre Européen de Recherche Archéologique de Bibracte, indicated that the settlement was abandoned before the date of the battle of Gergovia. In addition, they observed that the topography of Corent does not correspond with Julius Caesar's account. More recent excavations at Corent by LUERN (Laboratoire Universitaire d'Enseignement et de Recherche en archéologie Nationale), however, have indicated that some of the buildings on the site were erected in the post-conquest Gallo-Roman period, accordingly proving that Corent was not, in fact, abandoned before the battle of Gergovia.

Gondole, in the commune of Le Cendre, whose spectacular discoveries of human and horse burials in 2002 are discussed in chapter 3, also once was considered as being the site of the battle of Gergovia. In the mid-nineteenth century, it was suggested that Gondole was the site of a camp of Julius Caesar as a result of discoveries made during the construction of the railway line between Clermont-Ferrand and Issoire (both Puy-de-Dôme), although more recent research suggests that it was an oppidum. However, the topography of Gondole does not match Julius Caesar's account of the battle site.

The officially recognized site of the battle is Gergovie, in the commune of La Roche-Blanche (Puy-de-Dôme), situated on the plateau known for many years as Gergovie. The village, known until 1865 as Merdogne, had been suggested as the site of the battle as early as 1560, and in 1755 the first archaeological excavations were conducted by La Société littéraire de Clermont-Ferrand (Puy-de-Dôme). As at Mont-Auxois, the excavations were conducted by Colonel Eugène Stoffel at the behest of the emperor Napoleon III. Stoffel believed that his excavations of 1862 had revealed two of Caesar's camps at Gergovia, and in 1865, an imperial decree renamed the village of Merdogne as Gergovie. The topography of Gergovie corresponds to Julius Caesar's description, but finds from the site generally were considered to be from the later first century BC, from the reign of the emperor Augustus. However, in 1995 and 1996, the University of Sheffield collaborated with ARAFA (l'Association de Recherches sur l'Age du Fer en Auvergne) on a project titled "Iron Age in the Auvergne." The aim was to investigate whether Gergovia should be identified with the location of Napoleon III's investigations or one of the other oppida in the locality. The finds from the excavations at Gergovie in 1996, including catapult projectiles and fragments of amphorae, are contemporary with the battle of Gergovia and support the suggestion that Gergovie should be identified as the battle site.

ACCESS TO ARCHAEOLOGY: PALEOLITHIC CAVE REPLICAS

The increasing demand from the public to view caves that were decorated during the Paleolithic period, as discussed in chapter 2, has caused severe conservation problems from the 1960s onward. The most famous of the decorated caves, at Lascaux, was opened to the public in 1948 but closed again in 1963 due to the deterioration caused by the number of visitors. By the early 1960s, visitors to Lascaux totaled some two thousand per day during the summer months with a total of about one hundred thousand per year, affecting its microenvironment.

The discovery of new mold growth in the cave resulted in its total closure in January 2008 for a period of three months. Current access is limited to one person for a few minutes per week to monitor the environmental conditions in the cave. However, the seventieth anniversary of the discovery of the cave in September 2010 was marked by a highly controversial visit by Nicolas Sarkozy, then president of France, with his wife, Carla Bruni; Fréderic Mitterand (then culture minister); and five other colleagues. The presidential party was allowed to spend thirty minutes in the cave, the result of which, as reported in the press, was that routine security checks were canceled for two weeks to compensate for their visit.

To cater to public interest, a facsimile of the cave, known as Lascaux II, was constructed in a disused quarry two hundred meters downhill from the entrance to the original cave. The concrete building of Lascaux II has been covered with earth in an attempt to blend it into the landscape. The project to build and decorate Lascaux II was begun in the early 1970s, and the replica was opened to the public in 1983. Reconstructions have been made of two of the galleries: namely, La Salle des Taureaux and Le Diverticule Axial, representing around 40 percent of the cave. It has been suggested that some elements of Lascaux II do not feel authentic and, in particular, the floor is made from black rubber. To permit a wider appreciation of the paintings from Lascaux, an exhibition, known as Lascaux III was devised and built by AFSP (Atelier des Fac-similés du Périgord). Lascaux III is a portable exhibition with a floor area of eight hundred square meters, which displays over a wall area of 120 square meters four painted scenes from Le Nef and one from Le Puits that were not included in the Lascaux II replica. The exhibition initially opened in Montignac (Dordogne) and subsequently transferred to the nearby commune of Thonac before traveling to several destinations worldwide, including the United States, Canada, Belgium, Switzerland, South Korea, and Japan, returning to Europe.

The Centre International d'Art Pariétal (CIAP), more colloquially known as Lascaux IV, is a new facsimile of the cave that opened in December 2016 at the foot of the hill at Montignac where the original cave is situated (figure 5.1). One of the reasons for constructing Lascaux IV, which is designed to cater to around four hundred thousand visitors per year, were concerns regarding the location of Lascaux II. The entrance to Lascaux II is on top of the hill, close to the original cave, and any increase in visitor numbers potentially could cause damage to the original. The opening of Lascaux IV has not resulted in the closure of Lascaux II, although groups are restricted to a maximum of twenty people, who are offered an in-depth visit of an

Figure 5.1.   Centre International d'Art Pariétal (Lascaux IV), Montignac. Paul G. Bahn

hour and a half on two tours per day. The Lascaux IV building, which is made from glass and concrete, provides eighty-five hundred square meters of visitor space its various exhibition areas linked by means of indoor and outdoor paths. It houses a full replica of the cave, together with six galleries that provide the visitor with information on the discovery of the cave, its relationship to other cave art, and interpretation of its decoration. Within the cave facsimile, the environment of the time of discovery in 1940 has been re-created: the temperature, air pressure, damp smell, and sounds. The walls of the cave were reproduced using natural materials; their decoration, which comprises six hundred animal images and four hundred signs and symbols, was produced by around fifty artists and sculptors. In contrast to Lascaux II, where only paintings were replicated, Lascaux IV also includes engravings.

On discovery of the Grotte Chauvet-Pont d'Arc (Ardèche), a decision was made not to open the cave to the public in the interests of its preservation. In addition to the publication of images from the cave, the documentary film *Cave of Forgotten Dreams* by Werner Herzog was released in cinemas in 2010. A building containing a partial replica of the Grotte Chauvet-Pont d'Arc, known as the Caverne du Pont d'Arc, opened in April 2015 at Saint-Remèze (Ardèche). Rather than attempt to re-create a cave in the manner of Lascaux, the architects designed a modern circular building, clad in concrete, situated above ground (figure 5.2). The original cave was considered too extensive to replicate in full, and the designers selected what they considered to be its highlights. The limestone walls of the original cave were reproduced in concrete, with geological features such as stalagmites and stalactites made from resin. Paintings were created off-site by projecting images onto a resin background. In addition to the Caverne du Pont d'Arc, the building also includes La Galerie de l'Aurignacien, which is a museum with displays of objects, interactive displays, and a small cinema.

The replicas of the Lascaux and Chauvet caves, along with Altamira and Ekain in northern Spain, are the only full-sized replicas of painted caves. There are, however, in France replicas, and full-sized two-dimensional images, of individual elements of decoration. A facsimile of the sculpted frieze at Le Roc-aux-Sorciers, the most impressive sculpted frieze from the Ice Age, is displayed at the Centre d'Interpretation de la Frise Magdalénienne at Angles-sur-l'Anglin (Vienne). The Musée de la Préhistoire in Le Mas d'Azil (Ariège) has a display of reproductions of paintings and engravings in parts of the Grotte du Mas d'Azil that are not open to the public. In particular, many of the elements of the Parc pyrénéen d'art préhistorique at Tarascon-sur-Ariège (Ariège), which opened fully in 1995, were based on

Figure 5.2. Caverne du Pont-d'Arc, Saint-Remèze. Paul G. Bahn

art from the Grotte de Niaux, discussed in chapter 2. The team who created the Parc pyrénéen d'art préhistorique, which included the prehistorian Jean Clottes, have not attempted to re-create the Grotte de Niaux by building an artificial cave set into the ground. The gallery known as the Grand Atelier includes a room the same size and proportions as the Salon Noir, decorated with a a full-scale reconstruction of the paintings, depicted in their original appearance. There is, however, no intention to present the gallery as a real cave and, in addition, not all of the areas of the Grotte de Niaux are reproduced. The aim of the Parc pyrénéen d'art préhistorique is the same as at Lascaux II, Lascaux IV, and the Caverne du Pont d'Arc: namely, to cater to public interest without damaging the original cave.

Another approach has been taken at the Grottes de Saulges Musée de Préhistoire, which opened in Saulges (Mayenne) in spring 2017, unifying collections from a group of museums in the region. Although visitors to the museum can buy a ticket "package" that includes admission to the Grotte Margot in the nearby commune of Thorigné-en-Charnie (Mayenne), which has both paintings and engravings dating between 23,000 BC and 10,000

BC, the main attraction in the museum is a virtual reconstruction of the Grotte Mayenne-Sciences. The Grotte Mayenne-Sciences, which was discovered by a caving team in 1967, has been scientifically investigated since 1999 by a team led by Romain Pigeaud. Although the cave is not open to the public, it is possible for visitors to see in virtual reality its decoration, which comprises figures, mainly of horses, in black outline as well as engravings.

La Grotte Cosquer near Marseille, discussed in chapter 2, is in a somewhat different position, as the underwater entrance to the cave has prevented any public access, and it would seem logical to construct a replica. Indeed, the city authorities of Marseille proposed such action and were given permission by the French Ministry of Culture to conduct a photogrammetric survey of the cave. A survey of part of the cave using a 3-D laser system was undertaken in 1994 by Electricité de France (EDF), using technology that transferred from maintaining EDF's installations to recording the shapes and colors of the walls of the cave. A diver introduced a sensor into the cave, and the data collected by the sensor were then converted into a virtual textured model. Accordingly, the survey used photogrammetric and laser techniques to create a virtual copy of part of the cave, and the intention was to use the data to create a replica. The city authorities of Marseille apparently are still keen to have a facsimile of the Cosquer cave, with suggested venues being either the Villa Mediterranée or the Fort d'Entrecasteaux in the Vieux-Port of Marseille. However, in early 2017 it was announced that the former would be used to house the Parliament of the Mediterranean, and the focus has now shifted to the Fort d'Entrecasteaux. Reports in the press have mentioned the idea of recreating a replica that would be fifty meters long, twenty meters wide, and ten meters high. However, planning is at a very early stage, and "Cosquer Two" is far from being a reality.

The public's reception of the replica caves of Lascaux and Chauvet generally has been positive, given that visits to the original caves are no longer possible. In particular, the designers of the Lascaux IV replica have learned from criticism of the appearance of the building that houses the Caverne du Pont d'Arc by ensuring that the Centre International d'Art Pariétal was designed to blend into the hillside. Furthermore, it will become even less conspicuous in the landscape as it is concealed by vegetation. Comments have been that the size of the groups visiting the Caverne du Pont d'Arc, at up to twenty-eight people, are too large and, in addition, are at too frequent intervals. This criticism has been recognized at Lascaux IV; although the maximum group size is up to thirty-two people, tours per day are far fewer.

EXPORT OF ANTIQUITIES FROM FRANCE

The Paleolithic rock shelter known as the Abri du Poisson is on the right bank of the river Vézère in the valley known as the Gorge d'Enfer, close to Les Eyzies (Dordogne). The popular name of the rock shelter is derived from the sculpted relief of a fish, a meter long and originally painted red, identified as a male salmon. Although the rock shelter was found in 1892 by Paul Girod and Elie Massénat, the relief of a fish was not identified until 1912, when it was noticed on the upper part of the rock shelter by Jean Marsan (usually called Maurice) from the nearby commune of Manaurie (Dordogne). The site was classed as an ancient monument the following year, when it was excavated by Denis Peyrony. A series of holes around the fish, made in the twentieth century, are evidence of attempts to remove it. In his guidebook to Les Eyzies, published in 1928, Denis Peyrony wrote that the relief had been "sold in secret to the Germans" by the mayor of Manaurie. Peyrony reported that the relief was about to be detached and sent to Berlin when the Ministère des Beaux-Arts stopped the work. For many years, the person frequently blamed as the intermediary in the removal of the sculpture was Otto Hauser, a Swiss antiquarian, who apparently first was implicated in a 1952 publication by Henri Breuil. This view recently has been challenged, as documentary research does not link Hauser to the intended removal of the relief.

In his autobiography, published posthumously in 1944, Carl Schuchhardt, director of the department of prehistory of the Berlin Ethnology Museum (Museum für Völkerkunde), gives a very different account. Schuchhardt wrote that shortly after the discovery of the sculpted fish, he was in Les Eyzies with several German scholars. They secretly conceived a project to purchase the sculpture, remove it, and send it to Germany; and, indeed, Schuchhardt made a drawing of the fish. However, before the fish was able to be removed from the rock shelter, the site was declared an ancient monument and, accordingly, the property of the state. Therefore, Peyrony's 1928 account, which does not name Hauser, is correct. The suggestion that Hauser may have been linked to the removal of antiquities from France is likely to have been made because he is known to have removed the Neanderthal skeleton known as Le Moustier 1 from the rock shelters at Peyzac-le-Moustier (Dordogne) and the skeleton, recently dated to the Mesolithic period, from the site of Combe Capelle in the commune of Saint-Ait-Sénieur (Dordogne).

The skeleton known as Le Moustier 1, together with the skull fragment known as Le Moustier 3, were excavated in 1908 by Otto Hauser. Le

Moustier 1 was the name given to a deliberately buried fossilized skeleton of a young male, aged about eleven, that was attributed to the species *Homo neanderthalensis*. The skull from Le Moustier, together with another skull from the site of Combe Capelle, also found by Hauser, were sold to the Museum für Ur- und Frühgeschichte in Berlin. The skulls, together with a necklace of pierced shells that accompanied the burial at Combe Capelle, apparently were transported to the Soviet Union around 1945. In 1965, staff from the Museum für Ur- und Frühgeschichte located the skull Le Moustier 1, to which they gave the accession number Va 3858a, as well as the necklace from Combe Capelle, among art objects returned by the Soviet Union to the German Democratic Republic. As discussed in chapter 2, the skull from Combe Capelle was not located until 2001. The skeleton Le Moustier 2 was found in 1914 by Denis Peyrony. The individual, an infant aged four months or less, also was from the species *Homo neanderthalensis*, and his or her skeleton is now housed in the Musée National de Préhistoire at Les Eyzies (Dordogne).

THE RETURN AND RESTITUTION OF ANTIQUITIES AND CULTURAL PROPERTY

The return and restitution of antiquities and cultural property—that is, the return of objects and other material, such as human remains—has risen in prominence over recent decades. The UNESCO Convention on the Means of Prohibiting and Preventing the Illicit Import and Transfer of Ownership of Cultural Property, adopted in 1970 and ratified by 129 of 195 UNESCO member states, has reinforced this trend.

However, the repatriation of objects can be complicated, as the original location or ownership may not be straightforward. A historic example involving France is a bronze sculptural group of four horses, now in St. Mark's Basilica, Venice. Originally, they were part of a Roman monument whose location is not known. Subsequently transferred to Constantinople (modern-day Istanbul), the horses were displayed in the Hippodrome until 1204, when they were plundered during the Fourth Crusade by the Venetians. The horses were displayed on St. Mark's Basilica in Venice when the city was captured by forces of Napoleon Bonaparte in 1797. They were removed from the basilica and paraded in triumph along the Champ de Mars in Paris, alongside classical sculptures taken from the Vatican and Capitoline Museums in Rome. With the defeat of Napoleon, the horses were returned to Italy in 1815 and reinstalled on the facade of St. Mark's

Basilica, only removed in the 1980s to an indoor location because of fears of damage by pollution.

The Rosetta stone, one of the most popular objects in the British Museum in London, has an interesting history. It is part of an ancient Egyptian stela that is inscribed with a decree written in Hieroglyphic, Demotic, and Greek, dating to 196 BC. It was found in 1799, during the campaign of Napoleon Bonaparte in Egypt, by Pierre-François Bouchard. Bouchard was an engineer and officer in the French army who was put in charge of the rebuilding of Fort Julien, a former Mamluk fortification close to el-Rashid, also known as "Rosetta," on the Nile Delta. The text on the Rosetta stone had aroused academic interest since its discovery, as it was recognized immediately that the use of three languages in the inscription had the potential to allow the previously undeciphered hieroglyphic script to be read. The French troops in Egypt were defeated by British forces in 1801, and the Rosetta stone came into the possession of the British Crown in August of that year under the Capitulation of Alexandria, which brought the Commission des Sciences et des Arts de l'armée d'Orient, discussed in chapter 1, to an end. In 1902, King George III donated the Rosetta stone to the British Museum, where it has been on display ever since.

Indeed, the looting of works of art in wartime has an even longer attested history. The victory stela of Naram-Sin, king of Akkad in Mesopotamia (modern-day Iraq), is now in the Musée du Louvre in Paris. Its inscription records that it celebrated the victory of Naram-Sin over the Lullubi, a people who were living in the Zagros Mountains, in around 2250 BC. However, an additional inscription, added in the twelfth century BC, indicates that it was appropriated by forces of the Elamite king Shutruk-Nahhunte, who took it to their capital in Susa, in modern-day Iran. The stela was excavated in Susa in AD 1898 by the French archaeologist Jacques de Morgan and taken to Paris for display at the Musée du Louvre.

In more recent years, the demand has increased to repatriate works of art that have been removed from their original context. An example involving France has been the return to Egypt in 2009 of five fragments of wall paintings illegally removed from a tomb on the west bank of the river Nile at Luxor. The tomb, designated TT (Theban Tomb) 15, and situated in the so-called Valley of the Nobles at Dra Abu El-Naga, was of the official Tetiky, who died around 1550 BC, in the early eighteenth dynasty. The Egyptian Supreme Council of Antiquities reported that the paintings were documented in the tomb in 1968 and again in 1975. Apparently they were stolen some time between 1975 and 2000, when four of the fragments were bought by the Musée du Louvre; the fifth fragment was purchased in 2003. In May 2008, a researcher from Heidelberg University recognized the fragments in the Louvre's reserve collection as being from tomb TT15. The tomb was entered later that year, having been closed for some years as it is below a modern building. It was apparent where the painted fragments had originated, and accordingly they were returned to Egypt in late 2009.

A legal gap concerning the protection of cultural heritage of Native North American peoples outside the United States has been highlighted in the 2010s by several auctions in Paris that included objects sacred to various Native North American tribes, most notably the Hopi, which are protected within the jurisdiction of the United States. The Hopi people are recognized as an American sovereign tribal nation in northeast Arizona. In 2013, 2014, 2015, and 2016, auctions were held in Paris of Native North American objects, including katsinam. Katsinam are sacred to the Hopi and are sometimes referred to as "masks," although the Hopi do not use the term themselves. From the first sale onward, Hopi representatives had requested delays of the sales to enable research into the provenance of the objects, although this did not prove successful. An attorney for the Hopi tribe bought one katsina at each of the two sales in 2013, and the Annenberg Foundation bought twenty-four objects at the sale in December 2013, twenty-one for the Hopi and three for the San Carlos Apache. The Navajo Nation bought seven of the eight Navajo masks at the sale in December 2014. The Acoma Pueblo Nation in New Mexico and the Hoopa Valley Tribal Nation in California further protested at a sale in Paris in 2016, which also included Hopi katsinam, although in this instance, an Acoma Pueblo ceremonial shield was withdrawn from the auction. By contrast, it has been observed that other recent auctions in Paris that have included Native American objects, such as the sale of the collection of the surrealist painter André Breton, which took place in 2003, did not attract the protests seen in the 2010s. However, such protests serve to draw attention to the differences between the protection offered to North American indigenous cultural objects in North America and elsewhere.

The federation of French colonial possessions known as French Indochina was formed in 1887 from Cambodia and three Vietnamese regions, with Laos added in 1893. At this time, the art of the Khmer empire, which flourished in the northwest part of modern-day Cambodia from the ninth to the fifteenth centuries, was greatly admired in France. Removal of Khmer art to France occurred even before the formation of French Indochina. Between 1866 and 1868, the French archaeologist, artist, and art historian Louis Delaporte was one of the members of the Mekong Exploration Commission. Delaporte was said to have acquired seventy pieces of Khmer sculpture and architectural elements from King Norodom, although the exact terms are unclear. The objects largely were destined for the Musée Indochinois du Trocadéro in Paris, founded in 1882, where Delaporte was curator. After Delaporte's death in 1925, the objects were relocated to the Musée Guimet. During the early parts of the twentieth century, the temples at Angkor, the Khmer capital, saw a marked rise in visitors, many acquiring original objects. Although some of these were given or sold to museums, others remained in private hands or on the art market. As late as the 1920s, original pieces of sculpture and architecture were on sale in a pavilion in front of the temple complex of Angkor Wat by the Ecole Française d'Extrême Orient, for many decades heavily instrumental in the protection and conservation of the temples at Angkor Wat, and at the Albert Sarraut Museum in Phnom Penh, which has become the National Museum of Cambodia. Although it is clear that these sales may have been motivated to discourage vandalism of the temples, it is also apparent that the EFEO were at the same time facilitating the export of antiquities from French Indochina.

One of the greatest controversies regarding the removal of antiquities from French Indochina involved the author André Malraux, who subsequently became France's first minister of cultural affairs in the de Gaulle government. In 1923, Malraux had an official permit to study the architecture of Khmer temples but not to remove any fragments, which he was warned was illegal. However, Malraux and his friend Louis Chevasson removed sections of a stone figure of a goddess from the Banteay Srei temple in Angkor. Malraux and Chevasson were arrested, put on trial, and convicted, and the fragments of sculpture were returned to their original location. The theft from the Banteay Srei temple may have been the catalyst for the adoption of new legislation regarding the classification, protection, and conservation of historical monuments and art objects from French Indochina, which was adopted in 1925.

Malraux, however, was involved in further scandal regarding his acquisition of Buddhist sculpture while in Afghanistan in 1930. Malraux was unwilling to commit to how and where the sculptures were found, although it is clear that they were acquired outside the official excavations of the Délégation Archéologique Française en Afghanistan, founded in 1922. In 1931 Malraux exhibited in Paris fragments of Buddhist sculptures, mostly heads, dating from the fourth and fifth centuries AD that he had acquired in Afghanistan. Some of these subsequently were exhibited in New York, and several entered North American museums, including the Museum of Fine Arts in Boston.

THE GRAND CONGLOUÉ SHIPWRECKS

In the early days of underwater archaeology, interpretations of shipwrecks by scholars unfamiliar with this type of site could be erroneous. Misinterpretations often occurred because archaeologists themselves did not dive, a practice that now is considered to be unprofessional. An example of misinterpretation in the 1950s in the then emerging discipline of underwater archaeology is the site at the rock of Grand Congloué, south of Marseille (Bouches-du-Rhône).

The presence of a shipwreck first had been reported in 1936, when fishermen's nets brought up Roman amphorae with their maker's stamps. However, further investigation was not possible and had to await the development of the AquaLung by Jacques-Yves Cousteau and Emile Gagnan in the 1940s. Between 1952 and 1957 the site at Grand Congloué was excavated by Cousteau and Fernand Benoit, a noted terrestrial archaeologist who was director of historic antiquities of Provence and Corsica. Using Cousteau's well-known ship *Calypso* as their base, 90 percent of the site was excavated and produced many finds. However, as Benoit did not dive, he had to rely on interviewing divers and used their verbal accounts to prepare an archaeological plan of the site. Cousteau attempted to record the site, but he was not a trained archaeologist. The excavation was resumed by Yves Girault in 1961, the same year that Benoit published a report on the excavation concluding that a single shipwreck was at Grand Congloué.

The records relating to the discoveries at Grand Congloué were reexamined in the 1980s by Luc Long at DRASSM (Le Département des recherches archéologiques subaquatique et sous-marine) in Marseille, who identified two shipwrecks on the site, indicated by two distinct periods of finds.

The earlier shipwreck, Grand Congloué 1, carried a cargo of four hundred Greco-Roman amphorae, with around thirty from Greece. There were seven thousand pieces of Italian "Campanian A" black-slipped fine ware. Stamps on Rhodian amphorae date the cargo between 210 and 180 BC. The second shipwreck, Grand Congloué 2, dated from about 100 BC, around one hundred years later than Wreck One. It carried more than one thousand Dressel 1A type wine amphorae from the villa at Settefinestre, close to Cosa in central Italy, which is estimated to have produced more than four thousand amphorae of wine per year. The wine from Settefinestre was carried in amphorae stamped with SES, indicating the family of P. Sestius, who owned land near Cosa. Long also attributed other finds to this wreck, namely, later Campanian black-slipped fine ware, lamps, and coarse ware. The finds from the shipwrecks at Grand Congloué are in the collection of the Musée des Docks Romains in Marseille, on the site of a Roman commercial warehouse.

THE THEFT OF THE "TREASURE" OF KING CHILDERIC I

In 1653, a chance find was made during building work near the Church of Saint-Brice, Tournai, in modern-day Belgium, of the tomb of the Frankish ruler Childeric I, father of Clovis I, the founder of the Merovingian dynasty. The occupant of the tomb was identified as Childeric, who died in either AD 481 or 482, by an inscription on a ring in the burial. Childeric had been buried with rich grave goods, the most novel feature being around three hundred insects, usually identified as bees, made of gold with garnet cloisonné decoration, perhaps used to decorate clothing. The grave goods in the tomb were recorded by Jean-Jacques Chifflet and published in 1655. The grave goods, today commonly described as "treasure," initially were sent to the Habsburg court in Vienna, as Tournai was part of the Habsburg Empire. In 1665 they were given to King Louis XIV of France and housed in the Bibliothèque Royale (Royal Library), which later became the Bibliothèque Nationale de France (National Library of France). The "treasure" apparently was greatly admired by Napoleon Bonaparte, who was crowned emperor on 2 December 1804 wearing a cloak decorated with golden bees, perhaps using this motif in the same manner as Childeric, and emphasizing a wish to associate himself with the Merovingian king.

On the night of 5 to 6 November 1831, thieves entered the Bibliothèque Nationale, stealing, among other objects, the "treasure" from the tomb of Childeric. Some of the objects apparently were hidden by the thieves in the river Seine and were recovered the following year. Comparison with Chifflet's drawings reveals that only a fraction of the objects were recovered. These include the fittings from a sword, made from gold with cloisonné decoration (figure 5.3), and two of the golden bees. The retrieved items were returned to display at the Cabinet des Médailles at the Bibliothèque Nationale in Paris, where they reside to the present day.

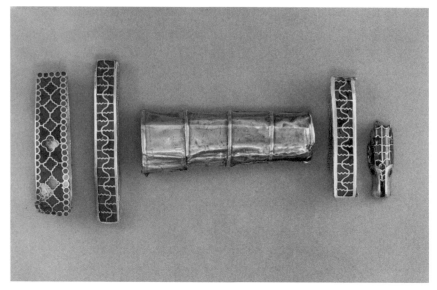

Figure 5.3.   Fittings of the sword of Childeric I. Alamy

THE DESTRUCTION OF ARCHAEOLOGICAL SITES IN FRANCE

Underwater Sites

Although the commercial development of the AquaLung in the 1940s enabled the development of the discipline of underwater archaeology, the ability to explore underwater encouraged a large number of amateur divers, not all of whom respected archaeological sites.

One of the earliest examples was the wreck of the Roman vessel known as the "Titan," discovered off the l'Ile du Levant, one of the Iles d'Hyères (Var). The wreck initially was surveyed in 1954, and it is believed that the publicity generated by the publication of color photographs of the wreck on the seabed led to its subsequent looting before it could be excavated by Philippe Tailliez in 1957 and 1958. Similarly, in 1955 when a wreck that sank off Cap d'Antibes (Alpes-Maritimes) in the sixth century BC was excavated, it was found to have been partially looted by amateur divers. Looting still was prevalent even in the 1970s; the small wreck found off the coast at Dattier, west of Cap Cavalaire (Var), in 1971 was found already to have been looted, although fifteen amphorae were noted. Unfortunately, the majority of these were themselves looted during the course of excavation before they could be raised to the surface.

Destruction and Damage to Neolithic Sites in Brittany

The Neolithic monuments found in Brittany and elsewhere are very visible in the landscape, which has resulted in the destruction and damage of some of the monuments. Indeed, it is said that the earliest known excavation in France, of the dolmen tomb at Cocherel (Eure), discussed in chapter 1, had resulted from the tomb being stripped for building stone. Damage to megalithic monuments in the early nineteenth century was noted by Prosper Merimée when he visited Brittany in the course of his time as Inspecteur général des monuments historiques, observing that monuments were being destroyed through reuse of their stone for road and bridge building.

However, destruction of important megalithic monuments still was occurring in the middle of the twentieth century, most notably the cairns at Barnenez in the commune of Plouézoc'h (Finistère), memorably described by André Malraux when French minister of culture as the "Parthénon mégalithique" (megalithic Parthenon). Ancient remains had been noted at Barnenez as long ago as 1807 and again in 1850. The two monuments, referred to as Barnenez North and Barnenez South, Kerdi Bihan and Kerdi Bras, respectively, in the Breton language, were around one hundred meters apart. Privately owned until the mid-1950s, they were exploited as a stone quarry by their owner, a public works contractor. Subsequent investigation of the remains of Barnenez North, which was destroyed in November 1954, indicates that it was between twenty-five and thirty meters long. The archaeologist Pierre-Roland Giot found the remains of a passage grave consisting of a roofed passage and a circular chamber with a large capstone. On the site of the chamber, Giot found sherds of Neolithic pottery and a few stone tools.

The quarrying of Barnenez South began in spring 1955 and was observed by the writer and journalist Francis Gourvil, who alerted Pierre-Roland Giot. Giot contacted the authorities, who instructed the quarrying to cease. Although four chambers were partially destroyed, with the contractors cutting a section through Chambers B and C, around 75 percent of the monument was saved, being classed in 1956 as an ancient monument. The site was excavated by Giot, Jean L'Helgouac'h, and Jacques Briard, followed by consolidation and restoration work that continued until 1968. They discovered that the monument consisted of two cairns, built in two consecutive phases, containing a total of eleven chambers approached by irregular passages, significant because of the variety of their construction, set in a row opening along the southern side of the cairns. The initial cairn, constructed around 4500 BC, was around thirty-five meters long and twenty-five meters wide and contained five chambers. Some of the stones approaching the chambers were decorated with engravings and paintings, and the recent research on this aspect is discussed in chapter 6. Around three hundred years after its construction, the original cairn was extended by a further forty meters to include six further chambers.

Destruction of Neolithic monuments is not limited to damage to the fabric of the structure. Researchers studying engravings and paintings in Neolithic tombs on Breton sites noted that some of the engravings at the dolmen tomb of Mané Kerioned in the commune of Carnac and the passage grave of Mané Lud in the commune of Locmariaquer (both Morbihan) had been damaged by the addition of modern painting, infilling of the engravings, and reworking of some of the designs.

The "Rodez Scandal"

In January 1997, French rescue archaeologists took strike action to protest at the destruction of Iron Age, Gallo-Roman, and medieval remains at a construction site in the town of Rodez (Aveyron). The protest was the result of the news that the then French prime minister, Alain Juppé, had authorized continuing construction despite the significant archaeological discoveries. It was claimed by the archaeologists that Juppé violated historic preservation codes and called for tougher laws. The scandal led to the establishment of a working party to consider a law on preventative archaeology and a new body to take over the responsibilities of AFAN (l'Association pour les fouilles archéologiques nationales), which resulted in the establishment of Inrap (Institut national de recherches archéologiques préventives) in 2002.

FAKES AND FORGERIES

The Crystal Skull in Paris

The collections of the Musée du Quai Branly-Jacques Chirac in Paris include a "crystal skull," a piece of quartz carved in the shape of a human skull. It is smaller than life size, measuring eleven centimeters high but weighing 2.75 kilos, and once was believed to have been of pre-Columbian Mesoamerican origin, most likely Aztec.

The skull was presented in 1878 to the newly founded Musée d'Ethnographie du Trocadéro in Paris by the French traveler and collector

Alphonse Pinart. The skull had been sold to Pinart by Eugène Boban, a French collector and antiquities dealer. Boban had lived in Mexico City from the 1860s, being associated with the Commission scientifique de Mexique of 1864 to 1867, sent to Mexico by Napoleon III during the French intervention in Mexico at this time. Indeed, Boban loaned to the Commission much of his pre-Columbian collection for exhibition in Paris from 1867 to 1868. Boban subsequently exhibited Mexican objects, including the crystal skull, at the Exposition Universelle in Paris in 1878, where it was purchased, along with other artifacts, by Pinart.

Archival research shows that Eugène Boban owned both the crystal skull now in the Musée du Quai Branly-Jacques Chirac and a similar skull in the collections of the British Museum in London, as well as being involved in the sale of three others. The British Museum skull apparently was acquired by Boban between 1878 and 1881, when he was based in Paris. In 1885 he offered it to the Museo Nacional de México, which rejected it as being a modern European object. Despite this, Boban sold the skull to Tiffany & Co., the New York jewelers, from whom the British Museum acquired it in 1897.

The crystal skulls in the Musée du Quai Branly-Jacques Chirac and the British Museum, as well as another in the Smithsonian Institution, Washington, D.C., were subject to analysis in the 1990s and 2000s, and all revealed the use of modern tools. It was concluded that the skulls in Paris and London likely were made in the nineteenth century, and the larger skull in Washington, D.C., made as late as the 1950s.

Paleolithic Portable Art: Real or Fake?

The discovery of Paleolithic portable art in the nineteenth century perhaps inevitably led to the copying of objects and presenting them as genuine. The objects that have led to the greatest suspicion are "galets peints" ("Azilian pebbles") and representations of females.

The objects popularly called "galets peints" ("Azilian pebbles") are small, flat pieces of stone decorated with simple dots and lines, probably with a finger or brush, using a pigment made from red ochre. The pebbles date from between 9000 BC to 7500 BC, the end of the Upper Paleolithic period in Western Europe. The name is derived from the Grotte du Mas d'Azil (Ariège), discussed in chapter 2, where they first were identified by Edouard Piette, who excavated the cave between 1887 and 1897.

Edouard Piette (1827–1906) trained as a lawyer and soon after became interested in geology and archaeology, financing several excavations. In

1869, Piette and Edouard Fleury excavated the cemetery known as Les Dessus de Prugny in the commune of Chassemy (Aisne), where they discovered both Neolithic and Early Iron Age burials, including a chariot burial. Piette's interest grew as the result of visits to several caves, including La Grotte de l'Eléphant in the commune of Gourdan-Polignan (Haute-Garonne), which he excavated between 1871 and 1875. In addition, from 1873 Piette worked with Emile Cartailhac and Eugène Trutat, curator of the Muséum d'histoire naturelle in Toulouse (Haute-Garonne), at the Grotte de Lortet (Hautes-Pyrénées) and La Grotte d'Espalungue in the commune of Arudy (Pyrénées-Atlantiques). In 1880, during construction of the railway station at Eauze (Gers), where Piette served as a justice of the peace between 1879 and 1881, he discovered several inscriptions on stone from the Gallo-Roman site of Elusa. The excavations that Piette financed often were conducted in his absence, as at the Grotte du Mas d'Azil (Ariège) and the Grotte du Pape at Brassempouy (Landes). Piette donated his collection of antiquities to the Musée d'Archéologie nationale in 1902, on condition that it was displayed according to his instructions in a room named after him.

Piette announced the discovery of the "galets peints" in the late 1880s, a time when the date of Paleolithic cave paintings had not been established. One of the reasons for this was a common belief that pigment could not have survived on cave walls for so long, so, similarly, pigment could not have survived on pebbles. Although Piette's claims initially were refuted by many archaeologists, Marcellin Boule and Emile Cartailhac, both noted prehistorians, found painted pebbles in archaeological contexts, and by the end of the nineteenth century many "Azilian pebbles" were identified in museum collections.

The majority of the pebbles from Le Mas d'Azil are between 30 and 130 millimeters long, up to 60 millimeters wide, and between 3 millimeters and 25 millimeters thick. The majority are blue-grey schist, although a few are limestone or quartzite. The decoration, which sometimes is on both sides, is red ochre; the usual motifs are dots, lines, and borders, occasionally chevrons or crosses. Most are painted, although a few are engraved. The French researcher Claude Couraud's study of the pebbles identified sixteen different signs, used in forty-one combinations. In addition, certain numerical groupings of signs were preferred, indicating that the decoration probably signified a type of notation.

Although this type of painted pebble has been found at several sites in Western Europe, it has been estimated that more than 70 percent from the total of around two thousand known examples are from Le Mas d'Azil.

A handful of sites in Spain and Switzerland, together with around thirty French sites, have produced painted pebbles, most notably at l'Abri de Rochedane, in the commune of Villars-sous-Dampjoux (Doubs). Although the site first was identified in 1877, followed by subsequent sporadic investigations, more excavations were conducted by André Thévenin between 1966 and 1976. The site has produced 77 engraved and 122 painted pebbles, most of which were decorated with transverse stripes.

However, the authenticity of some of the pebbles first was challenged by Adrien de Mortillet, partly caused by Piette's direction of the excavations at Le Mas d'Azil. Piette was known to have been absent frequently from the excavations he directed, leaving assistants in charge, and the suspicions were raised that some pebbles were painted by unsupervised workers who were paid for each individual find they made. It is apparent, however, that most Azilian pebbles are authentic and, indeed, spoil heaps from Piette's excavations were re-excavated to find any pebbles missed in the original excavation. Nevertheless, a willingness by collectors to pay high prices for painted pebbles undoubtedly led to a market for fake as well as genuine objects, bought by museums and collectors both in France and overseas, to the extent that there was a major trade in Azilian pebbles, both ancient and modern, by the early decades of the twentieth century.

Claude Couraud devised a methodology to identify both authentic and fake objects. This was aided by the knowledge that some fake Azilian pebbles had been kept by Henri Breuil at the Institut de Paléontologie Humaine in Paris alongside authentic examples. Couraud observed that pebbles painted in the Paleolithic period can be identified by a calcite formation on the painted surface. In addition, the coloring of many of the fake pebbles is not natural ochre and has been made using a modern colored pencil rather than a finger or brush. In addition, given that those who painted pebbles in the past would have had an ample supply of intact pebbles, any found with pigment on a fracture almost certainly are fake.

The authenticity of the carved head of a female made of ivory and known as the Dame de Brassempouy, or Dame à la capuche, discussed in chapter 2, has been questioned. The object, which has some very unusual features, has no real provenance. It was found in 1894 at a site where workers were rewarded for individual discoveries and, as at La Grotte du Mas d'Azil, frequently were left unsupervised by Edouard Piette. Furthermore, Piette recorded that he found large quantities of unworked fossilized ivory. As the material from which the Dame de Brassempouy is made undoubtedly is ancient, whether it was carved in ancient or modern times is difficult to establish.

Another female image, the "Venus" from the Abri Pataud in Les Eyzies (Dordogne), has raised questions regarding its authenticity. The rock shelter first was excavated in the 1950s and 1960s by a team led by Hallam L Movius of the Peabody Museum, Harvard University, in collaboration with the Muséum National d'Histoire Naturelle in Paris. The "Venus," a figure around twenty centimeters tall, is carved in relief on a piece of limestone. The carving, which cannot be dated, was discovered in 1958 by a student working on-site on the day after a violent thunderstorm. Doubts arose partly due to the circumstances of discovery, and rumors arose that it was planted on-site as a student prank. This was contested by Movius, who believed the confusion had been between the "real" Venus and another figure that, indeed, had been a student prank.

Glozel

One of the greatest and most enduring puzzles in French archaeology concerns the mystery of objects found close to the small village of Glozel in the commune of Ferrières-sur-Sichon (Allier), at the foot of the Auvergne mountains. The circumstances of the discovery of these objects and their date proved controversial for half a century following their discovery in the 1920s.

The objects were from a field owned by a farming family named Fradin. The field was said to have contained a tomb, found during clearance in 1924, although the structure, apparently a paved area with heavily vitrified walls, was destroyed.

The following year, Antonin Morlet, a doctor and amateur archaeologist from nearby Vichy, visited Glozel and offered to pay the Fradins for any finds made. The field, by now known as the "Champ des Morts," apparently produced a massive quantity of finds, which fell into three main categories: namely, carved bone objects, very well preserved pottery, and bricks or tablets inscribed with an unknown script. Morlet claimed that finds from the site were evidence of the beginning of the Neolithic period in France.

Morlet's claims were supported by the eminent French archaeologist Salomon Reinach. This not only gave credibility to the authenticity of the finds from Glozel, but led to the site becoming a tourist attraction. However, more scepticism came from the United Kingdom, and in an article published in 1927, O. G. S. Crawford stated that he believed that most of the Glozel finds were forgeries. Despite this, excavations continued at the site, and more than three thousand objects were recovered from 1924 until 1930, although no archaeological features were found.

In 1927, the International Anthropological Congress sent a team to Glozel to visit the site and see the finds, which they determined to be modern. Pottery was removed for further study by the French police, who concluded that the pottery was modern, as it could not otherwise have survived in such a good condition. Their report of 1928 stated that the excavation at Glozel had been disturbed and the sole archaeological find, an inscribed tablet, was discovered below freshly dug soil. Reinach initiated another investigation with a separate study team known as the Comité des Etudes (figure 5.4). In 1928 this team concluded that the site was early Neolithic in date with no later material. Despite this, Emile Fradin, aged seventeen when the field first was dug, was indicted for fraud, although the charge was overturned in 1931.

By the 1930s, most archaeologists believed that Glozel was a fraud, the consensus expressed in an article published by the French archaeologist André Vayson de Pradenne in 1930. Vayson de Pradenne reported that when he was allowed to dig on the site at Glozel in the company of Fradin, an inscribed tablet was found, but he was sure that the ground in which it was found had been disturbed. When Vayson de Pradenne returned to dig alone, in undisturbed ground, he found nothing.

Accordingly, Glozel generally was forgotten until 1974 when Emile Fradin announced in the magazine *Paris Match* that all of the finds from Glozel were authentic. A few objects from Glozel had been tested using the then new, albeit well-accepted, scientific method of thermoluminescence,

Figure 5.4.   *Excavations at Glozel by the Comité des Etudes, 13 April 1928. Alamy*

and the results indicated that the last firing of the ceramics was about two thousand years before. Independent testing in Denmark and at the National Museum of Antiquities of Scotland produced very similar results. The conclusion was that at least some of the objects from Glozel were ancient. However, the observation was made that the finds from Glozel did not appear to include Gallo-Roman artifacts, which would be expected given the thermoluminescence dates, casting doubts on Fradin's claim.

Further thermoluminescence testing was undertaken in the late 1970s and early 1980s. The results of the testing in 1979 fell into three main chronological groups: namely, Iron Age/Gallo-Roman (about 300 BC to AD 300), medieval (thirteenth century), and more recent. The thermoluminescence tests in 1983 produced very similar results (fourth century BC to the medieval period); in addition, carbon-14 testing of bone fragments suggested dates between the thirteenth and twentieth centuries. Further carbon-14 testing in 1984 revealed more objects to be medieval in date (charcoal from the eleventh to thirteenth centuries, and an ivory ring fragment from the fifteenth century), although a human femur was dated to the fifth century AD.

A reassessment of the site was made in the 1990s, and further thermoluminescence testing showed that although many of the ceramics were recent, others were fired around two thousand years ago. Further, the engravings on the stone tablets were made with steel tools and, accordingly, clearly were a modern addition. The bones almost certainly did not come from the site. Furthermore, the description of the "tomb" as a paved area with vitrified brick walls suggests it may have been a medieval glassmaking furnace.

The consensus is that the discoveries from Glozel were entirely fraudulent, where archaeological material may have been deliberately planted on a site that did not exist in antiquity, even though some of the material apparently is ancient. Despite the controversy, with the view expressed as far back as the 1920s that the objects from Glozel were intended to deceive, the small site museum in Glozel that displays the finds from the "Champ des Morts" is supported by the regional archaeological service. The "Champ des Morts" can also be visited, signposted from the village, although it is not certain whether the continued interest is as an archaeological site or as the scene of a notorious fraud.

It seems apparent that some of the debates, controversies, and scandals involving archaeology in France have had a positive effect on archaeological practices. However, it is clear that debates, such as the replication of archaeological sites, are set to continue for many years.

6

ARCHAEOLOGICAL RESEARCH IN FRANCE IN THE TWENTY-FIRST CENTURY

The twenty-first century has been marked by several discoveries that have made a significant impact on our knowledge of the archaeology of France, from the Paleolithic to the early medieval period. In addition to research excavations, generally conducted by universities, many of these discoveries have been driven by archaeological excavation in advance of infrastructure projects, such as the construction of new roads and railway lines or new building projects. The "Valetta Convention," discussed in chapter 1, with its requirement to undertake an archaeological evaluation before development begins, has been responsible for an increase in new discoveries. Many of these excavations have been under the auspices of Inrap (Institut national de recherches archéologiques préventives), founded in 2002, discussed further in chapter 1. However, the archaeological research has not been limited to new sites but includes reevaluation of previously known sites and reconsideration of objects from earlier excavations.

The chapter generally groups the discoveries according to the age of the site rather than the date of the archaeological work. However, a separate section presents the archaeological discoveries resulting from the extensive development of the high-speed railway network in France.

PALEOLITHIC

The past two decades have witnessed new discoveries in the archaeology of the Paleolithic period, as well as the opportunity to reevaluate older excavations and finds.

Information on the earliest settlements in Europe was gained in 2012 from excavations at the commune of Etricourt-Manancourt (Somme). The excavations took place in advance of the construction of the Seine-Nord Europe canal, over an area of thirty-two hundred square meters. The open-air site produced evidence of five prehistoric levels dating between three hundred thousand and eighty thousand years ago. The oldest level produced flaked flint tools, attributed to the Acheulian culture of the Lower Paleolithic period.

A rare and unusual discovery at the commune of Tourville-la-Rivière (Seine-Maritime), on the banks of the river Seine, has shed light on pre-Neanderthal occupation of France. Archaeologists found three long bones from the left arm of a single individual, perhaps an older adolescent or adult, who lived between 238,000 and 185,000 years ago, who studies suggest was a predecessor of Neanderthals. Other faunal remains found on the site indicated that animal species in the area were plentiful and included large mammals such as deer, aurochs, boar, rhinoceros, wolf, fox, bear, and panther as well as smaller mammals, including wild cats and rodents. It has been suggested that the arm from the pre-Neanderthal individual, together with the other faunal remains, were carried by the river Seine before being deposited at the foot of the chalk cliffs of Tourville-la-Rivière. Stone tools also were found on the site, many made using the sophisticated technique called the Levallois method, which would have been particularly useful in processing animal carcasses.

Archaeologists also have had the opportunity to revisit the well-known Neanderthal sites of the Bouffia Bonneval and La Ferrassie. A new excavation of the Bouffia Bonneval near La Chapelle-aux-Saints (Corrèze) took place in 2011 and 2012. As discussed in more detail in chapter 2, the cave originally was excavated in 1908; the main discovery was the skeleton of a male, designated La Chapelle-aux-Saints 1. The new excavations in the Bouffia Bonneval have led to reconsideration of the burial of La Chapelle-aux-Saints 1. The archaeologists concluded that the burial was intentional and conducted quite rapidly. In addition, the excavations produced more fragments of La Chapelle-aux-Saints 1, together with the remains of a second adult and two young individuals.

At La Ferrassie, the area adjacent to the findspot of the skeletons designated La Ferrassie 1 and 2 was re-excavated between 2010 and 2014. The application of recent scientific techniques suggests that the skeletons most likely date to between forty-five thousand and forty-three thousand years ago. A separate project reconsidered the partial infant Neanderthal skeleton, designated La Ferrassie 8, which had been found during archaeological work at the site between 1968 and 1973. In 2013, additional fossil remains and excavation notes from the 1968–1973 project were rediscovered at the Musée d'Archéologie nationale and at the Muséum national d'Histoire naturelle in Paris. These discoveries, which amounted to forty-seven new fossil remains, included fourteen cranial fragments, six mandible fragments, thirteen rib fragments, and two hand remains. Accordingly, the skeletal remains now consist of fragments from the head, thorax, pelvis, and four hand phalanges.

New discoveries are not limited to human remains; in 2012, during the excavation at Changis-sur-Marne (Seine-et-Marne) of a Gallo-Roman site, an almost complete skeleton of a mammoth was found in a quarry. This was a very rare find and the first since the "Mammoth of Choulans" in Lyon in 1859. The mammoth from Changis-sur-Marne probably was a *Mammuthus primigenius*, more commonly called a "woolly mammoth." The mammoth lived between two hundred thousand and fifty thousand years ago, the same time as Neanderthals. A flake of flint found near the mammoth is evidence of the presence of humans, a particularly significant find, as evidence of human activity and mammoths previously has been found together at only two Middle Paleolithic sites in Western Europe, both of which are in Germany.

Recent discoveries of art from the Aurignacian period have increased our knowledge of representational art from this time.

In 2003, excavations were conducted at the open-air site designated La Cantalouette II, in the commune of Creysse (Dordogne) in advance of the construction of the eastern Bergerac bypass route. These brought to light a wide range of stone tools dating from the Middle Paleolithic to the Neolithic periods, which has led to the site being interpreted as a flint knapping workshop. The most unusual find is a flint flake, which would have been discarded during flint knapping, engraved with a naturalistic depiction of a bird, possibly a quail or partridge. The engraving likely was made between thirty-five thousand and thirty-one thousand years ago.

Another Aurignacian engraving was found in 2012 at the collapsed rock shelter known as the Abri Blanchard, close to the commune of Sergeac (Dordogne). The engraving was found in situ on a limestone slab, already broken in antiquity, which had been carved with an image of an aurochs, surrounded by rows of dots. The carving was dated to around thirty-eight thousand years ago. Abri Blanchard is a large site, some 20 meters long and 6.5 meters wide. It has been interpreted as a domestic site, producing thousands of objects, largely tools, and personal ornaments made from stone, bone, antler, and ivory. This was not the first engraving to have been found at the Abri Blanchard; the rock shelter was first excavated between 1910 and 1912 by Marcel Castanet, directed by Louis Didon, a hotel owner and amateur archaeologist. Didon and Castanet found several examples of engraved and painted stone blocks, now dispersed in museums in France and the United States, although the methods used at the time meant that stratigraphical data were poor. The new excavations, which were led by Randall White of New York University, took place between 2011 and 2012 and found more than twenty-five hundred stone tools of different types, twelve objects made from bone or antler, an ivory bilobate bead, a pierced fox tooth, and three unworked plaques of ivory.

A discovery from the Gravettian period was the Grotte de Cussac near the commune of Le Buisson-de-Cadouin (Dordogne), found in September 2000. Archaeological study began in 2009 by a team led by Jacques Jaubert from l'Université Bordeaux 1. The cave, which was found by Marc Delluc, a caver from the Spéléo Club of Périgueux, is notable for its engravings, almost 150 in number. The majority of the engravings show animals, particularly mammoth, rhinoceros, deer, bison, and horses, although a few images of women are included. Color largely is absent from the engravings, but a few show finger tracings in red pigment. An unusual feature is human remains, although they apparently were not directly associated with the decorated panels. Archaeologists found the remains of at least six individuals, including an adult represented by an almost complete skeleton. Sediment under some of the remains was colored red with ochre, suggesting that the bodies were positioned deliberately. It is estimated that the engravings and burials were made around twenty-five thousand years ago, in the Gravettian period.

Research projects have centered on the method used to produce hand stencils rendered in pigment, generally made between 40,000 and 12,500 years ago, which are discussed in chapter 2. In the 1990s, experimental research conducted by Michel Lorblanchet, formerly director of the Centre national de la recherche scientifique (CNRS), indicated that the simplest method of producing hand stencils was by spraying pigment from the mouth at a distance of around seven to ten centimeters. In addition to re-creating hand stencils, Lorblanchet replicated the image of two horses surrounded by images of stencils of human hands from La Grotte du Pech Merle (Lot) and a bichrome horse from La Grotte de Lascaux (Dordogne) using charcoal and red ochre (figure 6.1). A more recent project at Durham University in England re-created hand stencils by using watered-down pigment blown through hollow tubes, with bird bones and shells likely to have been used for this purpose in the Paleolithic period. The team's aim was to

Figure 6.1. Michel Lorblanchet with his replica of a painting from La Grotte de Lascaux. Paul G. Bahn

study the position and context of hand stencils in caves in Spain and France, the latter at La Grotte du Pech Merle. It was discovered that only three or four individuals, all of whom were female, created hand stencils in each of the caves. In addition, in all of the caves, the majority of hand stencils were associated with specific features of the walls of the caves, such as small bosses or natural cracks.

Another aspect of the location of images within caves has been a project by Iegor Reznikoff from the Université de Paris X to investigate how the decoration of painted caves may have been influenced by the locations within the cave where human voices resonated in the most effective way. The sites investigated by Reznikoff included caves at Niaux (Ariège), Arcy-sur-Cure (Yonne), and Isturitz in the commune of Saint-Martin-d'Arberoue (Pyrénées-Atlantiques), the latter being noted for discoveries of artifacts interpreted as sound makers. Around 20 percent of known discoveries of these objects, made from bird bones and pierced with a series of holes, have been found at Isturitz. Reznikoff's conclusion was that the more resonant the location, the more paintings or signs are located there.

MESOLITHIC AND NEOLITHIC

New archaeological discoveries from the Mesolithic and Neolithic periods in France have not been plentiful, although all have been highly significant.

In 2008, excavation by Inrap of a site in rue Farman in Paris, close to the river Seine, prior to a new development revealed evidence of hunter-gatherer camps dating to the Mesolithic period, around 8200 to 7500 BC. In addition to microliths, the very small stone tools characteristic of Mesolithic technology, the archaeologists found fragments of the skeletons of one or two adults.

Recent archaeological discoveries have provided gruesome evidence of violence within Neolithic society. In 2012, archaeologists working at a site in the commune of Bergheim (Haut-Rhin) found the skeletal remains of two men, a woman, and four children who had been killed and their bodies dumped in a circular pit around 4000 BC. The pit also contained seven left arms; although the reason for the dismemberment is not known, it has been suggested that it was the result of warfare. Although other pits on the site contained human remains, none showed signs of violence. Four years later, in 2016, a Neolithic village was excavated at the commune of Achenheim (Bas-Rhin). Around three hundred pits were found on the site that had been used for the storage of food. At the bottom of one of the pits, which measured almost 2.5 meters across, the archaeologists discovered a group of skeletons. The deceased were all male, five adults and one adolescent, aged between fifteen and nineteen. All of the bodies had many fractures and most likely were thrown into the pit between 4400 and 4200 BC.

In Brittany, a project was undertaken in 2007 to record the depictions of axs and axheads in the passage grave at Gavrinis (Morbihan), with further projects begun in 2010 whose aim was to record the engravings, undertake a complete survey of the tomb, and, crucially, obtain dates for the construction and use of the tomb interior. Previously only one radiocarbon date had been obtained, in the 1980s, which related to the final use of the tomb between 3300 and 3000 BC, at the start of the Final Neolithic period. The more recent radiocarbon dates from the interior of the tomb suggest use between 3900 and 3770 BC, accordingly also dating the nearby Locmariaquer passage grave ("Table des Marchands"), discussed in chapter 2. Another radiocarbon sample indicated that construction of the Gavrinis tomb began between 4200 and 4000 BC. Testing of dark coloring on one of the engravings indicated that it dated from modern times, most likely from Zacharie le Rouzic's research in the 1920s. It is suspected that he colored the carvings with carbon to help in tracing the engravings.

Another recent project in Brittany has investigated the use of painted decoration in Neolithic tombs. To detect the paint, the team used various photographic techniques, with several different lights and filters. Analytical methods were used to study the pigment, involving a portable X-ray diffraction tube as well as direct sampling; research is continuing on their findings.

At Barnenez in the commune of Plouezoc'h (Finistère), most of the decoration is found in Chamber H, part of the oldest tumulus on the site. In addition to decorative carvings, several of the orthostats were painted with zigzag or wavy lines in red or black pigment. Elsewhere, remains of carving and red pigment were found in Dolmen 2 in the tumulus Saint-Michel in the commune of Carnac (Morbihan). On the Presqu'île de Rhuys, Dolmen 2 at Le Petit Mont in the commune of Arzon (Morbihan) was decorated with engravings and vertical motifs painted in red. Further to the west, the tomb at the site of Goërem in the commune of Gâvres (Morbihan) was decorated with both engraving and painting.

BRONZE AGE

Current research on the Bronze Age in France has focused on both reevaluation of objects from earlier excavations and information from recently discovered sites. Some of this research is included in the section at the end of the chapter on discoveries arising from the construction of the LGV railway network.

Excavations in the Ferrié district in the town center of Laval (Mayenne) prior to redevelopment in 2017 have produced evidence of occupation during the Neolithic and Bronze Age periods. Mostly notably, a circular enclosure, nine meters in diameter, dating from the Bronze Age, was identified. The initial suggestion is that it served as a funerary structure, originally surrounding an earth mound that no longer is present. Bronze Age funerary circles are rare in the region of western France known as Les Pays de la Loire; the only known examples were recorded in the commune of Cholet (Maine-et-Loire) and Auzay in the commune of Auchay-sur-Vendée (Maine-et-Loire).

An unusual underwater discovery from the transition between the end of the Bronze Age and start of the Iron Age is the site of La Motte, in the commune of Agde (Hérault). Although the site is now on the bed of the river Hérault, originally it would have been on the riverbank, now eroded away. The site, which lies at a depth of between four and seven meters, was found in 2003 during an underwater survey and excavated the following year. Fresh excavations began in 2011, and again in 2013, continuing on an annual basis, by a team directed by Thibault Lachenal and Jean Gascó of the Centre national de la recherche scientifique (CNRS). Pottery found at La Motte dates the site between 900 and 750 BC. Other finds include animal bones and organic material such as ropes and fragments of fishing nets. Groups of stones and lines of wooden piles indicate the remains of rectangular dwellings. However, the most spectacular discovery was made in 2004 of bronze ornaments and jewelry, which were retrieved in two large blocks of soil cut from the riverbed, their contents meticulously excavated at the Laboratoire de Vienne (Isère). The blocks were found to contain a deposit of more than three hundred bronze objects, pieces of female ornaments and jewelry, in all likelihood representing ceremonial dress, which originally were inside a box decorated with bronze discs. Included also were amber beads, some of which would have decorated torcs, and a few tin pendants. When worn, the jewelry would have appeared to cover all parts of the wearer's body, including earrings, torcs, an elaborate necklace, bracelets, and leg rings. The finds suggest that the wearer's clothing also would have been decorated, including ornaments for the skirt and hem of her dress, as well as an elaborate belt. In 2013, the Musée d'Ephèbe in Agde installed an impressive new display of the jewelry and ornaments.

Recent scientific study of bronze objects has been facilitated by the foundation in 2005 of LEACA: Laboratoire d'Etude des alliages cuivreux anciens (Laboratory for the study of ancient copper alloys), led by Anne Lehoërff from the université Charles-de-Gaulle-Lille-3. Since 2006, the team has been studying weaponry, including the cuirasses from Marmesse, discussed in chapter 3. They also have been studying the helmets from Bernières-d'Ailly (Calvados), which date between 1000 and 800 BC. The helmets, nine in total, were found in 1832 during agricultural work. The majority of the helmets still are in museum collections in Normandy, although one is in the University of Pennsylvania Museum of Archaeology and Anthropology in Philadelphia, and another is in the Palazzo Venezia in Rome, Italy.

IRON AGE

In recent years, northeastern France has been the site for significant discoveries of burials dating from the Early Iron Age, the so-called Celtic period.

In the commune of Buchères (Aube), the development of the modern-day storage and distribution area known as the Parc Logistique de l'Aube, occupying an area of about 250 hectares, has been the subject of regular excavations since 2005. The site has produced evidence of occupation from the Neolithic period onward, although the most significant discovery came in spring 2013, when the archaeologists unearthed a series of graves from the fourth and third centuries BC, still intact, with their contents undisturbed. The archaeologists found a total of twenty-seven burials, both adult men and women, but no child burials were found. Some of the men were buried with weapons, an iron sword and spear, and the remains of a shield. The women wore a torc and jewelry made of bronze and jet. On the chest of both males and females were found fibulas of bronze or iron, sometimes decorated with coral.

An even more spectacular discovery was made in 2015, during an excavation conducted by Inrap archaeologists Bastien Dubuis and Emilie Millet in advance of the development of an industrial zone in the commune of Lavau (Aube). The excavation revealed a very lavish burial dating to the fifth century BC, which has been compared to the discoveries from Vix, mentioned in chapter 3. The burial was covered by a tumulus, forty meters in diameter, within which was a large burial chamber, fourteen square meters in size. The deceased was buried with a two-wheeled chariot and lavish grave goods, including an Etruscan bronze cauldron, a meter in diameter, its four handles decorated with a head of the river god Acheloos and the cauldron rim decorated with the heads of eight female lions. Inside the cauldron was a Greek oinochoe (wine jug), decorated in the black-figure technique with a Dionysiac scene. Other objects associated with banqueting were a wine strainer and silver goblet. The deceased wore jewelry, including a gold torc weighing more than five hundred grams and decorated with a winged creature, gold bracelets, and an armlet made of jet. The archaeologists also found an ornate fibula and finely decorated belt. Amber beads found close to the neck of the deceased may have been from a necklace or hair ornament. Fragments of clothing have been preserved, including two hooks, made from iron and coral, from a garment of which a few pieces of leather and a decorative row of rivets from the collar remain, together with fragments of shoes that had bronze hooks. Although it is assumed that the deceased was male, no detailed study has yet been made of the poorly preserved skeletal remains. The rich nature of the burial, inevitably, has led to suggestions in the popular press that the deceased was a "prince."

The grave offerings from the burial at Lavau are being analyzed at the Centre de recherche et de restauration des musées de France, usually referred to as C2RMF, in the Paris region. The aim of the analysis is to learn more about the materials used and the way the objects were made. Although research of the grave assemblage will continue until 2019, early findings suggest that the fibula found in the grave was decorated with silver wire, and high resolution three-dimensional scanning showed evidence of wear on the torc and gold bracelets, indicating they were not made especially for the funeral.

A program by Inrap began in 2001 to excavate the Gallo-Roman sanctuary at Tintignac in the commune of Naves (Corrèze). The remains of the sanctuary had been excavated between 1842 and 1884, and the aim of the new project was to verify the plans drawn up in the nineteenth century and subsequently to present the site to the public. The archaeologists confirmed the presence of a temple, a semicircular building, a theater, and another building likely to have been linked to cult practice in the sanctuary. From 2004 the team began to excavate below the Gallo-Roman archaeological levels and discovered the remains of an Iron Age sanctuary dating from the first and second centuries BC. The most spectacular finds deliberately had been buried in a pit, roughly square, with sides around 1.1 meters long, and comprised almost five hundred fragments of iron and bronze objects. They included iron weapons and the remains of animal figures made from sheet bronze. However, the most rare and spectacular discoveries were bronze helmets with crests either in the shape of a bird or interlocking rings, and fragments of seven examples of the type of war trumpet made from bronze known as a carnyx. A carnyx was made in an elongated S-shape with the bell, from which the sound emitted, in the form of an animal head with its mouth open. Further excavations at the site in 2009 revealed the remains of an aqueduct that supplied water to the sanctuary.

Evidence of river transport along the river Marne was found during an Inrap excavation in 2007 at Chelles (Seine-et-Marne) with the discovery of a wooden quay, which apparently was constructed around 100 BC on a now silted-up branch of the Marne. The well-preserved remains, made from oak timbers, consisted of planks supported by a series of posts. The quay continued in use after the conquest of Gaul by Julius Caesar in 52 BC, but it was abandoned in the late first century BC because of silting of the river Marne.

GALLO-ROMAN

The majority of new research on the Gallo-Roman period is from both new sites and reinterpretations of sites in southern France.

An example of the latter is the site of Castellas in the commune of Murviel-lès-Montpellier (Hérault). The site has been known for many years, the first excavation having taking place in the nineteenth century at the behest of the Emperor Napoleon III. Subsequent excavations were conducted from the 1950s, initiated by Paul Soyris, an amateur archaeologist after whom the site museum is named. Since 2001, a team from the Université Paul-Valéry in Montpellier (Hérault) and Inrap have been conducting new excavations on three different parts of the site. The various excavations have revealed that occupation began at the start of the second century BC. The settlement expanded to occupy an area of thirty hectares by the end of the first century BC and had been fortified with a wall almost two kilometers long. The city was divided into two zones, one on top of the hill and the other on the slopes, and apparently was abandoned by the third century AD. The latest excavations have revealed a previously unknown Gallo-Roman sanctuary situated on a slope facing the settlement. The remains of the sanctuary include a temple, buildings with porticos, and a monumentalized spring. The temple, which was constructed in the first century BC, was approached by a porch with a mosaic floor whose remains consist of black-and-white meander decoration. The open area close to the temple is sixty-two meters long and twenty-five meters wide, bordered to the south by a portico.

Also in southern France, Roman houses from the second century AD had been found in the 1980s during the excavation of an eighteenth-century glassworks in the Trinquetaille district of Arles (Bouches-du-Rhône), but no further excavation took place. Archaeological work on the site recommenced in 2014, when an excavation was carried out below one of the Roman houses found in the 1980s. The remains of a property dating to 46 or 45 BC, shortly after the foundation of the Roman colony at Arles, known to the Romans as Arelate, was revealed. The archaeologists discovered wall paintings in August Mau's "Second Style," which are rare in Roman Gaul, although relatively common in the sites around the Bay of Naples, Italy, in this period. The lower sections of the paintings have been preserved on a section of wall about 1.5 meters high. Some were still in situ, although most were retrieved as fragments from debris during excavation. The reassembly of these fragments, more than twelve thousand in total, will take many years. By 2016, two rooms decorated in the first century BC had been excavated, one identified as a cubiculum (bedroom). This is painted with architectural designs that imitate marble columns and paneling. The area where it is believed the bed would have been located had a separate decoration of stripes and rosettes. The paintings in the adjacent room, interpreted as a reception area for important guests, were large-scale figures, half to three-quarters life size, painted on a red background. One of the fragments depicts a young woman playing a harp that had been painted in expensive Egyptian blue and red vermilion pigments.

Another important discovery at Arles were several Roman sculptures, found in the river Rhône by a team led by Luc Long, curator at DRASSM (Le Département des recherches archéologiques subaquatique et sous-marine).

Diving conditions in the Rhône are difficult, hampered by poor visibility and strong currents; despite this, discoveries of pottery and amphorae, in addition to the Arles-Rhône 3 barge, discussed in chapter 3, are evidence of a thriving trade along the river. In September 2007, Long and his team made an important discovery of marble sculptures depicting Neptune, Asclepius, and the life-sized bust of a man they believed to be Julius Caesar, together with architectural fragments and bronzes, including a gold-plated figure of Victory. Although the identification of the individual depicted on the bust is disputed, the discovery is considered to be one of the most important finds of Roman sculpture in France since the 1960s.

Discoveries of the remains of ships from the Roman period continue to be made. In 2011, the remains of a large Roman ship were found in the cove known as the Baie de la Baumette in the modern-day holiday resort of Agay (Var). Investigations of the ship, which was at a depth of between three and five meters, were made by Anne and Jean-Pierre Joncheray between 2011 and 2013. The ship, designated Agay C, was thirty meters long and is notable for the extensive remains of its elaborate double hull and its keel. Its cargo consisted of Dressel 1B wine amphorae, characteristic of the second and first centuries BC. As at the shipwreck discovered at Madrague de Giens, discussed in chapter 3, the presence of ballast stones used by divers may suggest that the wreck had been salvaged in antiquity.

In May 2012, the remains of the hull of a Roman ship were found no longer under water but on land at Pré des Pecheurs, Antibes (Alpes-Maritimes) between two and three meters below ground level. Excavation of the well-preserved hull was undertaken by Inrap, who discovered that the ship originally had been twenty-two meters long and between six and seven meters wide, made of conifer wood. The archaeologists concluded that it had been a merchant vessel that sank in either the second or third centuries AD. No cargo was found aboard the ship, suggesting that it had been retrieved, or perhaps that the vessel had been sunk deliberately. The hull timbers, of which fifteen meters had survived, were lifted for conservation. The excavation site, which was part of the harbor at Antibes during the Roman period, also provided plentiful archaeological deposits, attesting to the diverse nature of maritime trade between 400 BC and AD 600. The discovery was particularly fortuitous, as it has been estimated that 90 percent of the Roman port had been destroyed during the 1970s when the modern marina at Antibes was built.

The Gallo-Roman barge designated LSG4 (Lyon-Saint-Georges 4) has joined the collection of the Musée Gallo-Romain Lyon-Fourvière in Lyon. LSG4 was found during archaeological work undertaken between

2002 and 2004 in the Saint-Georges district of Lyon in advance of the construction of a parking facility. The archaeologists discovered sixteen vessels in total, six Gallo-Roman, two medieval, seven from the sixteenth century, and one from the eighteenth century. All of the Gallo-Roman vessels dated between the first and third centuries AD, had a shallow draft, and were made from oak and fir. Four of the ships apparently had been abandoned. The original length of LSG4, which dated to the second century AD, was 28 meters, of which 15 meters were recovered, 4.85 meters wide and 1.35 meters high. It has been estimated that it would have been able to carry a cargo weighing around fifty-five tons, with a draft of 0.85 meters, making the barge ideally suited for the long-distance transport of heavy cargo. Three of the Gallo-Roman vessels were selected to be preserved by reimmersion in water, of which two remain in temporary storage. In 2014, LSG4 was removed from immersion and transported to l'Atelier Régional de Conservation Nucléart (ARC-Nucléart) in Grenoble (Isère), where it was conserved and reassembled, work completed in 2016. It is expected to be on display in the Musée Gallo-Romain Lyon-Fourvière by 2020. The excavation team also found several architectural fragments on the site, including columns and doorsills, which seem to have been from one or more temples or monuments originally, perhaps reused in the Late Roman period.

The Roman settlement of Mediolanum Santonum, which has become the modern-day town of Saintes (Charente-Maritime), was founded in the late first century BC. Its notable monuments include the Arch of Germanicus and a large amphitheater, both dating to the first century AD. Excavation of a building plot at Saintes in 2014, some 250 meters west of the amphitheater, revealed part of a cemetery with around one hundred Gallo-Roman graves, including some double burials and a multiple burial pit, measuring 2 meters by 1.3 meters, containing the remains of five people, including two children and two young women. Of the burials that were excavated, few produced grave goods, an exception being the burial of a young child, who had two coins on its eyes, accompanied by pottery vessels from between AD 150 and 200. However, the most unusual feature of this cemetery was that a few of the deceased seemingly were restrained in some way. Four of the adults had shackles on the left ankle, and one man was shackled around his neck. A child also had a riveted object around his left wrist. It has been speculated that the location of the cemetery may suggest that the deceased were killed in the amphitheater, although this has not been proved. It appears that the oldest burials were situated alongside an ancient road whose existence was hitherto unsuspected.

On the island of Corsica, Inrap excavations at Mariana, in the commune of Lucciana (Haute-Corse), have revealed the first known evidence of the cult of Mithras on Roman Corsica. The discovery was announced in early 2017 of a Mithraeum, a sanctuary to Mithras, found on the outskirts of the Roman settlement at Mariana. The remains of the sanctuary consisted of a large complex of rooms comprising an antechamber and a rectangular assembly hall, 11 meters long by 5 meters wide, with marble benches, 1.8 meters wide, running along both long sides. Opposite were two brick-built niches, one of which still contained three intact oil lamps. In addition to the typical architecture of a Mithraeum, at the end of the central corridor of the assembly hall was a marble sculpted relief depicting Mithras killing the bull with which he was associated, three fragments of which were recovered. The Mithraeum shows evidence of violent destruction in antiquity, perhaps as a result of the decree of AD 392 by the emperor Theodosius I, which suppressed non-Christian religious practice. Around AD 400, a large Early Christian complex, with a basilica and baptistery, was constructed in Mariana. Mithraea have been found elsewhere in France, at Bordeaux (Gironde), Strasbourg (Bas-Rhin), Biesheim (Haut-Rhin), Septeuil (Yvelines), and Angers (Maine-et-Loire), the latter found only in 2010. Archaeological work on the site of a former clinic in Angers discovered a building whose architecture identified it as a Mithraeum. Finds from its excavation included around two hundred coins, complete oil lamps, and a terra sigillata cup dating to the third century AD, with an inscription added before firing indicating it was a dedication by a man called Genialis to the "undefeated god Mithras."

Excavations at Uzès (Gard), which began in October 2016, have revealed part of what is believed to be the Roman settlement of Ucetia. Although the name "Ucetia" was known from an inscription found at Nîmes (Gard), only a few fragments of mosaic had been archaeological evidence of Ucetia. Most of the remains date between the first century BC and the seventh century AD, although none are from the third and fourth centuries AD. The most striking discovery is a large building constructed in the first century BC, with four rooms, one of which has a magnificent polychrome mosaic floor. The mosaic is in two panels, both with similar elements of design. The larger panel has a central medallion consisting of a sun-ray design within a concentric band of black-and-white checkerboard pattern. At the center is a floral design made from red tesserae. In the four corners are polychrome images of animals and birds, namely, an owl, a duck, an eagle, and a fawn. A second, smaller panel also had a central sun-ray medallion, although it is flanked by two concentric bands of black-and-white tesserae arranged in a checkerboard pattern, and has a much less elaborate border. The richly decorated building, including its mosaic floor, went out of use in the first century AD, and subsequent decoration was much simpler. Another discovery was a well-preserved house, which was built in the early first century AD. The building later was remodeled with the addition of a hypocaust, a mosaic floor with dolphin motifs, and a portico added to the central courtyard.

EARLY MEDIEVAL

The Arab-Islamic conquest of the seventh and eighth centuries AD, which included part of the western Mediterranean coast of modern-day France, has left few traces in the archaeological record. An exception is the discovery of an early Muslim presence in France in Nîmes (Gard). In 2006 and 2007, Inrap excavations by Yves Gleize in advance of the construction of an underground parking garage revealed domestic architecture and around twenty graves. The bodies of three males, which may have been wrapped, had been placed in an extended position directly into burial pits rather than in a coffin. All had been placed on their right side, facing southeast, the direction of Mecca, in accordance with medieval and modern Muslim burial customs. In addition, two of the burial pits had been dug with a lateral niche known as a "lahd." Radiocarbon dating suggests that the men had been buried between the seventh and eighth centuries AD, corresponding to documentary evidence, especially the Moissac and Uzès chronicles, which attest to a Muslim presence in Nîmes between AD 719 and 752. Paleogenetic analysis suggests that the men had a North African ancestry, and researchers suggest they may have been Berber soldiers in the Umayyad army, recruited during the Arab expansion in North Africa. The burials provide rare archaeological information regarding the Muslim presence in the Visigothic territory of Septimania, the area defined by the Massif Central to the north, the Pyrenees to the west and south, and the Camargue marshes to the east.

As mentioned in chapter 1, Inrap is also involved in archaeological projects in French territories overseas. An excavation of a site that was occupied at a time corresponding to the Early Medieval period in Europe is at Pointe du Cannonnier, a cape on the extreme west of the island of Saint-Martin, in the French area of the island. Saint-Martin, which is one of the Caribbean island group known as the Lesser Antilles, is a "collectivité d'outre-mer," an overseas administrative division of France. Archaeological work on the site, which is now around two hundred meters from the current shoreline, began in 2002 and culminated in excavation in 2012, prior to construction of a private villa. The various archaeological projects revealed a pre-Columbian village, which was occupied between AD 660 and 960. The village occupied an oval-shaped site of more than one hectare, at the center of which was a living area surrounded by refuse pits. The 2012 excavation focused in the northern part of the pre-Columbian village on an area of refuse pits that included marine shells, revealing a diet based largely on shellfish.

CONSTRUCTION OF THE LGV (LIGNES À GRANDE VITESSE) RAILWAY NETWORK

The extensive development of the high-speed railway network in France, known as the "lignes à grande vitesse," usually abbreviated as LGV, has resulted in the discovery of a large number of archaeological sites along the route of the new railways. This is reminiscent of the many discoveries made in the nineteenth century during the construction of the first railways in France. The section focuses on the most recent railway lines, in particular the second phase of the LGV Est européenne, which opened in 2016; the extensions of the LGV Atlantique known as the LGV Bretagne-Pays-de-la-Loire and the LGV Sud Europe Atlantique, both of which opened in 2017; and finally the Contournement Nîmes-Montpellier, expected to be open by 2018.

Like all other infrastructure projects in France, there is a legal requirement to undertake archaeological investigations of the site before construction commences. In the case of new railway lines, the area under archaeological investigation can be several hundred kilometers long, such as the LGV Sud Europe Atlantique, which runs for more than three hundred kilometers but is sometimes as narrow as twenty meters. There is a legal requirement for such projects to use, and fund, specialist organizations and public bodies to undertake archaeological surveys and excavations, and to write reports.

LGV Est européenne

The LGV Est européenne, designed to link Paris with Strasbourg, opened in two phases, the first being between Vaires-sur-Marne (Seine-et-Marne) and Baudrecourt (Moselle) in 2007, the second between Baudrecourt (Moselle) and Vendenheim (Bas-Rhin) in 2016. Construction of the second phase alone between 2010 and 2015 revealed forty previously unknown archaeological sites along its route of 106 kilometers, dating from the Early Neolithic period (around 5400 to 4900 BC) to the modern era.

A cemetery dating from the Early Neolithic period (5400 to 4900 BC) was found at the site of Bannenberg in the commune of Ingenheim (Bas-Rhin). Thirty burials and six cremations were found, associated with a settlement around fifty meters away. Evidence of the Late Neolithic period (4100 to 3500 BC) has been found at a handful of sites along the route. The largest is the site of Gingsheimer Feld in the commune of Gougenheim (Bas-Rhin), where the archaeologists excavated almost one hundred storage pits over an area of around four hectares. Thirty-six of the pits contained a total of forty-six burials. The adjacent sites of Burgweg Rechts and Burgweg Links in the commune of Eckwersheim (Bas-Rhin) have produced archaeological evidence from two separate periods. Burgweg Rechts was the site of a cemetery from the Bronze Age, when it was in use for cremation burials between 1400 and 1300 BC, until the Gallo-Roman period. One of the Bronze Age cremation burials dating to around 1250 BC was accompanied by amber beads, indicating the high status of the deceased. Two of a group of Iron Age tumulus burials, dating from the eighth to the seventh centuries BC, were excavated. Both were aristocratic in nature, with one containing a bronze vessel known as a situla, from Italy; the second, which contained a large burial chamber, was used for two individuals, one of whom was buried with a razor. The cemetery continued in use in the Gallo-Roman period, with five funerary enclosures in use between the late first century BC and the later second century AD. The grave goods of cremation burials were distinguished by the presence of very well preserved glass vessels dating from the first and second centuries AD. In addition, very early evidence of metallurgy during the Neolithic period, from between 3850 and 3600 BC, was present at Burgweg Rechts. The archaeologists found fragments of a ceramic crucible and a small piece of copper ingot, which, when analyzed, revealed that it was from the foothills of the modern-day Austrian Alps.

One of the most significant finds from Burgweg Links is a blue glass bead with white spiral decoration, of a type known in Italy. Its date, between 1350 and 800 BC, makes it among the earliest known glass in the region. Burgweg Links was also the site of a Merovingian necropolis, in use from the late sixth century AD until the late seventh century AD. Around sixty tombs were found, of which thirty-eight were investigated. Many of the dead were accompanied with rich grave goods: women with jewelry and men with weapons. One of the women, who was buried in the late sixth or early seventh century AD, wore a necklace made from gold medallions alternating with amethyst beads. She wore a chatelaine at her waist, terminating in an openwork bronze disc encircled with an ivory ring, and also had offerings of food in the burial.

The site known as La Tête d'Or in the commune of Bassing (Moselle) is one of the most informative Iron Age sites discovered along the route of the LGV Est européenne. A high-status rural settlement, built within an enclosure, developed between 150 and 120 BC. Large quantities of pottery and metal objects were found, the most notable of which were fragments of a bronze wine strainer. Found alongside large quantities of sherds of wine amphorae, they suggested the affluent activity of wine drinking. Other metal objects are interpreted as military in character, including fragments of chariots and war trumpets. Small scraps of metal suggested a workshop engaged in the making of fibulas. The settlement seemingly was unaffected by the Roman conquest, and metalwork continued into the Gallo-Roman period. A spectacular find was a large deposit of almost twelve hundred coins, buried between 40 and 20 BC, minted in several parts of Gaul. The estate was reorganized in the second century AD, by which time it extended to three hectares and included a luxurious villa and an underground aqueduct that fed a bath complex. Several pieces of the artificial blue pigment known as "Egyptian blue" were found on the site, suggesting that the villa had been decorated with wall paintings, although no trace has survived. The agricultural estate included the remains of wooden buildings likely to have been used to house farmworkers. The villa was destroyed by fire in the third century AD and its stone removed for use in later buildings. The site was not abandoned, however; wooden buildings were erected in the fourth and fifth centuries AD, and occupation continued in the Merovingian period, the sixth and seventh centuries AD. A very rare discovery at Bassing was a gold ring, made using the techniques of filigree and granulation, familiar from Etruscan gold working. Unfortunately, the ring was found without a secure archaeological context, preventing further knowledge regarding its use.

The majority of Gallo-Roman discoveries along the route of the LGV Est européenne were villas, which began to appear in France in the first century AD. Eight sites were found along the route, including La Tête d'Or, previously mentioned, and a large villa at the site of La Guéren in the commune of Conthil (Moselle). The villa, in use between the first and third centuries AD, was built around a central courtyard and had a separate bath complex. The building was abandoned in the fourth century AD. A small Merovingian necropolis was in use at La Guéren in the seventh and eighth centuries AD.

Evidence of Gallo-Roman cult practice was found along the LGV route, including a temple to Mercury, in use in the second and third centuries AD, at the site of La Rothlach in the commune of Eckartswiller (Bas-Rhin). The association with Mercury was established through recognizable depictions of the god and, crucially, a dedication to Mercury inscribed on a stone slab. The cult of a deity characteristic of the northwestern provinces of the Roman Empire is attested by the discovery in the commune of Sarraltroff (Moselle) of a terra-cotta statuette of a woman suckling two children, interpreted as an image of one of the mother goddesses known as Matres. The statuette, which dates between the first and third centuries AD, is of a type known from other sites in the area.

The LGV Atlantique high-speed railway line has been extended by the construction of two branches, namely, the LGV Bretagne-Pays-de-la-Loire and the LGV Sud Europe Atlantique.

LGV Bretagne-Pays-de-la-Loire

The LGV Bretagne-Pays-de-la-Loire runs from Rennes (Ille-et-Vilaine) to Le Mans (Sarthe), a total length of 214 kilometers. Forty-five excavations were conducted during the course of its construction, revealing evidence from the Paleolithic period until modern times.

The excavation of the site of Château-Gaillard-La Mercerie in the commune of Fontenay-sur-Vègre (Sarthe) produced evidence from the Middle Paleolithic period, with almost eighteen thousand flint tools typical of Mousterian technology. The open-air site, which was on a flint deposit, was in use between sixty thousand and fifty thousand years ago. The site has been interpreted as either a tool "workshop" or a Neanderthal hunting camp.

The site along the route of the LGV Bretagne-Pays-de-la-Loire that produced the best new evidence of occupation during the Bronze Age is La Salmondière in the commune of Cesson-Sévigné (Ille-et-Vilaine). The archaeologists found small wooden buildings from the Late Bronze Age, dating between 1190 and 1000 BC, including an oval-shaped building that was nine meters long and six meters wide. A discovery in one of the postholes used in the construction of the oval building was a small glass bead made in Italy, which indicated links outside the immediate area. La Salmondière developed during the Iron Age, and between 250 and 80 BC a large farm was on the northwestern part of the site. During the first century AD, evidence of agriculture and industrial activities indicated that the site was part of the estate of a Gallo-Roman villa.

The discoveries along the route of the LGV Bretagne-Pays-de-la-Loire suggest an increase in rural settlements from the third century BC onward. Wooden buildings, probably for the storage of cereals, were found in Iron Age levels dating between 770 and 480 BC at the site known as La Poterie in the commune of Ruillé-le-Gravelais (Mayenne). This activity clearly continued into the Gallo-Roman period, shown by the discovery of a first century AD granary. Good evidence of Iron Age agricultural activity also was found at other sites in Ruillé-le-Gravelais. The neighboring sites of La Gachottière and Les Guimbertières were the site of an Iron Age farm in use between the second century BC and first century AD. As well as a large system of enclosures, the residential area of the farm was discovered at Les Guimbertières. Similar in date is the farm at the site of La Clairaserie at Ossé, in the commune of Châteaugiron (Ille-et-Vilaine). The archaeologists found several wooden buildings, some of which may have been used for food preparation. Like other similar farms, La Clairaserie was abandoned in the first century AD. This was also the case at the Iron Age farm at La Massuère in the commune of Brielles (Ille-et-Vilaine). The farm had been in a highly favorable position, with views of the surrounding area and close to a stream, a location that had been occupied since the Neolithic and Bronze Age periods. The farm included a large oval building, constructed in the third century BC, as well as granaries for the storage of cereals. Contact with other communities is suggested by fragments of wine amphorae from Italy. The site was abandoned at the time of the Roman conquest and apparently was not inhabited again until the thirteenth century.

However, other Iron Age farmsteads continued to thrive in the Gallo-Roman period. For example, Le Grand Coudray in the commune of Bonchamp-lès-Laval (Mayenne) was established as a farmstead in the Iron Age and continued in this form until the first century AD. In the second century AD, it appears that the wooden buildings were replaced with stone construction, including a large building with a porch, which may have served as the entrance to a Gallo-Roman villa.

Evidence of Gallo-Roman cult practice was found at the site of La Grillière in the commune of Saint-Denis-du-Maine (Mayenne). The site previously had been occupied by a large farm, established in the third century BC and abandoned at the end of the first century BC. It was replaced by a sanctuary, extended in the AD 70s by substantial buildings, including a temple. The sanctuary itself was abandoned during the third century AD.

A very unusual discovery from the beginning of the Early Medieval period was a small deposit of weapons, probably buried in the fifth century AD, at the site of Bas Bray in the commune of Fontenay-sur-Vègre

(Sarthe). The weapons, which had been buried close to an enclosure several centuries old, consisted of a shield boss and short sword, together with its scabbard.

A domestic site occupied during both the Merovingian and Carolingian periods was an unusual discovery. Its presence was indicated by a pottery kiln in use in the Merovingian period, in the sixth and seventh centuries AD, at La Liberderie in the commune of Gennes-sur-Seiche (Ille-et-Vilaine). The kiln, which was dated by archaeomagnetic analysis as being in use between AD 516 and 648, produced a wide range of pottery, most typically with impressed decoration. Other Merovingian pottery was found deposited in a ditch at l'Ouillère in the commune of Ruillé-le-Gravelais (Mayenne). The ditch, which contained fragments of several pieces of pottery dating between AD 600 and 650, suggested that they originated in a nearby domestic site that has not been located.

LGV Sud Europe Atlantique (SEA)

Archaeological work on the LGV Sud Europe Atlantique, abbreviated to SEA, which runs a length of almost 302 kilometers from Tours (Indre-et-Loire) to Bordeaux (Gironde), began in 2009. Fifty sites were excavated, twenty-four alone in the Inde-et-Loire département, revealing evidence from prehistory until the present day.

Some of the oldest evidence along the route was found at the site known as Le Bois Clair, in the commune of Montguyon (Charente-Maritime). At this open-air Paleolithic site, the archaeologists found stone tools characteristic of the Middle and Upper Paleolithic periods. At Villiers and La Roche in the commune of Maillé (Indre-et-Loire), they found only a few pieces of flint tools and debitage from their manufacture dating from the Magdalenian period, around 16,000 to 11,000 BC. However, the conclusion was that the site had been a source for flint to manufacture such tools.

Two prehistoric cemeteries, from different phases of use, were discovered at the site of Le Vigneau in the commune of Pussigny (Indre-et-Loire). The earliest, with more than eighty burials from the Middle Neolithic period, about 4500 BC, is a unique find from this period in western France. Grave goods with the burials generally were stone tools and pottery, although a few contained the remains of small animals. The second phase of use of the cemetery was the final phase of the Bronze Age, around 800 BC. Most of the burials were inhumations, but some were cremations. Occupation of the site continued after the prehistoric period, and a large sanctuary was constructed in the Gallo-Roman period, including a temple and ancillary buildings. Other significant evidence from the Neolithic period along the route was at the site of Bois Adrien, in the commune of Maillé (Indre-et-Loire), where archaeologists discovered a large Late Neolithic village.

One of the most significant Iron Age sites along the route of the LGV SEA was the site known as Les Noëls in the commune of Pliboux (Deux-Sèvres), where a small part of a large rural establishment was revealed. The part of the site that was excavated was occupied at the end of the Iron Age, from around 60 BC to the beginning of the first century AD. The archaeologists discovered twenty wooden buildings within an enclosure, with evidence of metalworking on the site. The inhabitants raised animals for their meat or milk: namely, pigs, cows, sheep, and goats. The high status nature of the establishment was indicated by the presence of fragments of amphorae containing wine imported from Italy and subsequently from Spain. However, the most striking feature of the site was a complex system of water management, involving channels and cisterns. Its precise function is unknown; it could have been used for domestic, industrial, or agricultural activities.

The Gallo-Roman period also was well represented along the route, including two sites in the communes of Colombiers and Marigny-Brizay (both Vienne). Archaeologists working at the site of La Genestrière, which extended over five hectares in Colombiers, discovered the remains of two well-constructed buildings, rectangular in plan, dating from the first to the second centuries AD. Some of the masonry suggested the presence of a heated room, possibly a bathhouse. At the site known as Les Champs de la Grenouille at Marigny-Brizay, a small farm was replaced in the second and third centuries AD by a villa equipped with a bath complex. At the sites known as Villiers and La Roche in the commune of Maillé (Indre-et-Loire), agricultural activity in the first century BC is in evidence; it was succeeded in the first to third centuries AD by a large Gallo-Roman farmstead. The archaeologists discovered the remains of a building with finds of terra sigillata pottery, amphorae, and grindstones. The site of l'Ouche-Torse in the commune of Luxé (Charente) initially was identified through field survey. Excavations revealed the remains of a large Gallo-Roman villa dating from the first and second centuries AD.

A Merovingian cemetery, in use in the sixth and seventh centuries AD, was discovered at the site known as La Garde-Le Temps Perdu in the commune of Migné-Auxances (Vienne). Forty-nine graves were found; as only one of the burials was accompanied by grave goods, one of the skeletons was carbon-14 dated, producing a date between AD 540 and 650. The general absence of grave offerings perhaps was the effect of the spread of

Christianity at this time. In addition, it has been suggested that the cemetery may have been used by an extended family group.

Contournement Nîmes-Montpellier

The Contournement Nîmes-Montpellier is a high-speed railway line bypassing Nîmes (Gard) and Montpellier (Hérault), which connects to the LGV Méditerranée. Its construction between 2012 and 2014 revealed twenty-eight archaeological sites along its route of eighty kilometers, of which twenty-one were investigated.

The oldest, and arguably the most significant, was found adjoining the farmhouse known as Le Mas de Vouland, south of Nîmes. Excavation of the site, which occupied eight thousand square meters, produced rare evidence of Upper Paleolithic activity on an open site, as opposed to a cave site. Around five hundred stone tools were found, including a biface made from quartzite. Although a few similar tools previously had been found, particularly in the 1970s, they were all surface finds, the result of agricultural activity. The tools cannot be dated more precisely than between six hundred thousand and thirty thousand years ago, as they were not found in their original context but had been deposited by glacial action around twelve thousand years ago.

Fifteen Neolithic sites were discovered along the route of the Contournement Nîmes-Montpellier, particularly from the Final Neolithic period. Excavation at the site of La Cavalade, south of Montpellier (Hérault), revealed a village from this time. The remains, which date between 2900 and 2700 BC, included ceramics with relief or incised decoration. Objects that indicated contact with external communities included fragments of knives made from flint originating in the Gard department; a polished stone ax, originating south of the Alps; and a copper ax, of the type known from northern Italy. A collective burial of seven individuals, mostly children or adolescents, was also found. Elsewhere on the site, the archaeologists identified a group of fourth-century AD burials, at least seven adults and five children, and an enclosure dating to the middle of the sixth century AD. The site was crossed by a road that perhaps was used from the Iron Age until the medieval period, linking Lattes and Castelnau-le-Lez (both Hérault).

Iron Age cremation burials from the fifth and fourth centuries BC were found at the adjacent sites of Saint-Pierre Nord et Sud in the commune of Lattes (Hérault). It is apparent that the cemeteries were used for a small number of individuals only. In particular, at Saint-Pierre Sud, the cremated remains had been buried with lavish grave goods, which included bronze vessels and jewelry made from precious metals. In particular, one of the men whose remains were buried at Saint-Pierre Sud was accompanied by two bronze vessels of Etruscan origin, a knife, a fibula, and a ring. A woman was buried in a similar manner, with jewelry made from gold, silver, bronze, amber, and coral. Pottery included local wares, as well as Greek amphorae and fine wares imported from Athens. The archaeologists also found evidence of a small vineyard adjacent to the cemetery, perhaps indicating the high social status of the deceased.

Good evidence from the Gallo-Roman period was discovered at the site known as Castelle GR in the commune of Lattes (Hérault), which was occupied from the Final Neolithic period until the end of the seventh century AD. In the Gallo-Roman period, it was a farmstead that included a vineyard from the first century AD. Among the most interesting finds was a deposit of iron agricultural tools dating from the third century AD, including a cattle brand with the letters L and S separated by a fish. Also from this period was the top of an altar dedicated to Jupiter, evidence of religion in a domestic setting. The farmstead continued to be used in the Merovingian period, indicated by the discovery of fifteen silos, in use in the sixth and seventh centuries AD, one of which contained iron weapons and tools.

The archaeological work conducted in France since the beginning of the 21st century has largely been the result of new building projects, linked to the statutory requirement, in line with the European Convention for the Protection of the Archaeological Heritage, generally known as the Valetta Convention (1992) and the French Heritage Code (2001, 2016) to undertake comprehensive archaeological evaluations and excavations, paid for by the developer. Alongside this preventive archaeology, more traditional 'programmed' archaeological projects have continued. The surge in preventive archaeology has led to the number of archaeologists in France increasing to more than 4,000 and has also enhanced the visibility of the social relevance of archaeology. In addition, this has led to the discovery of a large number of archaeological sites which were previously unknown, many of which are the result of major infrastructure projects, such as the new LGV railway lines. In addition, the refinement of scientific techniques in recent decades has led to archaeologists re-visiting both projects and artifacts, some of which were brought to light many years previously. Ongoing construction projects will continue to pose threats to the archaeological heritage, but, with appropriate funding and the reinforcement of legislation, these projects will undoubtedly lead to new discoveries in the future, which will increase our knowledge and understanding of the archaeology of France.

SELECT BIBLIOGRAPHY

The following are a selection of some of the sources that were of particular use in preparing this book.

Amy, R., 1970. "L'inscription de la maison carrée de Nîmes." *Comptes rendus des séances de l'Académie des Inscriptions et Belles-Lettres*, 114 année, N. 4, 670–86.

Audouze, F., 1999. "New Advances in French Prehistory." *Antiquity* 73:297, 167–75.

Aujoulat, N., 2005. "The Gravettian Sanctuary of Cussac (le Buisson-de-Cadouin, Dordogne, France): First Results of a Team Research Project." *INORA* 65:7–19.

Bahn, P. G., 2008. *The Cambridge Illustrated History of Prehistoric Art*. Cambridge University Press.

——— (ed.), 2014. *The History of Archaeology: An Introduction*. Routledge.

———, 2016. *Images of the Ice Age*. Oxford University Press.

———, 2010. *Prehistoric Rock Art: Polemics and Progress*. Cambridge University Press.

Bahn, P. G., and C. Couraud, 1984. "Azilian Pebbles—An Unsolved Mystery." *Endeavour* 8:4, 156–58.

Bakker, J-A., 2010. *Megalithic Research in the Netherlands, 1547–1911*. Sidestone Press.

Bayard, D., and A. Nice, 2009. "Le Musée des Temps Barbares de Marle (Aisne) et son parc archéologique. Présentation du hameau merovingien." *Revue archéologique de Picardie* 1–2, 17–26.

Benoit, F., 1958. "Nouvelles épaves de Provence." *Gallia* 16:1, 5–39.

Billaud, Y., et al., 2014. "Acquisition 3D et documentation multiscalaire de la grotte Cosquer." *Karstologie* 64:7–16.

Bourguignon, L., et al., 2016a. "Bois-de-Riquet (Lézignan-la-Cèbe, Hérault): A Late Early Pleistocene Archaeological Occurrence in Southern France." *Quaternary International* 393:24–40.

———, 2016b. "The Stone Tools from Stratigraphical Unit 4 of the Bois-de-Riquet Site (Lézignan-La-Cèbe, Hérault, France): A New Milestone in the Diversity of the European Acheulian." *Quaternary International* 141:160–81.

Bourrillon, R., et al., 2017. "A New Aurignacian Engraving from Abri Blanchard, France: Implications for Understanding Aurignacian Graphic Expression in Western and Central Europe." *Quaternary International*, 1–19.

Boyer, R., et al., 1987. *Vie et mort à Marseille à la fin de l'antiquité.* Atelier du patrimoine, Marseille.

Bueno Ramirez, P., et al., 2016. "Decorative Techniques in Breton Megalithic Tombs (France): The Role of Paintings." In L. Laporte and C. Scarre (eds.), *The Megalithic Architectures of Europe*. Oxbow.

———, 2012. "Paintings in Atlantic Megalithic Art: Barnenez." *Trabajos de Prehistoria* 69:1, 123–32.

Cassen, S., et al., 2014. "The First Radiocarbon Dates for the Construction and Use of the Interior of the Monument at Gavrinis (Larmor-Baden, France)." *PAST* 77:1–4.

Catsambis, A., B. Ford, and D. L. Hamilton (eds.), 2011. *The Oxford Handbook of Maritime Archaeology*. Oxford University Press.

Chenal, F., et al., 2015. "A Farewell to Arms: A Deposit of Human Limbs and Bodies at Bergheim, France, c. 4000 BC." *Antiquity* 89:348, 1313–30.

Closmadeuc (de), G., 1892. "Dolmen des Pierres-Plates en Locmariaquer." *Bulletins de la Société d'anthropologie de Paris, IV° Série* 3, 692–710.

Clottes, J., and C. Chippindale, 1999. "The Parc Pyrénéen d'Art Préhistorique, France: Beyond Replica and Re-enactment in Interpreting the Ancient Past." In P. G. Stone and P. G. Planel (eds.), *The Constructed Past: Experimental, Archaeology, Education and the Public*. Routledge, 194–205.

Coles, B., 1987. "Archaeology Follows a Wet Track." *New Scientist* 1582:42–48.

Cornu, M., 2013. "About Sacred Cultural Property: The Hopi Masks." *International Journal of Cultural Property* 20:451–66.

Costambeys, M., M. Innes, and S. MacLean, 2011. "Villages and Villagers, Land and Landowners." In M. Costambeys, M. Innes, and S. MacLean, *The Carolingian World*. Cambridge University Press, 223–70.

Couraud, C., and P. G. Bahn, 1982. "Azilian Pebbles in British Collections: A Re-Examination." *Proceedings of the Prehistoric Society* 48:45–52.

Craddock, P., 2009. *Scientific investigation of copies, fakes and forgeries*. Elsevier.

Crawford, O. G. S., 1927a. "L'Affaire Glozel." *Antiquity* 1:1, 100–101.

———, 1927b. "L'Affaire Glozel." *Antiquity* 1:2, 181–88.

Daniel, G., 1960. *The Prehistoric Chamber Tombs of France*. Thames and Hudson.

Delporte, H., 1972. "L'Aurignacien et le «Bayacien» de la Gravette: mise en oeuvre statistique et problèmes posés." *Bulletin de la Société préhistorique française.* Études *et travaux* 69:1, 337–46.

Delluc, B., and G. Delluc, 1997. "L'Affaire de l'abri du Poisson aux Eyzies: Otto Hauser non coupable." *Bulletin de la Société Historique et Archéologique du Périgord* 124:171–77.

Driard, C., 2015. "Des aménagements hydrauliques dans les fossés de l'enclos laténien des Noëls à Pliboux (Deux-Sèvres)." In F. Olmerand R. Roure (eds.), *Les Gaulois au fil de l'eau.* Editions Ausonius, 407–22.

Effros, B., 2012. *Uncovering the Germanic Past: Merovingian Archaeology in France 1830–1914.* Oxford University Press.

Eluère, C., 1984. "Two Unique Golden Helmets." *Gold Bulletin* 17:3, 110–11.

Firmin, G., 1984. "Agriculture expérimentale dans la vallée de l'Aisne." *Revue archéologique de Picardie* 1–2. *La néolithique dans le nord de la France et le basin parisien,* 95–102.

Garrod, D., 1938. "The Upper Palaeolithic in the Light of Recent Discovery." *Proceedings of the Prehistoric Society* 4:1–26.

Gleize, Y., et al., 2016. "Early Medieval Muslim Graves in France: First Archaeological, Anthropological and Palaeogenomic Evidence." *PLoS ONE* 11(2):e0148583.

Gómez-Olivencia, A., I. Crevecoeur, and A. Balzeau, 2015. "La Ferrassie 8 Neanderthal Child Reloaded: New Remains and Reassessment of the Original Collection." *Journal of Human Evolution* 82:107–26.

Gran-Aymerich, E., 2007. *Les chercheurs du passé, 1798–1945.* CNRS Editions.

———, 2004. "Jane Dieulafoy, 1851–1916." In G. M. Cohen and M. S. Joukowsky (eds.), *Breaking Ground: Pioneering Women Archaeologists.* University of Michigan Press, 34–67.

Gran-Aymerich, J., 2013a. "Etruria Marittima: Massalia and Gaul, Carthage and Iberia." In J. M. Turfa (ed.), *The Etruscan World.* Routledge, 319–48.

———, 2013b. "Etruscan Goods in the Mediterranean World." In J. M. Turfa (ed.), *The Etruscan World.* Routledge, 373–425.

Grosjean, R., 1967. "Classification descriptive du Mégalithique corse. Classification typologique et morphologique des menhirs et statues-menhirs de l'île." *Bulletin de la Société préhistorique française.* Études *et travaux,* 64:3, 707–42.

———, 1961. "Filitosa et son contexte archéologique." *Monuments et mémoires de la Fondation Eugène Piot,* 52:1, 3–96.

Guérin, G., et al., 2015. "A Multi-Method Luminescence Dating of the Palaeolithic Sequence of La Ferrassie Based on New Excavations Adjacent to the La Ferrassie 1 and 2 Skeletons." *Journal of Archaeological Science* 58:147–66.

Guérout, M., 2002. "France." In C. V. Ruppe and J .F. Barstad (eds.), *International Handbook of Underwater Archaeology.* Kluwer Academic/Plenum Publishers, 433–48.

Guipert, G., et al., 2011. "A Late Middle Pleistocene Hominid: Biache-Saint-Vaast 2, North France." *Comptes Rendus Palevol* 10, 21–33.

Guyon, M., and E. Rieth, 2012. "Wreck of the 1st-Century AD Lyon Saint-Georges I (Rhône, France): A Ferry or Lighter from the River Saône?." In N. Günsenin (ed.), *Between Continents. Proceedings of the Twelfth Symposium on Boat and Ship Archaeology, Istanbul 2009.* Ege Yayınları, 195–202.

Jaubert, J., et al., 2016. "Early Neanderthal Constructions Deep in Bruniquel in Southwestern France." *Nature* 534:111–14.

Jordan, P., 1978. "Glozel." In R. Sutcliffe (ed.), *Chronicle.* British Broadcasting Corporation, 67–81.

King, A., 1990. *Roman Gaul and Germany.* British Museum Press.

Kleiner, D. E. E., and F. S. Kleiner, 1982. "Review of Amy, R and P. Gros, 1979. La Maison Carré de Nîmes." *Journal of the Society of Architectural Historians* 41:1, 56.

Lawson, A. J., 2012. *Painted Caves: Palaeolithic Rock Art in Western Europe.* Oxford University Press.

Lehoërff, A., 2015. "Le métal archéologique du côté du laboratoire: mythes et réalités d'un matériau/The Archaeological Metal in the Laboratory: Myths and Realities of a Material." In S. Boulud-Gazo and T. Nicolas (eds.), *Artisanats et Productions a l'âge du Bronze.* Association pour la promotion des recherches sur l'âge du Bronze/Société préhistorique française, 97–108.

———, 2008. "Les armes anciennes de la collection Odescalchi." *Jahrbuch des Römisch-Germanischen Zentralmuseums* 55:43–79.

Lejeune, M., J. Pouilloux, and Y. Solier, 1988. "Etrusque et ionien archaïques sur un plomb de Pech Maho (Aude)." *Revue archéologique de Narbonnaise* 21, *Epigraphie et numismatique*, 19–59.

Levine, G. P. A., 2011. "Malraux's Buddha Heads." In R. M. Brown and D. S. Hutton (eds.), *A Companion to Asian Art and Architecture.* Wiley-Blackwell, 629–54.

Long, L., 1987. "Les épaves du Grand Congloué. [Etude du journal de fouille de Fernand Benoit]." *Archaeonautica* 7:9–36.

Maclaren Walsh, J., 1997. "Crystal Skulls and Other Problems." In A. Henderson and A. L. Kaeppler (eds.), *Exhibiting Dilemmas: Issues of Representation at the Smithsonian*, 116–42.

Marquet, J-C., and, M. Lorblanchet, 2003. "The Proto-Figurine from La Roche-Cotard, Langeais (Indre-et-Loire, France)." *Antiquity* 77:298, 661–70.

Mason, D. J. P., 2003. *Roman Britain and the Roman Navy.* Tempus Publishing Ltd.

Masset, C., 2002. "Review of Boulestin B. (1999) Approche taphonomique des restes humains. Le cas des Mésolithiques de la grotte des Perrats et le problème du cannibalisme en Préhistoire récente européenne." *Bulletin de la Société préhistorique française*, 99:2, 398–99.

Menéndez Iglesias, B., 2008. "The Chalcolithic and Ancient-Bronze Age Engravings of the Mont Bego Region." *Annali dell-Università degli Studi di Ferrara. Sezione di Museologia, Scientifica e Naturalistica.*

Mussi, M., 2015. "Encoding and Decoding the Message: The Case of the Mid Upper Palaeolithic Female Imagery." In F. Coward et al. (eds.), *Settlement, Society and Cognition in Human Evolution: Landscapes in Mind.* Cambridge University Press, 275–78.

Ortega, I., et al., 2015. "A Naturalistic Bird Representation from the Aurignacian Layer at the Cantalouette II Open-Air Site in Southwestern France and Its Relevance to the Origins of Figurative Art in Europe." *Journal of Archaeological Science: Reports* 4,:201–9.

Pétrequin, P., 1999. "Lake Dwellings: Archaeological Interpretation and Social Perception, A Case Study From France." In P. G. Stone and P. G. Planel (eds.), *The Constructed Past: Experimental, Archaeology, Education and the Public.* Routledge, 217–28.

Pettitt, P., and P. Bahn, 2015. "An Alternative Chronology for the Art of Chauvet Cave." *Antiquity* 89:345, 542–53.

Peyrony, D., 1928. *Les Eyzies et les Environs.* Eyboulet & Fils.

Reich, G., and D. Linder, 2014. "Experimental Archaeology in France: A History of the Discipline." In J. Reeves Flores and R. P. Paardekooper (eds.), *Experiments Past: Histories of Experimental Archaeology.* Sidestone Press, 67–84.

Rendu, W., et al., 2014. "Evidence Supporting an Intentional Neanderthal Burial at La Chapelle-aux-Saints." *Proceedings of the National Academy of Sciences,* 111:1, 81–86.

Renfrew, C., and P. Bahn, 1999. "Garrod and Glozel: The End of a Fiasco." In W. Davies and R. Charles (eds.), *Dorothy Garrod and the Progress of the Palaeolithic.* Oxbow, 76–83.

Reznikoff, I., 2008. "Sound Resonance in Prehistoric Times: A Study of Palaeolithic Painted Caves and Rocks." *Journal of the Acoustical Society of America* 125(5): 3603, 4137–41.

Rieth, E., 2011. "L'épave du chaland gallo-romain de la place Tolozan à Lyon: approche d'une tradition régionale de construction «sur sole» en relation avec l'architecture navale maritime méditerranéenne/The Shipwreck of the Gallo-Roman Barge of the 'Place Tolozan' in Lyon: Approach of a Regional Tradition of 'Bottom Based' Construction in Relation to the Mediterranean Maritime Naval Architecture." In G. Boetto, P. Pomey, and A. Tchernia (eds.), *Batellerie gallo-romaine. Pratiques régionales et influences maritimes méditerranéennes.* Editions Errance, 61–72.

Sackett, J., 2014. "Boucher de Perthes and the Discovery of Human Antiquity." *Bulletin of the History of Archaeology* 24:2, 1–11.

Sax, M., et al., 2008. "The Origins of Two Purportedly Pre-Columbian Mexican Crystal Skulls." *Journal of Archaeological Science* 35:10, 2751–60.

Scarre, C., 2011. *Landscapes of Neolithic Brittany*. Oxford University Press.

Schnapp, A., 1984. "France." In H. Cleere (ed.), *Approaches to the Archaeology Heritage*. Cambridge University Press, 48–53.

Schulting, R. J., 1996. "Antlers, Bone Pins and Flint Blades: The Mesolithic Cemeteries of Téviec and Hoëdic, Brittany." *Antiquity* 70: 268, 335–50.

Spigola, B., 2016. "Barbegal. A Roman Watermill Complex in Gallia Narbonensis." *Auctor* 1:96–105.

Trigger, B., 2006. *A History of Archaeological Thought*. Cambridge University Press.

Vayson de Pradenne, A., 1930. "Glozel Forgeries." *Antiquity* 4:14, 201–22.

Verger, S., et al., 2007. "Le dépôt de bronzes du site fluvial de la motte à Agde (Hérault)." *Jahrbuch des Romisch-Germanischen Zentralmuseums* 54:85–171.

Wells, C. M., 2009. "Alésia and Kalkriese Compared and Contrasted: Local Chauvinism, Nationalistic Fervor, and Sober Archaeology." *Journal of Roman Archaeology* 22:674–80.

White, R., 2006. "The Women of Brassempouy: A Century of Research and Interpretation." *Journal of Archaeological Method and Theory* 13:4, 251–304.

GLOSSARY

Articulated skeleton: A skeleton whose bones are in the same relative position as in life. If a skeleton is articulated, one normally assumes that ligaments and flesh were still present when it was buried.

Biface: A type of stone tool worked on both sides.

Bilobate: Having two lobes.

Black-figure technique: A technique employed in Greek painted pottery first found in the seventh century BC. Figures are painted in a slip that fires black, and details such as anatomy and clothing are incised through the slip.

Carbon-14 dating: See *Radiocarbon dating*.

Carolingian: The name of a dynasty of Frankish kings that was founded in AD 714 by Charles Martel. The term "Carolingian" derives from "Carolus," the Latinized form of Charles.

Chateleine: A female decorative ornament worn at the waist, with a series of chains suspended from it.

Cloisonné: A decorative technique whose name is derived from the French word "cloison," meaning "cell." A pattern of small cells was made using thin gold strips, a paste, possibly beeswax, and was put at the bottom of each cell, supporting a piece of textured gold foil and a thin piece of garnet, both of which had been cut to the shape of the cell.

Commune: The smallest territorial division of the French Republic for administrative purposes.

Crouched burial: A burial position in which the deceased's legs have been pulled to the chest in a fetal position.

Cup mark: See *Cupule*.

Cupule: A motif found in prehistoric rock art consisting of a roughly circular hollow or hollows sometimes surrounded by one or more concentric rings.

Debitage: The waste by-product resulting from the manufacture of stone tools. Debitage in the form of chips or flakes of flint normally is found in large quantities in areas in which the tools were made.

Département: An administrative division of France. There are ninety-six mainland départements, including two on Corsica. In addition, there are five "outre-mer" (overseas) départéments.

Dionysiac: Relating to the Greek god *Dionysus*.

Dionysus: The Greek god of wine and the theater. *Dionysiac* scenes on Greek painted pottery often show Dionysus with his companions, known as maenads and satyrs.

Dolmen: A tomb constructed from upright stones supporting a capstone.

Dressel: A system for classifying the shape of ceramic amphorae, mainly covering Roman types. It was developed by Heinrich Dressel (1845–1920) and published in 1899.

Etruscan: The name given to the people who dominated central Italy, with a distinctive material culture from around 800 BC. The rise in the power of Rome resulted in the Etruscan cities being in decline from around 500 BC.

Extended burial: A burial position in which the deceased has been placed lying flat, with arms or legs straight, or with arms folded on the chest.

Fibula: A brooch in the form of a pin with a catch, sometimes highly decorated, assumed to have been used for fastening clothing.

Franks: A Germanic people who settled in northern France in the post-Roman period. Their leader from AD 480 to AD 511 was Clovis, who became the dominant ruler in what had been Gaul and the first king of the *Merovingian* dynasty.

Gallo-Roman: The material culture of *Gaul* under provincial rule during the Roman Empire.

Gaul: For much of the period between 600 BC and AD 486, the region of modern-day France was considered by ancient writers as "Gaul," an area separate from modern-day Spain, Italy, Britain, and Germany.

Hypocaust: A Roman architectural feature that heated houses and bath complexes. A floor was supported on pillars made from tiles, with air, heated by a furnace, drawn beneath the floor and up through vertical flues built into the walls.

Martyrium: A church or other structure, especially a tomb, associated with a Christian martyr or saint.

Massaliot: Relating to Massalia, a colony founded in around 600 BC on the southern coast of France, now modern-day Marseille.

Meander: An ornamental motif often used in Roman mosaics consisting of a continuous band of rectilinear forms in a series of successive half turns.

Menhir: A single standing stone.

Merovingian: The name of a dynasty of Frankish kings who ruled from the late fifth to the mid-eighth century AD. It is named after Merovech, the semilegendary figure who was the father of Childeric I, king of the Franks. The last Merovingian king was Childeric III, who was deposed in AD 751.

Mithraeum (plural Mithraea): A building devoted to the cult of *Mithras*, recognized from its distinctive architecture of a rectangular assembly hall that had benches running along both long sides.

Mithras: A male deity whose cult was prominent in the Roman Empire, from the first to the fourth centuries AD, and was particularly associated with soldiers. Mithras, who wears distinctive headgear, usually is depicted in the act of killing a bull. Mithras also appears in Iranian, Hindu, and Zoroastrian traditions.

Oinochoe: The Greek term for a wine jug.

Oppidum: The word used by Julius Caesar to describe hill forts as well as large defended settlements that were not in an elevated position. Accordingly, the term "oppidum" often is used by French archaeologists to describe pre-Roman settlements.

Passage grave: A type of tomb in which the burial chamber is accessed from the edge of a covering mound by means of a long passageway.

Pre-Columbian: The period in the Americas before contact with Europe.

Radiocarbon dating: Also known as carbon-14 dating, a dating technique used for determining the age of carbon-bearing materials, including wood and other plant remains, charcoal, bone, peat, and shell.

Red-figure technique: A technique employed in Greek painted pottery first used in the late sixth century BC. The background is painted in a slip that fires black, leaving figures "reserved" in red. Details such as anatomy and clothing are painted in slip using a brush.

Romanesque: A style of European art that emerged around AD 1000 and was predominant until around AD 1150, when the Gothic style of art emerged. The preceding period is known as pre-Romanesque.

Scaenae frons: The architectural background of the stage of a Roman theater, often elaborately decorated.

Situla: A container in the shape of a bucket, with a single movable handle.

Terra sigillata: A type of Roman pottery whose surface is covered with a slip that fired to a glossy red, made in *Gaul* between the first and third centuries AD. The name of the maker sometimes is stamped on the vessel.

Torc: A metal neck ring, with a small opening at the front.

Type site: An archaeological site that produced objects that are considered as defining the characteristics of a particular period or technology. This is often the site on which the distinctive material culture was first recognized.

Villa: A large agricultural establishment from the *Gallo-Roman* period, which began to appear in the first century AD. Villas consisted of domestic buildings, often of high status, within an estate that frequently included industrial as well as agricultural activities.

INDEX

ABOUT THE AUTHOR

Georgina Muskett is an Honorary Fellow of the Department of Archaeology, Classics, and Egyptology at the University of Liverpool, where she taught Aegean and classical archaeology. Dr. Muskett was formerly curator of classical antiquities at National Museums Liverpool, where she continues to research the classical collections. One of her research interests is Roman mosaics, and she is a member of the executive committee of the Association for the Study and Preservation of Roman Mosaics.

Dr. Muskett is the author of numerous publications, including *Greek Sculpture* and *Mycenaean Art: A Psychological Approach*, and is coauthor of *Catalogue of Etruscan Objects in World Museum, Liverpool*. In addition, she has published articles on aspects of Aegean, Greek, and Roman art and archaeology.